The Dialectical Self-Concept of Symbolic Being

# The Dialectical Self-Concept
# *Of* Symbolic Being

An Ontology of Post-Industrial Aesthetics,

The Abstract Conceptual Transcendental Social Subject

### Jeffrey B. Holl

I.C.H. Publishing Inc.

©2018, by Jeffrey B. Holl

Produced in affiliation with the Freedom of Expression component of the Canadian *Charter of Rights and Freedoms*, **Canadian Heritage** directive (see *fundamental freedoms* section (2b)).

Edited and typeset in Canada

I.C.H. Publishing, Wpg., MB.

Library and Archives Canada

ISBN 978-1-7752848-0-2

Published in accordance with the laws of The Commonwealth for World distribution under the provisions set forth by the Canadian Copyright Act, and in liaison with the forces administered by the author and publisher in a binding agreement to proliferate and foster literary culture in the United Kingdom, Canada, Australia, and other Commonwealth nation states held under the same principles of intellectual property rights and privileges.

Cover image © Shutterstock

The author hereby soundly declares full ownership to the copyrights held herein. All rights reserved. No part of this publication may be reproduced, distributed, or transmitted in any form or by any means, including photocopying, recording, or other electronic or mechanical methods, without the consent or prior written permission of the author and the publisher, except in the case of brief quotations embodied in critical reviews and certain non-commercial uses permitted by law.

# Contents

Introduction  13

**Chapter One**  *The Dialectics of Noumenal Freedom*  19

The Absolute Determination  22

Thought and Being  24

Representations and the Lifeworld  27

Objectivity and the Absolute  33

Modes of Being 36

Consciousness and Essence/the Socio-Naturalistic World  39

Totality-in-itself  42

Subjectivity and the Transcendental Identical  48

On Being and the Lifeworld  50

**Chapter Two**  *The Primacy of Metaphysical Forms*  53

Ego, Representations and Appearances  57

The Transcendentally Knowable 'is'  60

Subjective Identity and the Self-Positing Objectivity  63

Emancipatory Measures  66

The Totalization of the Ego  67

Phenomenality  69

Causality and Reflexive Duality  71

**Chapter Three** *The Historicity of Vernunft*  77

Conceptual Synthesis of the Self-Identical  78

Essence Mediation and Abstract Subjectivity  80

Otherness in the Post-Industrial Age  82

Collective Substance/Objective Essence  85

The Triad of Being  91

The Assets of Reason  94

**Chapter Four** *The Enlightenment of Objectivity*  97

Conceptual Understanding of Objective Beings  101

From the Knower to the Known  103

Philosophizing of the Will a priori  104

The Otherness of Contingency  106

Objective Truth and the Self-Positing "I"  109

Judgment and the Objective Totality  110

The Question of Freedom  111

**Chapter Five** *Conceptual Signifiers and Symbolic Representations*  115

The Tetrad  116

Diachrony and Synchrony  117

The "Post-Industrial Dialectic"  118

Open System  121

Contingency  122

Nominal Signification  124

Symbolic Representation  125

The "Post-Industrial Aesthetic"  127

Social Abstraction of the Concept  128

Self-identification  131

Objective Self-Identification and the Emancipatory Social Being  133

The Other as Contingent Possibility of the Self-Identical  137

The Detachable Subject through its Ontological State of Corporeal Supersession Toward a Representational Other  140

Conceptual Universalism: Ontological Impossibility, or Ontico-Ontological Preservation of Reflexive Universal Self-Identity?  143

Metapsychological Coherence and the Socio-Symbolic Identity  152

Representative Collective Identification and the Ontology of the Real  159

The Projection of the particular Ontic identity and the Reflexive universal positing of its Ontological object  164

Grammatology, Semiotics, Ontological Dialectic and its Symbolic Nominal Significations 167

Self-Consciousness as an Interobjective Experience of the World Totality Throughout Our Dialectical Presuppositions 172

The Self-Concept and its Dialectical Limitations Upon the Otherness of Contingency 177

The Hypostatized Universality of the Existential Being Otherwise Known as Artist 183

The Real as a Fusion of Transcendental Subjectivity and Social Production and the Transcendental Social Subject 187

# Chapter Six

Monadic Symbolization and the *Aesthetics of* Transcendental Signification

Introduction: Symbolic Rigidification *of* a Transcendental Signifier 191

1  The Distantiation *of* World-Society *for* the Instantiation of Identical Singularity 195

2  The Return to Subjectivity: Socio-Ontological Existentiality 198

3  In Participation of the Existentiality Composing Aesthetic Experience: Semiotic Correspondence 201

4  The Tableau *of* Our Symbolic Thinking:

Ontological *Uniformity* and Ontical Differentia 205

5  Conclusion: Symbology and Transcendental Reproducibility 209

# Chapter Seven  Noematic Symbolization 213

Appendix A 228

Appendix B 244

Bibliography 247

*Index* 253

Dedicated to Reason without compromise

On a bridge to the horizons out there

# Introduction

Reflection upon the existence of the other is an extremely time-consuming and all-encompassing act—it may fuel contemplation for countless hours where speech never even enters into the equation: one is simply possessed to greet ontological endeavor with a fight or flight dynamic. The urge to flee the scene of one's own consciousness is indeed quite inconceivable, so invariably the idea is to engage in the positing of concepts—with the intention of gathering one's thoughts toward an arrival at what may be called *The Ontological Path Toward Human Understanding and free will*.

One is never quite sure how to attain this freedom, but without question it exists as both a function of our concepts and our reasoning. Subjectivity of course also benefits from the *sublation, negation,* and *metacritique* of all representations that appear with the intention to challenge subjective undertaking fruitfully. The question may in fact be: how does one arrive at knowledge if one is only ever greeted with the *objects-in-representation* as a function of negation? The meta-solution for this problem has long been undertaken by continental philosophy, and still there remains no clear answer as to how one must approach this without simply resorting to political upheaval, rebellion, or the flagrant use of a skewed pursuit of ethical conduct—*morality-in-itself* offers a broad range of very limited options to how one is expected to approach this *aporia* of consciousness where it appeals to the inane, the profane, the unjust—and the downright cruel performance of reason that excludes so many from the gifts of *post-industrial* living.

How we get by this is with the rational intent to conjure being as something intentional toward whatever relations we have that may suggest that our ego is truly being reduced by a nefarious *super-ego* with the purpose of appropriating the content of our own objects—these that do depart in the absence of the Other—yet seem to become enriched by representations that function as an adjunct to the very *ego-cogito* that finds itself *trans-subjective* and even more reduced to an *absence-of-object* while under the guise of no representational experiences whatsoever. The arrival of these multitudes outside the proximal manifold does indicate that one's presuppositions are intentional toward the world a priori, yet the demand for more positing that puts up ideas for an increasingly nominalist society becomes a function of a participatory democracy—the ideal that both culture and state could couple to form a Utopian society where the class structure is not so much the case; but what is the case moreover is the promulgation of ideas that would potentially constellate in one individual particularity. Universality itself is the inversion of rational subjectivity into a *monadological* stratification of self that is in appearance only before the world—through our *impressions, propositions and judgments, contingent identity, and absolute subjectivity*.

Yet we cannot be faced with this absolute knowledge without the inheritance of the produced world-society that exists in the beyond of our very subjectivity that would be without objects should it fail to transcend the subjective past by the assertion that existence is the genus that precedes our perceptions of the way things are in reality;—though it greets us in our own subjectivity as an *in-itself*—prompting the notion that the duality between subject and object has released an experience to the collective, we can never know whether or not we have *temporologically* traversed our own being into rational noetic strata that is represented to us as an *in-itself*; other than by way of the very conceivable notion that this is the very causality of our being.

The reason we exist is indeed this universality that moves us from the unfathomable realm of the ontological event of *existence proper*—the generative elements of nature that produce a habitat for us in which to dwell. But what is more generative of being is the concept of the One—be it as the Gnostics saw it, or as a function of an Absolute object-predicate that introduces inter-subjectivity to the *lifeworld*; this apparent objective being is the very truth event that has been sought in connection with so many movements in philosophy;—there can be no other more potent existent that forwards reason toward its absolute knowing—other than the contingencies of intelligible being (often false) and the understanding that results from *temporal* causality—the notion that our experiences can be subject to the judgments of others that hold a stake in what matters to us most.

Following this, the undertaking really does become a function of the consisting probity. The yet ever-elusive rapport that we may have with our own facticity and *lifeworld*, and the conditions posited a priori by our *habitualities* and non-immediate judgments. These do appear to us in reflection, but the *aporia* exists whereby the *subject is known in-itself, and distracted by a proposition that precedes the concepts that may lead to absolute knowledge* on a greater understanding of the very situation the subject may be in. As such *absolute identity* is integral to the freedom of the *noumenal* self—without this liberty to posit the subjective will, there can be no transcendental subjectivity, no transcendental correlation where state power regulates subjectivity *in-itself*.

It's part and parcel to a subject's identity that universality take both ontic and ontological positing to be redemptive of rationalism while in pursuit of epistemology and the abstraction of essence that a subject requires. Here a subject may self-determine what is already causal, thereby invoking the social forms to come to light as a function of both transcendental subjectivity, and societies that exist beyond one subject's identity. With this it would be that the *monadological* composition of a subject were itself transcendent *temporologically*, but that behind this substance as subject the multitudes and collective of one's objective social being could arrive at a reunion with one's object—as well as a prospective intersubjective relation observationally of the One: behind the pure self-reflecting subject that has lost its

## 16 The Dialectical Self-Concept of Symbolic Being

temporal constraints, exists the social forms—the conceptual realism that produces a subject's social being.

The phenomenological status of a subject is determined by the conditions of choice as a reflexive act of the free will, yet causally determined by representations that determine the choice of action only *a posteriori*. *This indicates that culture and technology have blended to make an effort to assimilate rational subjectivity to the authority*—or more accurately—the whims of the state. That pure being should be infected with the invisible universe that endeavors to force conformity of the subject to norms that limit the identity and free choice of any rational subject appears as a coercive force that must be sublated *in-itself*—or at the very least negated as a function of any onto-genetic composition whatsoever. These representations of otherness make efforts to—for instance—dictate objective sexual inference. As a function of the *id,* and within all judgments toward the necessity of emancipatory measures that must be taken to release both man, and woman from their chosen signifiers is a measure that has many political connotations—as it does delve into human nature, thusly pre-emptive of things such as the libido. The subject in his/her objective morally constituted self will only identify with the symbolic as a function of their own (libidinal) being—and with this it is that there must be no politicized distantiation; as it invariably stems from an *oedipal biogenesis of socio-symbolization*. Here being becomes liberated from its understood norms so as to pursue an emancipated rational identity—the life force of which will allow for the ontologically constituted self to engage the world of appearances without the *sui generis* of a negative, stigmatized socio-symbolic identity that cuts across both phenomenal being as it does *noumenal* freedom. Any subject will render their own substance a priori with the assistance of the mutually-produced society that presents objects that have no pre-conceived notion about what a subject *is* or is not. With this the emancipated rational being can appear and posit judgments *only*, and will objects that will allow for a more substantive sense of self—arguably the self that will eventually become what can only result from self-determination—this is the social role that is *co-extensive* within the choices that have already been determined by universality/genus *proximativa*. Both space and time, causality and socio-cultural class will determine the *habitualities* of subjective being; but these are determined by the subject's own praxis. Empirical/factual experience (all being determined ultimately by private interests) will invariably restructure the collective identity of one's personal selection—but only as it becomes engendered toward what will allow for the subject to find a place amongst its peers in the community—with hopes of ordaining causality out of an objective confusion as to the hostility of social norms, and into the necessity of what benefits may arise from undertaking to subdue bio-chemical processes with the intention of balancing acts of the free will where concern the substance of relations.

For instance, those that procreate at the same time may find themselves all becoming relations and entering into a constellation of representations and sharing—or, conversely—monopolizing properties, etc. The way by which the social norms constitute the conduct of the individual *forms* the reflexive appeal of causal identities *prima facie*, yet the enterprise to obtain one's own absolute subjectivity as identical and *noumenally* free, is to presuppose phenomenal entities that stem from a tactical world: the world that has no established concepts for a subject, yet may know the subject *in-itself*. It then rests upon the subject to pursue creative freedoms in order to preserve and reify the *sociologically symbolic world*—never verification as a function of the mere appropriation of an object's substance, yet the a priori reflection upon the content of objects that are inherently and mutually brought into the awareness of a subject by way of their subjective universality—only achieved by paying attention—and having an intentionality toward objects that are given through disciplined acts of contemplation.

# Chapter One

## *The* Dialectics *of* Noumenal Freedom

No one simply arrives at dialectic without first becoming aware of their own noumenal freedom—that can only come as a result of philosophy, trauma, a world event or *evental* truth (such as the collective or mass-consciousness of a movement or revolution). By way of the system, organized labour, governments, and corporatist organizations and institutions, a subject knows that looking out beyond a *for-itself-transcending self* has wielded this presence in the world—a *lifeworld* where we're bound to one another because of the very objects of our consumption. They all represent the opportunity for the having of substance (if for any reason the subject has been stripped of it) by the instantiated ordering of forms and crypto-faschoid corporations that chose the popular culture icons; not without enslaving thousands of unsuspecting consumers to their programmes—but certainly their consumers are *mutatis mutandis* also the representations that constellate in the common will of the thinker once power has been driven away by *noumenal* freedom. This exercise of praxis is bound to yield and constitute more authentic works of art—which leads us toward the notion that the causal network of objects presented by mass-culture is not altogether *as* an individuated totality. But what does require negation is the incendiary cancellation of all artistic merit by power that looks for the signifiers that meet with only the standards of collectives lacking in objective merit and substance.

There one can certainly imagine oneself on an island without masking the *culture industry* in the least. Its symbolic universe has already been reified and presented to the world as a function of the market economy, and this is what may deter a subject from pursuing their comportment toward their own subject-object interplay, as one's own object and its content may be appropriated by the networks presented as they are also in *representation*. They are apperceived but for the technological device, this constitutes a substrate for the technological world of appearance that invariably is self-positing and causes a subject to disengage capitalism either as a consumer, or as a participant. Invariably, the participant will also appropriate objective content as a function of their random praxis in connection with it;—but it will be determined by the social collective, and as such will take the form of something that is contemporary. In turn, this will blend with historicity—forming a synthesis between the cultural object and its historical origins. Historicity blends motifs with the arts and the sciences, which is why its movements have to them a natural flow. *Weltgeist* has a great deal to do with this phenomenon, as Western Culture in all of its traditions is ultimately dominated by intellectuals— not by political/economic power.

However, that being said, capital will always drop one in pursuit of their own private revolt that has no lawful leg to stand on,—and for this reason, the dominance of the *super-ego* can only be in part subdued by conformity to the *id*; and for this reason dialectic finds necessity in its pathic *noumenal* freedom as it perseveres through the vicissitudes of self-identity. Contingent representations that are self-identical to the subject are constitutive of Otherness unless the subject identifies the intersubjective relation that has become of this past self—only in *that* re-appropriation does the subject stand a chance to engage their absolute knowing without falsity being at the forefront of every conception. The concept needs to breathe within the pure "I"—without the *temporological* compromise shaking rational identity; and interfacing with the *potentia* of the subject as it is presented with *Dasein* (both as an entity and as ontico-ontological being).

There is a most notable difference in thoughts incurrent of the positing of the self-identical—the absolute subject—in terms of the transcendental constitution of being as a phenomenal object, but also as a reflecting subject and the ontological constitution that inheres of a speech act. Though this seems remarkably self-evident, it is of no coincidence that positing the self-identical yields both contingent self-same objects-in-representation, just as it does render the *symbolic universal* proximal—both as a concept and as a given; though it would seem that the judgments of the symbolic universal are to be questioned, and ultimately may fall prey to ontological verification before any speech act is in effect required. Though this is not to admit that the ontic being—the communication between subjects externally—may not in fact determine the proximity of the *cogito* at a later date that is a function of civil law and thereby enacts the constitution of a dialectical correspondence where actors are concerned with objects as reifications of symbolic identification—appealing to actuality and adhering to the subjective will as it either acts in accordance with the ethical substance, or acts within the sole purpose of appropriating the self-concept for reification of both *Symbolic Being*, and the content of an ontologically constituted existence which allows for objectification of a subjectively instantiated ownership of surplus-value. So the winner is most certainly basing his earning more upon the inherence of unrepresented extraneous negative value than what the *truth-in-itself* had actualized before its formative dialectical obfuscation.

This seems to be more based upon caprice than on the very concept of dialectical abstraction—but as far as the *symbolic universal* is concerned it is up to the subject to posit judgments that recognize the *monadological* substance within its transcendental constitution, entering into a dialectical realism with the concept as it determines the contingency of the *noumenal* act in projection of the will to bring into representation all relative absolutes. In other words, one must conjure the spirits to bring into being the objects that dwell within the truth event as it is in the process of forwarding content and subjectivity to the understanding multiplicities concomitant to the communal undertaking—the matter at hand. With this, ontology can win over action *prima facie*, but action must then follow in a very structured and organized way. Every subject is a pure being that has been transmitted from its own *transcendental constitution*, and it is not until acts of the free will that truth may enter the symbolic universal; as it corresponds directly with universality and the natural laws that determine objectivity, subjectivity, collectivity, and multiplicity. While collectivity stands a fair chance at the cancellation of multiplicity—as it is determined by a collectively transcendent constitutive apparatus of a virtual system—the materialist/nominalist universalism of multiplicity corresponds directly with the plurality of subjective wills that are constellated objectively a priori. Such as it is, this objectivity is a phenomenon of the One—and thereto unites a principle of absolute subjectivity/*noumenal* freedom with nature and its objective components. Though humankind does not engage in the materialist dialectic without the rational world as a contingent necessity, the inherent causality of nature and the macro universe affects us at the quantum level. Without question, the origins of the universe present consciousness with its ultimate determination—if ever there were any doubt that universal nature and mind/brain would be engaged in dialectics in a dichotomous relationship to the world—then contemplation has not yet reached its end and philosophy can continue to work its magic for many years to come.

## The Absolute Determination

The constitutive characteristic of universality is that it is in fact split into the absolute determination and the symbolic. This division is not to be confused with the subject-object dichotomy (subject=symbolic, object=absolute universality (determination)). What is different here is the symbolic may be in representation of a property of a subject that finds its being within the notion as a contingent proposition, or an evidently *false* judgement with which to deceive the subject—whereas the absolute determination is brought into being by the positing of the subjective identity dialectically. This becomes the only way to bring into being the construction of essence in an abstract universality that is necessary for the subject to further proceed. Hence, without free will as a function of intelligible being from entity (*Dasein*) and the symbolic universe, absolute determination may never come into existence. Therefore it is that the symbolic/transcendental constitution is advanced before the absolute determination. Then, and only then, does a subject enter into the process of dialectical reasoning and intersubjective being with all representations that have arrived upon the scene. Without which, there would also be no *ego cogito* as these are—at the very essence of the *transcendental constitution*. But it is not to be lost on the other-worldly examination of the possibility for self-awareness but to be the launch pad for a dialectic with the objective world. This world is constitutive of our own transcendental subjectivity and *monadological* self—thereby it can also present and be in representation of falsity—which is a most profound *aporia* of philosophic endeavor; but by any measure does represent properties that are constitutive of substance and preface all available free will with a potently binary *noumenal* projection. Beyond this projection exists the world.

One must summon all existing objective contingencies into collective representational being with this act of the subjective will;—and again elicit abstract determinations a priori. They may, in fact occur more as impressions than representations, but without question are properties that connect the subject to its universal symbolization and nature. As such it is merely a function of the *ego cogito* in its capacity to posit judgments that have universal validity claims that allows a subject to be both composed of phenomena as of *noumena*.

This is most interesting, as the phenomenon is more proximate to the subject than is the posited free will. This supports the theory that the *transcendental constitution* produces phenomena, while the objective world produces *noumena*. While both are part of a *totalization* of the self, they are also identical and only institutionally mediated. The process of self-mediation is a necessary contingency and only comes as a function of transmission. That is, one subject transmits being to another of immediacy. The yield on this is that subjectivity is so constituted both phenomenally and *noumenally* and may be won by *fiat*. Barring that, the subject is bound to necessity of projection of the self-identical and consistently in pursuit of it—should the subject ever fall into particularity without first engaging the concept:—having for its own possession control of what it judges or conceives, and when to approach a condition with affirmation or negation. The general rule-of-thumb is that the positing of concepts before judgments exist in representation of something that may be "up for grabs"—resolving a dispute without it ever coming to retaliatory violence or conflict. Yet, what seems more necessary is the evolutionary thoughts toward the constitution of a notion as can appear for both an intelligible being or object/thing, or symbolically. The imagination has within its grasp the real in both instances, though one may be based strictly upon the unconscious drives, while the other is based upon the concepts that have been posited. These concepts are often the result of practices that occur a priori or in a passive state of being—while the positing of concepts requires an objective world for any such recognition or acknowledgement of what has been therewith brought into being.

## Thought and Being

The *originary* concept of being has long been contemplated—from Parmenides to Badiou and Žižek—that its original aim was to establish a precept for what constitutes thought as a function of its correction to both the inner (ontological), and outer (material) realm. However this reflexive ontology allows for further postulates of what constitutes being as a thing, and thought as being. What we have here is a very basic dichotomy between the ontic and the ontological. Does matter (our physical existence) precede the thoughts that we have—or is mind-substance-spirit the source of what generates our intellectual capacities. Since temporality has a direct affect upon this equation I will begin with it as a foundation upon which to build my argument that *mind-substance-spirit* does in fact precede the *ontical* realm in many of its variations.

Firstly, we have the genesis of the human form (genus) as it relates to the necessary conditions produced by nature (the ecosystem) so as to preserve the very possibility of a sustainable organism. It is noted here that historicity has produced innumerable self-sustaining varieties of the primates (some of which became extinct) but that this generative nature of the necessary environmental conditions for what will eventually be human life—homo sapiens—was no accident in the development of reason. Clearly, the more industrious and civil *homo sapiens* are, the more we are able to sustain our existence;—with a combination of developed brute force and institutional reason. Without reason, humankind never would have sustained on this planet. The calamities with which we have been faced have nearly destroyed us many times throughout our history. But this reason has often times fallen to violence, crime, and acts of war—none of which will be discussed here in detail—but all of which have led toward similar conclusions. Man's impetus to promulgate the species—at the insistence of women's requirement to utilize their power both biologically and psychologically—have given birth to an extraordinary depth of reason that has struggled within the pursuit of rational identity, the maintenance of genetic substance, and the proliferation of ideas that would allow for a sustainable and egalitarian human race to occupy Earth; without the compromising of any political movements that jeopardize ethnological relations or sexual/gender barriers. As such, we find ourselves in a day and age where "being" becomes something that is in fact generated by all of us collectively.

We find the *Dasein* of being is this collective notion of subjective experience as it encounters the outside world; yet has been produced by forces which defy all rational/empirical ideas about how we did come into being. The notion that "conceptual realism" has generated our substance from some metaphysical realm is far-fetched enough to bring forth many opponents—yet it is fashioned so as to sustain the argument that form, content, substance all precede the thinking organism's experience at the level of universality. It is only that we as *thinking* beings must all coexist within the vicissitudes of our own particularity that truth is not an absolute before reason wills into being the objects that are in possession of this universality. In fact, *any constellation of objects for consciousness as they appear to the mind* denote universality.

These are the *originary* sources of all rational content within reason—being that they possess the content that can only become available to the thinking man. Yet, any subject that fails to adhere to the causality that determines the ability to fulfill the very notions of freedom will find the self cast aside these objects. If they are few, then they are many, and most will likely become constitutive while within one's own phenomenon. The very fact that the collective has broken free from its own subjective constraints and found a home in a symbolic universe a *master signifier* leads one to believe that the object or phenomenon is to become constituted by a passive collective of receptive objects,—or, the audient. Willing to be led by an objectivity that transcends the limitations of their own judgments. Thereby, the notion of class struggle is to a degree eliminated, as the master needs only provide objective content for the student—and therewith eclipsing all notions of the primacy of economics having a strangle hold over the minds of the subjects that would wish to engender themselves toward a greater level of performance.

Life after all is a performance, and without this being—transmitted from every intelligible and generative form of reason from a universal generality—there is to be no *progressus* of ideas beyond the *status quo*.

The Dialectics of Noumenal Freedom 27

And without the very accessibility of reason through academic institutions, there is to be no *compatibilism* with the causal universe at the quantum level. This necessary absolute of determinate self-causality stands to further both the contingent self-positing aspect of humanity—which furthers the pursuit of truth within subjectivity with a keen sense of democracy; and will ultimately proceed to render the reflexively causal chain of predicable universality more attuned to the strictures being posited and in creation of forms of the absolute (which is evolving as we do). The absolute is not to be confused with the historically perfect or divine—our notions of spiritual being evolve as we do, and this is how the human species will continue to sustain its "New Age of Reason" well into the next century.

## Representations and the Lifeworld

All things represented have for them the distribution of cultural objects in the form of mass media. Therefore, representations themselves are more than likely the result of stimulating the *lifeworld* from a standpoint that insures the neural net not only conforms to the causal chain of events that are circumscribed to the currency of the contemplation—but also representations themselves—as they have to do with the currency of what every subject has in pursuit. And thereby is the substance of any thinking being's rational constitution. Things reflected upon however, require an identity and must be posited in order to enact the predicate "world", or "society"; or "culture" within the mind in order to escape any lengthy analysis of what if anything is actually going on. As the truth sleeps—sometimes with its worst enemy—and must be awakened in order to fulfill its obligations to every subject that is in search of its own socio-cultural determinations. These moments all fall under the concern and consideration of those faced with the external source and control over objective being, yet do not conspire against the free will—other than by way of limitation and observational scrutiny. Truly, universality is such that we can and may be watched—even in solitude—for the purposes of an objective power "clinching" a property that would otherwise fall into our own particularity. This experience, however is quite different from the one defined in the Judeo-Christian tradition as "God watching"—it is in fact, living, breathing subjects that have found themselves in observation of the symbolic universe—though in this case it is in form of a mind's eye that can contemporaneously observe the activities of persons if only to judge them on their morality. This experience is overtly invasive, and interfered with the privacy of a subject; but it must be endured as a mere function of the quantum reality in which we all live.

It is "possible" to enjoy this *infinite regressus* of space-time as a function of remote viewing in the effort to "investigate" any particular individual—unbeknownst to them often times—yet still stands as a function of our human capacities as one of those human traits attainable only through reason that we endeavor never to want to part with it. In occurrence within this truth, the *absolute* allows for only the observation of any subject as it appears as an image-object within the mind; in order to grasp the object in its entirety with its content, one must part with the image in order to pursue more profound endeavors of objective speculation and awareness. All objective being conforms to the very same socio-psychological/metaphysical laws, and thereby is accessible to all those that pursue thought at an equal level. Thought *in-itself* precedes the knowledge of the body—as revealed in our dream state where we can only conceive of a body to make lucid dreams more enjoyable: however corporeal exits have been reported whereby a subject is fully psycho-physically constituted in their dream state a priori.

Given this, it should be noted that because our own *ego* precedes the arrival of our proximate thoughts as they are determinable by an absolute, outside of our *transcendental subjectivity* we may find that the very process of thinking *is* in fact the essence proper. Both at the *phenomenal* and at the *noumenal* level. The subject must not only *abstract* an essence, but also *claim* one—universal exchange-value becoming more constitutive of essence as the human ecology of planet Earth ceases to provide the necessary conditions for all life-forms (including humans). This *aporia* where concerns philosophy is *mutatis mutandis* the very consequence of our evolution into beings that do have a greater capacity for knowledge and invention than any preceding generations. What's missing is the algorithm that self-posits our subjective idealism. This is of course being replaced by machines themselves:—which we have been in the process of merging with since the discovery of radio waves. The stand still solution is to encourage the efficacious development of humans to not only participate in their own intelligibility—but to own it.

A functional *representationalism* of ownership over intelligible being is a move toward the becoming of a participatory democracy. This would be a condition of the state whereby multiplicity would become of its own *sub specie aeternitatis*; thereby creating no greater division between subject and object, but invoking the possibility of a greater unity between subject and the objective world,—as the democratic *lifeworld* state could be as emancipated from hierarchical controls, as it were determined by the absolute of nature, to which we all would become more responsible in pursuit of the preservation of threatened life forms. What will concern us further at this point is how to constitute our *lifeworld*—an objective world with the *symbolic transcendental* as it refers to any subject's agency in pursuit of the aims without which our substance would be reduced too much; and indeed subjectivity would be found in its necessary duty to perform the unification of substance/subject with objective world.

It is here elucidated that there is a clear demarcation between objective world and nature. Reason herself is more than anything else a function of the designs of Western Society as it is in a dialectic with nature; but what is here more the case is that the environment is populated by the phenomena of humankind as it does adhere to its own natural laws. Knowing that our reason itself affects the causality of "acts of God" reflexively adds fuel to the fire where concerns our conduct toward one another bio-economically, and this relational dialectic between particular subject and universal object can be seen as the dialectic between humankind and nature, society and exchange-value. What becomes of the problem here is that there are only the empirical solutions being offered as the resolution of what otherwise should be considered a philosophical *aporia*. The more humankind consumes objects/universality/nature, the more we step out of the confines of our own rational being and "into the will"— if only to capture more exchange-value from the consumption of dialectically abstracted objects.

The representations of epistemology reveal what counts to the subject as the determinable properties of rational and normative being; and most certainly objects present the subject with the potential of the having of content leading to the expansion of essence—but this turns out not to be the goal of dialectical subjectivity. The objects themselves are produced by a universalistic natural world, and without actually entering into dialectic with an "all powerful" totalitarian state as a rationally thinking subject, one would be without essence—unless it had been produced by a universe and planet that had produced the necessary conditions for evolutionary life forms to exist. As such, objects themselves that are not in fact dichotomous to the particular subject, universal object, use-value/exchange-value dialectic, are to be consumed as historical objects—objects of historicity; while all objects in-themselves that are universally produced should be *sublated* for the purpose of the preservation of human universality. A new *aporia* here is that, of course those objects will be appropriated by exchange-value:—it is only through the *deontic* evaluation of how they should be put to use that determines the *quid pro quo* of subject-object dialectics.

It is upon the very notion of the idea that the world presents itself to "May we change a light bulb?" that this very action of thinking and doing is what is represented in its objective necessity to the world that just simply *is*. By way of circumstance, one can only find oneself immersed in the process of reflection upon what the world is by way of the idea. This is what constitutes both being *and* essence before intelligibility or representation, as the act of doing the deed brings into reality the consequence of what will posit the notion of an understanding that presupposes the requirement or obligation of doing the deed. But one is more in need of further investigation here is how the idea has occurred—before any concept of the idea had actually been represented or brought into being. Well the short answer to this is, that it did not come into being before the concept, as the concept was the very event that preceded the very idea in question. This idea (of the world) has become of the very innocence of the undertaking to merely perform a menial task, the task at hand—yet still this notion of being "somewhere out there" advanced the idea of the world to the subject, in that being had already been disclosed to the world by way of the very act of doing. Thereby consciousness of self precedes the very act of doing as without the knowledge of what must be done, there would then be no "doing". It is by these very means and by way of which we arrive at our knowledge of the world; in that our presuppositions about what must be done are then realized to allow the world to represent itself to us as it is *in-itself*. The world *in-itself* is the horizon upon which all other matters that concern being and doing rest; and by way of which all knowledge of becoming is to find its footing—granting largely toward the essence of being and the grounding of essence. That essence is essentially grounded in the becoming of the world "as idea" is what advances the very notion of becoming to the subject before anything actually arrives on the scene representationally. This void of being *is* the idea of the world—and all encumbrances of *weltgeist* that come with it—most notably the externality of mass-revolution, and the internal consciousness of the horizon of Western democracy that constellates in a universal principle of being. That this being—the universalized being of substantive unity—has been constituted, is the very notion that all being of collective norms and unified identity may be so constituted. The upside of this is that all rational unity will precede institutional mediation of essence—which would only subtract from universality its higher understanding and contribution to thought and thinking; and that the organized mediation of essence would (and does) result in radical political upheaval,—as not only the *ego*, but the *id* is affected by the coercive powers that institute privilege to the handmaidens of objective universality:—which is what we are all in pursuit of in terms of its constitutive properties and the consummation of subject-object unity; yet inherently the thoughts that dwell in disunity with the notion may endeavor to rob the proportional unity of its provisions from rational doing in pursuit of more universality for its most preferred subjects. The argument lies within the very notion that the object had only separated from the subject insofar as it has found itself in an Otherness that represents the affirmation (positive negation) of its own camp;—while simply subtracting from a subject their own objective being, which leads to countless instances of dispute and falls under the guise of tortious law. One becomes fully aware of the loss of their own being in this moment, yet is acquainted with the more profound *notionality* of the existence of the objective world. The question one may ask oneself is: "Why do I exist within an objective world?"

For not only does a subject exist within an objective world, but the objective world exists within the subject. The very *transcendental constitution* of any subject's being is the fact that not only does one represent oneself to the world a priori, but the world is represented to us. It is only compounded by the knowledge that the universality of a noetic substrate cannot thereby possibly accommodate all subjects equally and still function as a democratic whole. The answer is that this objective world is *in-itself* beyond the subjectivity of anyone that does not have the sure "causal referent" as the pure "I" has in conception. Truly the notion of an objective world that has been *de-transcendentalized* will most certainly present nominalist positing that only has the objective world for an "arena" of thought, yet the transcendental/symbolic/representational world will be mediated by the concept itself that is advanced a judgment that precludes the impossibility of the pluralistic totality of contemporaneous subjects (otherwise experienced as mob psychology). This however is the very nature of the trans-subjectivity that proposes *lifeworld* causality—as without both the collective apparatus of the governed, or technologically collectivized, and the trans-subjective beings, there would be no "matter-at-hand" or contemplation of any given relevance. As such, being itself would be in jeopardy of its own self-mediating, self-positing, immediacy as it relates to the objective world/universality of concepts. It is by way of these universal concepts that being is transmitted over to the next subject as a historical object—being is in fact an object realized as a sensation of neural properties:—there the ontic takes precedence over the ontological once the process of transmission has occurred and presents the subject with a very necessary occasion of a well-founded "speech act" and becomes the *noumena* of what will ultimately arrive for the self-positing contingencies as necessary beings of both the subject and their relational counterparts.

## Objectivity and the Absolute

Objectivity exists for a purpose: that what it is, is a mysterious constellation of objective experience as a historical object that is antecedent to the determinations of every subject. What it does for subjectivity is based upon the substrate of all conscious endeavor, yet is within the necessary contingency of all objectivity—never to be relied on "absolutely"—though once a subject realizes their own *transcendency*, it is without question *of* an absolute. This is revealed through and only by way of the positing of subjective observations that occlude the symbolically direct and contemporaneous natures of collectivity and democratic endeavor. Because the world exists, society precedes the consciousness of self in terms of its self-relating properties towards its own realization of the transcendental properties that the subject has within grasp; and by way of this line of reasoning it is also that the determinations that come from outside the sphere of rational subjectivity be considered absolute from the causal perspective; and those that stimulate free acts of the will in self-determinations of an alternate outcome to the *antecedently* determined event. Since these events are universal, and historically based upon the genus model for human integrity, we will deal only with how a subject can posit substance that has been reflexively constituted, despite the causality of absolute determinations that do not confer with a subject's own *transcendency*.

Here, what we find is that the very motif of subjectivity and the experience of consciousness proper, is willing to grasp an object within its conception and thereby appropriate its content; but also that a content may be posited in order that a subject may find its being in its own object. This reflexivity is at the helm of all ontico-ontological causes and determinate upon the relational and proximate qualities inherent of the historico-political dynamics referential to the subject as it engages in its activities concerning the consciousness of the world or *weltanschauung*. The world view brings into play all subjective considerations, as the object of the self that has been posited based upon the perceived content (and the relative proportions of its truth content) is toward the realization of the objective world as a function of objective being posited by the very content that represents the circumstance of the very content that posits objective being. Truly, there is indeed a constellation of inter-subjective powers that operate outside of the system that have the *potentia* to realize the "truth" more than any measures of diplomacy or bureaucracy may ever hope to.

This phenomenon is the very phenomenon of objective idealism in its most pure form—that the unity with the object has brought into being objective forces that constitute subjectivity further as a function of its own contrariness. Its difference to the system is what brings to light the *lifeworld* representation that bridges the objective world with the symbolic—allowing the absolute determinations to proceed from nature through both the *lifeworld*, and the transcendental. Again this distinction will require clarification, but in terms of the dichotomous relation between universal and particular, societal and transcendental, and objective and subjective; it would seem quite clear that the given of dialectical reasoning between all of the aforementioned in pursuit of the rational subject that is still constituted by the symbolic universals and dreams of the unconscious is certainly not without the determinations of a certain natural environment that may account for what happens to the subject when faced with the predicate of substance. That it is both preceded by the natural world, the universal order, and society—all constitutive of the transcendental—reveals that space and time are *ex nihilo* external conditions of an internal ordering of the conscious mind—leading one to the realization that *noumenal* freedom in point of fact is thinking into its domain, the realm, of some apperceived Otherness that may be required to adjure to the conditions posited of our rational subjectivity—without these conditions, democracy would never be possible as our own (monadic) *transcendentality* is constitutive of others in a *post facto* fashion—as they are in commensuration of the free-act of rational subjectivity that has resulted in a "truth event". The phenomenological perspective being that a content that has been encountered has resulted in the positing of one's own object that has become within the currency of the objective world, and many then become contemporary as a *lifeworld* with intersubjective beings all reflecting upon the currency of their own determinations as understood through the universality of the symbolic (and in turn constituted within their own spatio-temporal causality and *transcendentality*).

The subsequent action or activity of the subject is to become engaged with an objective world insofar as their essence is no longer being mediated by the institutional order that negated the instance of any ordering of thoughts in pursuit of dialectical subjectivity—and has indeed engaged the necessary ordering of the external action to order an emancipation from the oppression of the very possibility of free-willing subjects that are able to constitute their very substance within the ordinance of the universality/objectivity only presented to those that become liberated from the *super-ego* that is a dominant force over the very functionalism of the constitution of all the aforementioned.

## Modes of Being

Modes of being tend to be interesting at a glance. It is that they are accessible as functions or capacities of the intellect much of the time; but also that they lead to the necessary pursuit of truth. As such, one may be led astray by the multitude of contingencies that one has as both self-identical representations that seem to be playing "language games" with a subject, but also be intersubjective relations in pursuit of their own *noumenal* freedom with a particular goal in mind. Modal logic certainly presents me with the opportunity to attain some sense of grounding while in pursuit of what is the case here, but from where I stand the *alethic* (truths in the world) and the epistemic (truths in the mind) are inseparable as functions of the intellect as the "truth event"— the ontological event that presents me with an epistemic occurrence is about something in the world—whether it refers to the subject a function of their relational particular facticity, or the *universalizable* world itself; the fact of the matter is that the truth is an event that is being understood—if anything its *alethic* quality is one of verification alone through the speech act, rather than a determination of validity of aural claims so as to reduce the subject into a blithering idiot (as would be in the aim of a cross-examination in court). The key element to the "truth claim" is in the very justification—that its components have not interfered with any *universalizable* laws that would bestow upon the subject the utter face of falsity and beliefs that have no verifiable means for the pursuit of a "speech act" or "validity claim". One settles the score best when justification is met by way of the *assertory* judgment as it meets with the *noumena* of concepts now engendered toward the opponent. The magnitude of verifiable truth is within the new validity claim that has been supported by the judgments that advance concepts to the subject—now the verification of the hypothetical judgment has been reduced to its component parts of "violation" and the "violated". The subject has become bereft its object by way of legerdemain and must establish both a validity claim for lawful action, and a judgment for re-appropriation of the contingency that has become a representation for the opponent. Simply put, the subject engages in combative dialectic with the other that has been found guilty of the crime. The status of the subject will then change from that of the "victimized" to that of the constitutionally resolute. And in constitutional resoluteness, the subject will find a concrete universality.

The differentia will virtually disappear as absolute determinations return and constitute the *performative* activity of the subject. This invariably will commensurate all of the subject's activities as the temporality of contingencies and necessities become realigned so as to support the very horizon of the symbolic that will then be once again produced by the idealistic reflections that are bound to occur. Then once again the pairing of universal/absolute and symbolic/transcendental will find an unmediated essence that calls upon its own identical subjective being to summon other beings that share constitutive awareness and the similar ideals of constellation of democratic ideation toward the purpose of attaining the goals that have been longstanding in the tradition of philosophy—the one perhaps, more likely a multiplicity that engages norms as their own modality; that is the world can function in its own variety and multiplicity without adjuring to one common will—a general will that unites everyone within a totality:—it is still attainable to exist as a monadic totality, due to the transcendental quality of subjective idealism as it refers to the symbolic universality; yet the *universalizable*, unmediated particularity is predicable of its own determinations from the societal *lifeworld*. Beyond that, the *pantheistic* notion of nature that produces absolute determinations for a subject is found to be tenable; and it is argued here that these function as our very grounding (of essence) where the *lifeworld* has been anthropologically developed within its own historicity in causation with nature. The dialectic here is also a function of the attainment of concrete universality and finds its subterfuge outside of the "institutional forms" that reduce subjects to their own self-determined particularities—unable to cope with the colossal inequity in the distribution of exchange-value. While as subjectivity finds its footing in its own creation, it becomes more necessary for humankind to engage axiology within the notion that *Dasein* is not particular to our religion, race, creed, colour, or gender—it is in fact the institutional object of an entity that is in appearance of all subjects once they have discovered their humanity as it is enveloped with its ontological conditionality as a human ecology. The planetary edification of entities that dwell *outside* of their own essence are bound to resort to the "subtraction" of truth from the world; invariably resorting to acts of deception and legerdemain in order to fulfill a perceived function in the world (most notably the appropriation of surplus-value). Granted, in this post-industrial age ideas are indeed *universalizable,* and thereby subject to various forms of legitimation—yet because every subject has within their grasp the possibility for both the collective will of a "truth event" and the *potentia* for a verifiable propositionally accurate validity claim, ideas stand a greater chance of reaching those in possession of necessary faculty of cognition and *pure synthesis of the understanding* that makes for the democratic distribution of the very organic unity that made the loss of the object result in whichever acts of dissent may have ensued.

## Consciousness and Essence/the Socio-Naturalistic World

An inheritance of consciousness is without a doubt of its representations that bridge the gap between subject and object (world) or subject and relation, etc. The epistemic quality of these representations is such that they often refer to properties that determine the *ousia* (substance/essence) of a subject. It is most notable that epistemology as a whole is the gauge of what proximate value is attainable to any given subject. Granted, there is of course (and always has been) some overlap with ontology—and they are in many ways always combined in the pursuit of both knowledge and being. What is not striking about epistemology is that it responds to the posited concepts with judgments and propositions, or further concepts that allow any subject to enhance the *ego cogito's* stance amongst the represented knowledge and further constitute its being. As such, there are three variations on the theme of the purely phenomenal object-in-representation worthy of consideration here. Hegel's first were the contingent; the second were the necessary; and the third the *assertory* (truth component). Though these are quite familiar to everyone in pursuit of the context of what one's own *ego cogito/possessio phaenomenon* might be telling them—its goes further into consideration to note that the temporality of every phenomenological thought or representation may be determined symbolically by the very schematization of the self-constituting apparatus of reflective thought;—or that judgments toward concepts may always yield the self-positing *ego* that is quite revelatory in its truth. Nonetheless, it remains *contingent* whereby it is identical with the truth of a past event—constitutive of the present concept that has been posited, and effectual to the horizon that lies beyond the pure "I" into what we may call here the *transcendental social being*. If I may leap toward this synthesis of the natural world and society, the *ego* and *transcendental subjectivity*, and the phenomenal with *temporal* subjectivity—I will do so with the intention of a further elaboration. While the necessary phenomenal content does indicate a connection to the rational world that includes society and nature as it constitutes our environment and the apparatus of reason, it displays a priori the significance of the synthesis between the *transcendental ego* and the social being more concerned with proximate value in relation to representations, ideas, properties. The world presents the subject with its being as a function of the universality of collective substance due to the order of nature—yet it is of course fractioned-off into its component parts as a measure of the proximate conditions of the subject-object dichotomy. Though the object is naturally produced by the natural world, it claims subjectivity *in-itself* as the *transcendental ego* that resolves to a symbolic absolute; not to be confused with the symbolic universal and the absolute determination,—but rather a fusion of the symbolic *with* the absolute that confers knowledge upon the thinking subject and bestows upon the subject its *temporological* properties. With this comes the third species of phenomenon that is only phenomenal when the subject is still undergoing its own *noumenal* determinations—the truth phenomenon, or *assertory* being is constitutive of the social being insofar as it connects directly with the *socio-naturalistic* media that have occasion to address both the status of a subject *in-itself*, but also as it has already acted for-itself in order to bring into play its own social being. This dialectic inherently bestows upon the subject its absolute determinations (once again) and its symbolic/transcendental universality. The properties themselves are more "out there" than the subject may desire—but for this reason it does become necessary to will the components that constitute the social being; that the use-value is first so derived as a function of thought and representations; and as follows a function of doing. Where this doing comes in is where the intersubjective *lifeworld* has reappeared (integration) and the subject can once again engage in not only validity claims, but also acts of folly and enjoyment (yet not without the danger of losing substance). To which I elucidate that the *universalizable* collective substance, and universality herself expresses an extraordinary dominion over the actual order of things—presenting *being-in-itself* with what could only account for its own *transcendental constitution*, but also making way for the unmediated appearance of its subjective substance that has been produced by not only "speech acts" but also "thought acts". The bottom line of *universalizable* use-value is its content in representation—without which the "absolute knowledge" or "concrete universality" or "institutional forms" would fall into particularities that had not already engaged in the process of synthesis with the intent of creating progress in terms of representative content; but also phenomenal truth, and the motility of properties. The more movable an object, the less available it is to those that do not produce value with thought acts; therefore on one hand it is unjust for the object to become available to those that may judge it and conceive of it (having the time to do so);—but on the other hand the proximity of an object where it has no calculable use may seem a waste to many. The middle-ground is not to *commodify* being—thereby rendering objective encumbrances the sole property of those that horde quality for their interminable benefit, while making what are democratically endowed subjects suffer the loss of the object; that it has come into being from the *socio-naturalistic* world and presents quality to many that have aspirations for its use beyond what any institution could possibly engender toward the subject. Yet without the institutions, the naturalistic order will be "thrown off" into revolt—which would in turn redirect all objectivity into socio-political upheaval—so rendering acts of judgment obsolete in pursuit of representations that have appeared from the *socio-naturalistic* world into the *transcendental ego*. At this juncture, the subject chooses to go beyond the "speech act" into further action as has occurred many times throughout history and led to the greater expansion of reason.

## Totality-in-itself

Should this now become likely is a truth beyond the *in-itself*. The notion that the state is responsible for the very systemization of thought brings one to the conclusion that ultimately the *in-itself* can only be known by the *socio-naturalistic* world—that the *lifeworld* has truly been uncoupled from the system. Time—temporality as both an experience and *as* experience of the past, present and future is twofold. Most certainly it is dichotomous between the transcendental/symbolic/temporal *ego cogito* and the *socio-naturalistic* world. Yet the symbolic universality is thrown out into the social network and has ties within the *socio-naturalistic* world as a function of *Dasein*—it is our own sense of temporality and the very essence of the historicity with which we exist. Correlatively, the *socio-naturalistic* world can represent *temporal* judgements that are particular to the subject, and as such are inherently dialectical between the transcendental subject and the *socio-naturalistic* world. This dialectic is inherently negative, yet responds positively to the positing of concepts that came before the judgments of intersubjective beings that are also thrown from their own temporality *in-itself* into the sphere of the now emancipated *socio-symbolic* being. This form of being is that which has come to terms with its own independence from the conceptual realism that had initially presented it with its own universality—a state of being that had objects for consciousness that it could do nothing but consume and enjoy—beyond this particularity (unmediated) and abstract universality however, exists the world as a *totality in-itself*.

Indeed, the world is a representation of itself as a function of ontological endeavor, and not only knows subjects in-themselves; but the subjects know the world *in-itself*; and with this engage in ongoing and never-ending dialectics which shape the very environment in which we live. We know the world to be as such not only as a global society or as a totality, but also as a discrete multiplicity of global communities; and as the human endeavor that engages implicitly with nature as a function of our capacity to utilize our resources with the intention of renewing and replenishing them within the measures of the capacity we have to do so. Yet, the finitude of being is reflected also in the finitude of our resource, hence the over-simplification of the dialectical relationship between man and nature. Our rapport with what is known is exhaustive within verifiable empirical data—yet still the consequences for reason as a function of our global enterprise toward the multiplicity of co-existent societies within the *socio-naturalistic* world would go unrecognized as an ongoing crisis to the species in terms of its abilities to choose factually and collectively within the natural interest of both the transcendental subject and the *socio-naturalistic* counter-agent to rational subjectivity. Thus the agency that humankind has over the outer-world is such that it need only to comply and adjure to the properties determined by the very forms of consciousness as presented and in representation of society's intractable natural determinations. For the *pantheists* were certainly not wrong within the realization that human endeavor is determined by the natural causes of the universe—and thus worthy of comparison to divinity, just as humankind's exertions had affected external powers formed from the constellations and collectivity of free acts of the will, so are the elements dialectically bound to our noumenal freedoms and ontological presuppositions.

The tell-tale of lightening never striking in the same place twice is to be constituted as a measure of assurance that the acts of subjects in collectivity have for their objects what dwells aboard something temporally *formed* of a greater causal nexus than any subject might imagine is to be discounted here. In fact, the very manner in which we assemble as a species has a greater degree of significance upon causality in-itself—the very notion that human activity is not only predicable of the concrete universality that provides us with our being, but also the idea that being itself is a predicate to the causality that determines the very outcome of *Being*. With this knowledge in mind, most certainly the nature of our actions is brought to task, but also the very origin of our agency that precipitates our actions. These fall once again to the necessary auspices of "absolute determinations" that only *become* of the constitutive nature of our rational subjectivity; but also how those very actions determine the *socio-naturalistic* world that determines our reflexive identity. Here, the activity that moves the subjects' causal identity inherently results in violations of their natural agency where concerns the *apriority* of the dialectic between subject and nature. The elements themselves respond within a societal manifold that represents the objective world as a trans-subjective whole. Thereby, objectivity (the object) is posited for a subject that then has within agency a connection to "Mother Earth"—as not only a thinking "I"—but also a doing "I" that must regard human activity as something that warrants ethical conduct that can never deprive the life-producing system (genus) of its accumulation of resource; this is self-evident and functional to every subject as a constitutive principle in the preservation of substance, being, and properties. The properties themselves are representations that emerge out of both the temporality of the *transcendental ego*, but also the *world-in-itself* that has already recognized within the subject their own rational freedom and identity. This identity is the *noumenally* produced "absolute subjectivity" that emerges from the transparency of the objective world's technological and cultural presence that advances rational freedom and engages in dialectic with the subject. The subject then has within its own capacity the *potentia* to will and create its own *phenomenality* which will forge the path toward an understanding of greater determinations than known previously. *Sui generis*, the subject then finds its individuation from the mediated essence that had before determined its facticity and causal necessity—not the absolute that is inherent of the dichotomous subject-object that has lost its object to the world-*in-itself*. *Quid facti*, the subject then receives its absolute determination from the *socio-naturalistic* world.

Insofar as consciousness (subjectivity) produces the *noumenal* identity in an act of projection absolutely as it engages from the transcendent self, so does the absolute determination recognize the identity of the subject not only as a concept *in-itself* (the subject-object), but also as a *phenomenal* being. This being is epistemologically *and* ontologically contingent—yet the very products of the conceptual reasoning of subjectivity itself. It follows from this that temporality is in question where concerns the content of the objective knowledge; but not in the form of which knowledge is experienced as an object. This object *knows* the subjective of its own determination *in-itself* as a function of the aprioristic *temporality* of the concepts that led to the positing of the *noumenal* identity at the forefront of conscious observation of the possibility of the *phenomenal* event. Without question, this would never render the subject's representations as an obfuscation of the *matter at hand*; but in fact would lead to a greater self-knowledge as subjectivity engages in the act of reflection upon the epistemic validity of the objective claims. These though, also purport to immerse the subject into "negative dialectics" with the conceptual self-identical object as it has managed to come into its status of judgment not only from the *noumenal* assertions of the subject—but also its other. This *Other* is a function of the absolute determinability of the world-*in-itself* as it resolves to the immediacy of being of all relational *temporological* subjects—yet at the same time is substantive of what might be a symbolic Being or guardian. The very nature of the other may be the other of antagonism, yet within the altruism of this universality produced, subjective experience of the transcendentally constituted *socio-naturalistic* world, can have its place both as a function of the very nature of rationality herself, but also as a function of the absolutes that have emerged out of the subject's use-value as it exists transcendentally in philosophic artefacts and temporal contingencies that have already been posited as a function of the subject's reflection.

The functionalism of this positing not only depends upon the *habitualities* of the agent/actor, but very much upon the ordering by which thoughts are produced. "The produced mind"—one that "sends" or "transmits" content from subject to object, or intersubjectively—is not only constitutive of substance on the individual; but also substance of the collective as the universal consciousness—everything *universalizable* of the "produced mind" and everything pro-generative of the collective minds is assembled into an "organic unity". The commonplace notion of which is a *symbolic* democracy—one whereby all agents/actions fulfill their duty to produce substance either through acts of the will, or by way of adding use-value to the production of goods and services that do not infringe upon the use-value of others. Any such democracy would of course be considered Utopian, and would rule out the disproportionate concentration of wealth that ultimately leads to oppression and politicization of the "death drive" and the *id*. Yet there is still room for the preservation of institutional jurisdiction of the juridical and the legislative—only without a hegemonic signification intervening in the pursuit of the absolutes that are a direct result of being that has been constituted by its socialization into the correlates that become what are presented by certain societal activities. The reason that being had been *sociated* into regulative over-arching administrative bodies, is not the same reason that *noumenal* freedom should be emancipated fully from centralized power. However, the existence of a regulative body is in order so as to preserve an objective world as it conjoins the transcendental subject with the *socio-naturalistic* world.

The duties and responsibilities of *noumenal* and *phenomenal* being must resort to collective aspirations from the standpoint of democratically realized freedoms, but also identification with the regulative body as it deals with the preservation of the very source of planetary life. Exchange-value in-itself can only provide the means by which an objective world can disperse its acknowledgement of the correlative use-value of thinking *and* doing subjects. As they relate in inter-subjectivity, there is "high demand" for the production of ideas—those that should not only fall into the hands of exchange-value—but must also be collectively and democratically assigned *to* the subjects themselves. This Utopian democracy would enhance the being of the collective, so as to put an end to the mere process of verification. However, modes of being that make material use-value in the course of the improvement of the conditions of the *shared lifeworld* will of course be compensated. Technology will advance in proportion with the distribution of human ideas and productivity. The minds that reflect upon a diminished objectivity and a loss of reason must practice *noumenal* freedom and thereby bring about the return to the naturalistic status of being that revolves around democracy, representation, and ideas. The network produced by the regulatory body is of course not responsible for subjective representation—the subject must adjure to naturalistic thoughts that are only *monadologically* normative in their impetus—but as it stands the individuated transcendental subject becomes collectively restructured in self-determination—aptly in possession of properties as a function of their "genus"—their *absolute determinability*.

Thereby, the *noumenal* representations become reflexive and predicable of *universalizable* correlative absolute knowledge. As a function of this, ideas are assembled into a constellation whereby they will be distributed in accordance with the "productive minds"—not only produced from "emancipatory structures" themselves, but from acts of restructured *noumenal* freedom that results from an ethical relation to the symbolized dialectical self-concept. As such, the *socio-naturalistic* world will have a constitutive representational presence within the mind of the subject—both epistemologically, and as an object of content ontologically that will allow for the natural progression of developmental being that is in pursuit of the ever elusive "absolute knowing".

## Subjectivity and the Transcendental Identical

The notion that subjectivity presents one with a particular truth is one that concerns itself with the world of appearances. Appearances themselves approach subjectivity before its experience of an objectively constituted essence—therefore they are integral to the way by which any subject understands society and the world in general. What is most striking regarding these appearances is the fact that not only do they unmask this by which a subject may be deceived, but also the very magnitude of one's contingent temporal being were concerns the events, memories and relativity to the historicity of the body politic as a fully integrated subject. What subjectivity takes away from its encounters with appearances is not the very speculation of what subjective truth needs to be "tweaked" in order to arrive at a greater, more positive, universal truth that will allow for the essence to be abstracted without the consistent posits of the confused loyalty to the notion that "2+2=4"—that one's subjective truth is subject only to oral verification, thereby rendering the "validity claims" of the subject hospitable to other gents that have an interest in the predicates that are at stake in the validity claim. This all comes down to the agency of the subject to negate the appearances—as painful as it may be to do so; within the pursuit of attainment of the *transcendental identical*. This is a correlative of objective intelligible being that goes hand-in-hand with the absolute determination—as it is self-positing of objective claims that prove to be more grounding of essence, and less disavowed by the proximate ontological validity claim that generates the self-mediation of essence that can only arrive at disasters for the subject. These "panic attacks" are a result of the very ruminations that dwell upon "unmasked" conclusions that require immediate clarification—but to the subject do not support reflection or may be causal of "episodic *epiphanical* thoughts"—simply rendering a long-term status of dialectical rationality within a subject—a status readily diagnosable and self-evident as the root and cause of erratic and irrational behavior. This function of objective truth is the very source of the *sublation* of the transcendent, representational truth that can only come from a democratic system that recognizes the necessity of not only collective universal laws,—but how the notion of objective being within the normative status of a rationally collected body politic would also lead to norms of subjective truth that do not "jump to conclusions" or "act out" in opposition of a perceived "wronging". It is not that the wronging has not occurred necessarily—it is that reflective verification of what legerdemain has taken place in order to enable the opponents of a democratically distributed objective truth (that have not been taken to task for swallowing the consciousness of the subject only in pursuit of understanding) is to arrive at the truths that will become predicable of the justly distributed properties. These properties are attributes of genus and the *socio-naturalistic* world—it is only what becomes available to the high-minded, the understanding, and the ethical. The substance that is thus produced, is one that is divided only between subject and object, *lifeworld* and system, *transcendental ego* and *socio-naturalistic* world. With this, the multiplicity of the body politic is found within the ontological *constituens*—affirmed in their own subjectivity by the rights of freedoms offered by an "institutional order". This order has been arrived at by way of a "participatory democracy" and institutes the organization of substance attained by reason, and by acts of doing that do not inflict harm upon other subjects/actors/agents. This is the only way to insure a *universalizable* civil system that does not place intersubjectivity into unity a priori, induce conflict, and perpetuate acts of war and violence in order to facilitate some sense of false security of the radical insurgency of the disobedient. Substance is produced by both the cosmological conditions that enable life to exist, but also by the thinking beings that employ their justly acquired "rational right" to have an existence while acting freely from their own identical truth. The moment this truth is identical to a contingency of falsehood and deception, the objective "institutional order" has finished the subject— in that reliance upon observable facts was put in place of verifiable empirical knowledge which requires the subject to depart from rational wisdom (philosophy) and engage in an investigation of the subjects that may be in violation of an "ethical agreement"—the universally binding status of an agreement not to deceive a subject—thereby depriving the subject of substance and fully in violation of their civil rights. The endeavor to clarify(truth) is a never-ending project that is determinable upon both the resiliency of the subject, and the breadth and scope of the *violative* act that has taken place, perpetual, indefatigable, obsessive rumination will never solve the dilemma—for which *will* is the institution of the *transcendental identical*. This is a mode of self-assurance that is objectively satisfactory toward the attainment of rationally produced subjective truths. As the identical is inherently contingent by its very nature—this relies upon everything that is *universalizable* of objective truth—yet everything that has been produced through the objective world as the *natural* object-in-representation of a subject; such that they are so constituted by their own rationally produced beliefs and valuations. So produced, would be a negotiable salient constitutive substance that could only increase collective value—subsequently enhancing the valuations of society and the objective world. Where the objects depart from the subject to become a thing within the constellations of collectively *universalizable* objects, in relations as a *phenomenon* through universal freedom, so giving possibility to the very attainment of rational subjectivity. Given the necessity of abstractly viable choices to the ethically produced collective substance, this will be achieved concomitantly to the presence of the "absolute knowing" of the *transcendental identical*.

## On Being and the Lifeworld

Being propagates awareness both as a formation of the *in-itself* of proximate substance—but also as a formation of its Otherness. Certain conclusions that have been arrived at where concerns the identity of determinate entities and representations lead themselves to the very notion of the essence of being itself, and in terms of its quantity. The quantity is determined by access to the objective world—arguably only possible though the very *process* of thought and thinking—which leads to greater conclusions regarding the origin of our very rationality and all of its encumbrances and properties. The quality, however is determined by relations to objects that possess a synthetic property that has been made available to the consumption of the subject. It is for this very reason that normativity and meta-ethics are widely discussed amongst philosophers and those concerned with distributive justice. Yet what lies at the very core of the meta-ethic, is this notion that a synthetic property may be mine through simple acts of the subjective will—that my very thinking is in direct contact with the notions of the will give a *concrete universality* to my very being. I will never be "a fish on dry land", I will in fact be constituted by the very substance of collective being. This sense of community and belonging is inherent of the notion of what one has for the societal representations that bridge the gap between self and symbolically constituted transcendental Being.

The *lifeworld* benefits more from a direct correlation between social being and cultural identification however, and this is structured most saliently throughout the symmetry of the technological apparatus. Given this inherent dialectical relation between subject and apparatus, it is found that the schematization of consciousness gives way to its image quality to the actuality of objective reality and the psychophysical tangibility of corporeal objects. Yet this brief flirtation with mere physicality will never be able to account for thousands of years in the development of instrumental reason that has allowed us to fashion these tools that allow for consumption of cultural objects—surely there are moments where reason gives way to material reality.

This self-evident truth proves to be a *deus ex machina* as the power that we have ascribed to technology,—where a *de facto* actuality is deified and responsible for the production of thoughts that otherwise would have fallen to the spirits—ideas that without these machines would never find concretion within our conscious minds. Yet how this affects the *transcendental* subject, is that it posits collectively what will only allow for *apriority* of the intelligible realm where naturalistic ideation has *found* its own singularity amidst the plurality of universal representations. From the side of *transcendental* identity and simplicity, these have all been collected into the collective identity of the subject—allowing for the subterfuge from a multiplicity of subjective wills all in pursuit of the same object and utterly divorced from their own subjective determinations. Those of which will always fall before any rational subject's judgments as their truth—allowing for the subsequent *symbolic collectivity* to act as a constitutive representation for all rational agents of collective subjectivity. As the world of appearances fuses with *transcendental subjectivity*, the *ego* merges with the world *in-itself* as a function or resultant of free-acts of the will; so the horizon upon which all objectively known collective facts are being established to further the causal relationship between subjectivity and the rational collective identity will reflexively coordinate an organization of free acting subjects as collectives that find both singularity and a collective purpose in pursuit of most determinate natural objectives that come under the scrutiny of the "popular spirits" as it were—not rulers but the very initiators of rationally causal action. The very activity of which secures the substance of all individuated subjects for the collective is grounding the essence of all being that is in pursuit of the democratically established course of action that resolves to civil acts of the emancipated subjective collectivity—motile forces in pursuit of the self-actualization of the non-collectively represented. As the objective world is apportioned to two essential sides in a dichotomous relation between subjectivity and a horizon of socio-historical reality, symbolic universality imposes its dialectical potency through a negation of the particular mediation of opposing factions, and ontological discourse distantiates the self-identical from its collective totality. Interobjective forces as "actors" and "doers" may now simply posit as ontological beings in pursuit of the self-concept to instantiate the dialectical impetus that reifies what objectivity may be as an essence.

# Chapter Two

## *The* Primacy *of* Metaphysical *Forms*

The primary focus of metaphysics has always been upon the nature of the human organism as a being that relates to other entities "in thought"—that is a function of the very consciousness that produces self-knowledge, the knowledge of the objective world, and the epistemological understanding, that allows one to relate one's subjectivity to the objective world. The nature of one's subjectivity is of course always in question, as it allows for the assertion or judgment of which properties are of the object's own substance, and which ones come from the objective world in the form of givens, or are appropriated by the subject, and taken to be of the self—its properties.

A question arises concerning this whereby a subject is faced with an all-encompassing Other or *super-ego* that seems only determinate upon the notion of subjectivity being deprived of objective natural properties. The clue to this resides within what has not yet founded or anticipated a dialectical position in the particularly reified *world-in-itself*—either as a self-positing Object or as a *noumenal* certainty. In other words, the subject is not yet a *being-for-self*—which is the only way to attain the normative status of subjective agency *to* the objective world. Without any claim to selfhood, the subject will merely be held in a recycle bin of property appropriation of another being in pursuit of its own interests. This is not to negate the inherent use-value of collectivity as a function of normative agency towards the attainment of communal goals; but rather a statement that portends to add to the equation the stipulation that a subject's voice is only heard when it finds its own totality as the transmission of collective agency to the individual in pursuit of actuality—the motif of an ontologically proximate entity such as *Dasein* (in its contingent sense) that may determine the cause of action of any subject in pursuit of active determinations.

These may defy the "absolute determination" to the degree that no actuality were more proximate to the subject upon said determinations than the representations of apodictic qualities *in abstracto* of the essence or *essential qualities* of the subject;—as such the subject continues to will upon the objective world from its own existential possibilities so as to find dialectical agency within the synthesis of society and nature. The subsequent universality that will result will be both an abstraction of *positive universality* or *concrete universality* as well as a universalization of all *ontical* components—now making the predicate the objective world. The result of this, is of course well within the domain of ethics, as *Dasein* must find its path to the ethical substance as an ontological basis for "pure concepts of the understanding", but also a basis for action that never destroys the environment in which *Dasein* has found itself—both as a contingent *alethic* modality, and as a *deontic* normativity.

One can only hope that the "institutional order" has found the subject well within its deontic normativity where concerns collective beliefs that are concerned with the well-being of the *socio-naturalistic* world, and not its ontological, and thereby ontic *diremption*. The more *Dasein* pulls apart the objective world of its collective substance that has been modally distributed based upon *noumenal* activity and institutional validity claims, the more possibility for destruction of the geopolitical substrate to the world—given that the world-*in-itself* is both a totality of global universality, and a *pure concept of the understanding* that has Reason as its ultimate authority. While knowing the subject as a *being-in-itself*, one can assert the necessity of the absolute determination's place amidst the rationally constructed reason of any given subject that has participated in the willing of an emancipation from the constraints of use-value appropriation where concerns the maintenance of the collective substance that had been achieved by way of participating democratic speech acts and validity claims toward the establishment of a Utopian state. Normativity is only possible given "equanimity"—a dialectical subject first pursues its free will in order to arrive at the safe haven of determinations that then project toward a more functional ordering of the affairs that make for "free thinking", self-positing objectivity, and responsibility for how not only material goods are produced, but more importantly the minds associated with them. These new fruits of mental labours are not lost, and will in fact develop reason so as to evict falsity from its own corruption—thereby instantiating truth as the key component of Being itself.

The concept and all content associated with it are indeed conceptual content, yet the concept that is in absence of any applicable subjective judgment *is* the object and essence or substance (the *ousia* of a subject). When one encounters this objective judgment that acts as a determination of the essence/substance of subjectivity itself, one is brought closer toward the Lacanian notion of the "big other". However, one still recognizes the self-positing objectivity of life *in* a reflecting consciousness that has its own determinations both as active judgments and as objective contingencies. This leads us closer to the *notionality* of substance-as-subject being composed of both its *being-for-self* and being-for-another a priori. The *in-itself* of the subject is reflected from itself into the Other as a function of duty or obligation according to Kant and Hegel—where the reciprocal effect of a return to self and the self-positing objectivity is instituted mostly as a function of dialectical positionality. As the subject pursues the matter further, it will however be found that other contingencies will be in pursuit of the substance that the subject now has in being—that *being* may have been constituted in "bad faith" and thereby subject to the judgments of a constellation of *self-same* others. It is for this reason that the substantive essence of being is thought to have "synthetic value". What this means, is that the grounding of essence is not only determined by the actuality of the subject, but also by its contingent counter-positionality. That they may all constitute a whole being is a *non sequitur*—the community of collective substance has been breached by a *being-for-self* that has certain fictitious claims toward the grounding of the essence of otherness—and the very foundations upon which the truth may lie. This continually abstract criminality is an ontological phenomenon that seeks to mislead rational agency "right out the door"—eclipsing "synthetic value" for the subject and appropriating its use-value for its own purposes. Any objective value faced with this legerdemain is well within its ethical substance to pursue the down-fall of these particular contingencies that threaten to universalize "bad faith"—making it commonplace and acceptable to all in pursuit of the reification of the ethical substance *for* synthetic value.

Property is produced by both mental and physical labours. It is, in fact, devoid of any process of monetization outside if its constitutive existentiality in the pursuit of the grounding of essence, and the substantive acts that result from its proximity to a subject. What follows from this, is the ordering of both thoughts and events into what may be further constitutive of a "participatory democracy". The outcome would be representational of an actuality of subjects—all respective of their universality and absolute identity into what may be indicative of a "truth absolute". As the subject has received its essence through its resolution of the incompatibility with the Other as a function of its duty to the unifying substance, the self-positing objectivity is in an act of synthesis with the *transcendental constitution*, as it creates (brings into being) the absolute determination that—given the *temporological* concept or judgment whereby the subject has been engaged—will yield the "truth absolute". This truth is the correlative *de facto* identity of the subject as it merges with its absolute identity—the two concur, and as such constitute the essence and substance of the subject. Both essence and substance are once again reunited as the "institutional order" has been uncoupled from the *lifeworld*—where the subject finds its metaphysical identity constituted into it and becomes a predicate for all others; *beings-for-self* that have the necessary conditions to identify the call-of-conscience that engenders being—that the grounding of essence for the subject does not ethically align with the principles concerned with the proximity of "synthetic value". As the subject has normatively met with personal or collective duty and obligation, it is found to be for both the statesman and the revolutionary perfectly ethical that the subject has substance and essence with which to engage in all *performative* activities associated with concrete universality. The subject now has its means to employ "synthetic value" for the good of collectivity, and "participatory democracy".

## Ego, Representations and Appearances

The fact that consciousness is in possession of an *ego* is oftentimes contingent to the representations and appearances that arrive at the mind of the subject. A consciousness is not inherently in possession of it is own *ego* until the content has been judged and is submerged in the actions of a subject's necessary approach to thinking both as an instrument of the faculty of cognition, but also as a doing that places concepts within the subject's grasp. The manner by which these concepts become attainable is not only through transmission from another source, but also as a function of the subject's monadic *ego*. As once representations confirm the *transcendency* of the subject, concepts begin to form and constitute the *ego* of the subject. In other words, the reflexive act of thinking is not only what arises from what has been posited, but also what *appears* to the subject—this which ultimately constitutes the *ego* of the subject. That this would become possible given the dynamics of any previous restructuring of the essence of the subject indicates that *temporological* considerations are also *monadological*—the subject has not failed to adjure to their own notions about what constitutes a Self by any stretch of the imagination. In fact, subjectivity itself has now become ensconced with the very idea of its own being as a *transcendental identical* before the copula of the objective world has intervened as a causal determination. At any length, the subject grasps existence as a function of the very self-determinateness that bestows any *ego* consciousness upon the subject a priori. It is only that the very phantasm of *transcendency* has thrown being from itself into the objective world—fostering the *apophantic* representations upon the subject in its pursuit of Self—not only that *being-for-self* has yet arisen—but that the intentionality has been established in connection with an object that has not yet become an object for consciousness:—in fact, it is yet to be determined in this case whether or not the object will ever become proximate to the subject, as it also has within its mind a *post-industrial* collectivity that constitutes transcendental being from the standpoint of absolute identity, while *obviating* and obfuscating the epistemic contents and composition of the rational identity of subjectivity. Such as it is, the unlimited *transcendency* of a dialectical subject posits the world as a function of its own transcendental *ego*, yet only as existence itself has been posited and has become known to the collectivity as a *being-in-itself*. The trajectory of dualistic positing establishes the subject both as a living and thinking being, which means the rational identity has been "caught". It is held "accountable" for having expressed modes of freedom that have contravened the directives of the established order—not yet aware of the "institutional order" which has given it its own powers of mediation where concerns the essence of subjectivity.

Hereto, where Being pursues emancipation from mediating authorities concerning essence, certainly representational facets of the "institutional order"—or a democratically mediating collective of contributing entities toward community substance—would be found to be well within the attainable goals of social existentiality. As entities are ontologically produced by the world, the genus and universality *of* Being has the potential to fill the primordial substrate of every living sapient creature with an abstract essence—one that becomes self-determined to posit outside of the *monadological* confines of harmonistic existence into the collective, constitutive elements of the objective world. While one can subsist in short order bereft of an object, it is most certainly that this division will only lead to more upheaval and dispute. Any subject is reflexively anointed with a necessary and thoughtful connection to Objective Being. Precisely where this falls apart is where the unconditioned, transcendental subject has achieved the status of having the world-*in-itself* for an object. This is not the goal of every post-modern actor in pursuit of emancipation from apodictic or problematic judgments, and releases the subject from an objective world *as* predicate as it becomes abundantly clear that there is still a division that has left the subject "in the lurch"—that is, without one's own objectivity—the ontologically allowable process of being and *performative* aspects of becoming falling sway to nothingness. As such, there would be no truth upon which the subject could lose any claims, nor would the judging of conceptual content become available. One looks directly to the concept, and its representational qualities to the monad as equally valid of what allows for a deterministic positing of the world as conceptually reflexive of the understanding—that we are here and have much to do in order to attain an absolute determination of collective subjective existentiality.

    In and throughout the pursuit of the subject's *noumenal* freedom, to become at the unification of transcendental cause and the a priori projection of the subject outside of its own moral agency—the phenomenal realm is borne, precisely where the subject finds moral agency that adjures to universal laws that perpetuate the collective identity of substance so as to allow for ethical acts to take place—both as a function of the ontological identity of the subject, but most importantly as a function of externality and the ability to engage in *performative* acts that are for the common interests of all participatory agents and subjects vulnerable to the causality of the collective ontology common to the rational whole. The currency of rational content is approximated by a dialectic between the reason of objectivity and a constellation of socio-symbolically intertwined city-states.

## The Transcendentally Knowable 'is'

This motif of consciousness lends itself to the currency of the transcendental unity of apperception between the symbolic universality and the determinations reflexive of reflective thinking—yielding an output to commensurate the contemporaneous *aprioristic* perceptions of knowable facts. The transcendentally knowable "is"—the copula that presents any subject with its object—also promotes the symbolic universal and the knowable other of consciousness a priori. For instance, the subject may ruminate upon certain facts that refer to the conditions of the weather, or cause of the mood, without ever encountering *the* very cause of the determinations that present rational and well-actioned agency with its presuppositions. This is precisely where the *pantheistic* phenomenal identity is encountered, as an absolute determination of the *socio-naturalistic* world. However, one can only measure the truth of the proposition based upon experience—most notably the representation is rational and based in reality. One can only expect that other truths concerning identity are also delimited by the same instruments of nature—often resulting in the collective panic of all citizens affected—but these calamities require the objectifying element of consciousness in order to precipitate action that justifies the needs of the parties that have been hit.

Collectivity itself is a pure function of the *in-itself* of substance of the community, and without the necessary care and concern for collective well-being, no longer will the being of the individual promote the autonomy that creates the necessary functionality that is able to become resilient of nature's potency. Herewith, called to arms are all the faces of good that engage in participatory democracy within the intention that the collective will be preserved as a function of the objective world. There is nothing more primitive than the expectation that "everything will be alright"—yet most certainly causality at times may indicate that this is a mere "pipe dream", and in fact events that will follow are to jeopardize the existence of not only one human being but many. This is precisely the moment where the *transcendental identical* comes into play as an objective for established truth, yet where pragmatic measures are instituted. In which case the will of any non-rational agent would of course act as a deterrent to the free agency of another subject in pursuit of its own necessity.

Here is where the gents must engage in binding agreements with the established order—the catalyst group that for collective agency is an interior ontological measure that creates the *necessary conditions of action* that will resolve all intersubjective *lifeworld* disputes that may jeopardize the outcome for the collective. The agency of the individual is never given toward the necessity of an outcome of economic *supervenience,* yet is solely interested in the benefit of their own rational agency toward the survival of the collective substance—as the objective world is correlative to the subjective activity that stimulates the "preponderance of the object"—ultimately responsible for all programmed activity that adjures to the framework of pure dialectical reasoning. Such reasoning is this that produces both spirit and matter that fuel our species with the products necessary for our collective survival—none of which have been produced by the mere pursuit of economic gain, but will most certainly assure the participatory democracy of its subsequent prosperity as it identifies with the collective benefits that have been realized in the preservation of all natural substance. The generality of the concept is revealed when what is thought—the conceptual content that has already been represented—also expresses socio-cultural determinations and the objective world. That these are, in fact, presuppositions about the nature of the world that the subject has as "what ifs" or this is "the way of the world"—

then the represented society is replete with objective being as it precedes the activity of subjective idealism.

The *meta-logical* rudiment of this is that the concepts that led to the very expression of the social being of the subject as an object already "out there" indicates the inherent transcendental unity of subject and object within the dynamics of dialectical reasoning. Subjectivity stands only to gain in its acts of the free will—as it adjures to the objective reality as it extends constitutively throughout being;—and in fact produces the experience of the subject where concerns the transmission of the *direct* immediate self as it relates to the inner world, and the *indirect* object that has produced a content for another subject at the other end of the ontological playing field. Two or more concepts and locality-specific proximities may in fact be the impetus for what presents the objective reality taking the form of all socio-cultural activity corresponding with the "shared" event—which ultimately produces the *progressus* to the new status of the subject as it embraces the object that has come about before the societal collective. By no means is this the manner by which essence is mediated institutionally, but the very elements that constitutively correlate the positing of the particular non-identical reasoning that returns the phenomenon to its former proximity—thereby lending itself to the synthesis between subject and object that may produce rational agency. Without this movement of conceptual content, the content of the socio-cultural, industrially represented world will be lost to instances of poor behavior and bad conduct—nullifying the *potentia* of the subject to engage in productive activity that synthesizes only subject and object, but objective content with subjectivity—based upon the *noumenal* and phenomenal posits in a dialectic with the objectively represented judgments; as these socially already reified forms are the constitutively productive elements of consciousness that may yield further activity, the negative component of the judgment is to be dialectically reduced as a function of its *being-in-and-for-itself*. This reduction becomes constitutive of the subject both logically and dialectically—juxtaposing the further conceptual content upon the subject who is now "pulling the strings" and fully able to engage in free acts of the will, or ethically productive conceptualization—proceeding toward a common goal for the subjects as for the collective. The "emergence" is in fact—under this conditionality—enhanced and enabled further toward aspects of the unified consciousness to embark upon greater, more enticing ventures toward a unification and synthesis of subject and objective conceptual content. As such, the limits upon free will are only those of which is the way to proceed toward an emancipatory unifying synthesis that allows the objective to continue to produce objects with content—that have no identity in the subject but their own. This self-identical object is productive of the historicity of socio-cultural content, but also promulgates justificatory reason to the collectives all engaged by the very same concepts that led to the represented world to begin with, and ultimately will be responsible for the social identity of the subject.

## Subjective Identity and the Self-Positing Objectivity

What is found to be the subject's identity as it comes from the understanding of the other tends to conflict with the Hegelian notion of a self-positing objectivity. That it may be the other is only revealed by the reflection upon an outer particularity that is fastened by a proximate *phenomenality* that judges in accordance with the a priori status of the subject appearing before consciousness. This apparent otherness may in all actuality be a contingent particularity of a self-positing objectivity as it seems to be apportioned to both sides of interiority—the subjective side of the other—and the objective side of the self resides as a moment of what may very well be a synthesis of the *transcendental identical* with the subjective understanding of a *noumenal* otherness; in fact the particularity of the care and concern of something such as a guardian or *syphogrant*. A platonic motif here indicates that it is in fact a contingency of the Other, and that one should abandon Fichte's notion that subjectivity posits itself in connection with the *apriority* of the understanding. What may in fact flirt more with the rationality of the self-positing identical phenomenon is the inter-subjectivity of the collective understanding. Granted, one will always respond to this mode of reflection with careful judgments—as only reflective judgments that may yield an output of rational agency are to become of these well-structured, constitutive judgments that pose no threat upon the Self, are neither coercive nor antagonistic, and seem to emerge from a source that is very becoming of the ethical substance;—without which one would be lost in pursuit of rational agency and the commensuration of identity as a product of the determinations that form causal relations between the objective understanding, and the *phenomenality* of reflexive subjective identity.

Without these two poles working closely to insure that the residue of every ontological undertaking never does yield falsity and the very legerdemain that leads to self-destruction, every subject welcomes this dialectic as a function of the synthetic a priori:—the judgments that advance knowledge to the subject and propose to shape the consciousness of the individual as a member of the social collective. By way of this, substance preserved for the subject is an advance of the *progressus* of ideas toward the modification of being so as to preserve the "sources of the self" beyond their perishable origins, into what may in fact become the edification of an essence that has no contact with the individual,—yet is in fact the production of an ontical subject that is creating something for consumption;—not that *onticality* may produce essence itself, but that the exertion of the intellect in the production of any work of substance will have the property of an essence that is to be found universally, and within the capacity of the *lifeworld* of a subject's abstract capabilities. This One, or collective objectivity is both responsible for the perception of the particularity of the understanding of otherness, as well as for the self-positing objectivity that results from intersubjective reflection in connection with this otherness as objective identity. What once again comes to the fore as a *meta-logical* function of consciousness is the totality of the *world-in-itself*, from the temporal locus of what understands subjectivity as a free and ongoing act of the produced mind: the absolute is brought into being as a methodological means toward attaining the end result of a constitutive process of thinking—found most notably with the *noumenal* projections that know collective identity, and on a much larger scale, the objective world as a forum for the assembly of representations and ideas. Without this outlet for the *res cogitans*, for the *ego*, the "I think", humankind would fade from existence, no longer employing reason in pursuit of man's capacity to undertake the propositions into forward movements of rationalistic endeavor—those that gave rise to the collective substance that birthed modernity at the same time it did anguish. The subject is prone to the anguish only when bereft of its responsibility to the object, as this is what gives it the rational agency that is needed to preserve our species as a whole—this is what makes subjectivity the particular otherness, and the phenomenal identity that will perpetuate the "synthetic value" associated with the ethical status of all agents respectful of the heteronomy that is advanced before subjectivity is granted its autonomy and collective responsibility. For the socio-institutional forms are givens that reflect the cultural and intellectual output of its citizens; and thereby are remarkably accountable for the participation in what serves cultural collectivity with the common good. This would of course be that the rational constraints upon the subject once having achieved the dual *phenomenality* of the identical otherness of its own phenomenon as a function of the understanding of the objective world, and its own actively positing *phenomenality* of both *contemporaneity* of thought and contingency have been collectively assembled into a totality of autonomous subjectivity. Here the subject may take empirical measures to preserve and protect themselves such as would be meritorious of a participatory democracy.

## Emancipatory Measures

The entire process of emancipation from the antagonistic/coercive nature of philosophy under established power may begin again once this ideal of justificatory representation has run into an empirical obstacle—yet the process remains the same. The subject cannot be responsible for its own being or the being of others when left entirely without free choice and free will. Furthermore, being-for-another that results ontologically on a much wider scale gives rise to greater concepts that have more potency and staying power; products of thought and rational *phenomenality* giving and adding value to the shared *lifeworld* of all participants of the collective consciousness. As such, it will be more likely for subjects and objects to attain unification, bridging the intelligible gap between individual and objective world that exists for some. Existence itself is pure to the nature of human understanding, and for this reason one consistently looks to the object for its origin and intentionality. What gives meaning to the *energeia* produced is the facticity that becomes apparent for the subjects in pursuit of identity. This makes the truth more a function of the temporal social determinations of the subject from both the side of intelligible being *and* empirical being. Where the value is recognized as a function of the intelligibility of a subject, is where the subject will find the availability of positive affirmations that will ultimately yield constitutive reflective judgments; then the negations are formed in connection with an infringement upon the liberty of the subject—which becomes necessary where the subject has not yet attained its status to the collective substance as an equal citizen. The usual reason for this is that the produced mind is not yet visible, and may be in bad conscience. The only way to turn this around is to affix heteronomy as an advance to the subjects and to rely upon the system of education to sort it out. Great lengths are needed to preserve all minds of the collective, and they need to be fed equal amounts of knowledge with their entertainment.

## The Totalization of the Ego

The *totalization* of the ego is a de facto *totalization* of a rational identity where concerns *all* ontological identity based signifiers of a socio-cultural absolute. These figure into the questions concerning, "What am I?" or "What is there?", and have profound consequents where concern both the concept and its Object. The conception itself is well put forward as an ongoing, active positing of the ego and summarizes the dialectical agency of a subject within all temporal and logical boundaries. In essence, the positing of the ego is what *becomes the dialectical identity of the subject* insofar as subjectivity is itself concerned. Where this falls short of socio-symbolization, is where there is no further pursuit of essence to be had outside of the opprobrious and over-arching consequential otherness that may ensue. Yet most certainly, this motif of active contemplation is responsible for a birthing process of ideas as of agency. The synthesis between subject and object is quickly recognized in the identity-based signifier—as it designates all relational identity within the given temporal conditions of the subject within the intentionality of the collective substance. That this may come from the socio-cultural absolute is without question, as it indicates to the plurality of intersubjective beings their own collective identity in the preservation of substance for the subjects that find themselves within the understanding of which *monadological* objective world has engaged their faculty of cognition. To cogitate objects whilst enraptured in other tasks always presents an *aporia* to consciousness, yet it is of course here noted that the dialectical reasoning is always at work, and what in fact preserves all objects of labour—not only those that result in fiat recognition—but also those that yield the production of the human intellect. Power seldom comprises this act of subjective will, unless it is in *violation* of the ontic/primordial being of the Other as it is found within the ideality of the "institutional order". The dialectical constraints upon the posits of the subject are nominally founded outer restrictions upon behavior—these which ultimately are borne alongside the impetus to pursue the *totalization* of the ego by way of the identity's signifier. The language is inherent of identity and meaning, and meaning is inherent of identity and language, so the signifier that proposes a concept that ties to the socio-cultural absolute may also surprise subjectivity with a determination that is not prohibitive of the (any) thinking subject—albeit a limitation upon collectivity—yet the copula to further representations; some of which may be philosophical artefacts, yet some of which possess the key elements of the preponderance of rational agency in pursuit of objectivity and reflection.

This does indeed allow subjectivity to glimpse into the *monadalogically* objective being of the Other—yet preserves the *temporological* being of the monadic subject in its being as it has no contemporaneous referent with which to follow the socio-cultural absolute. The Other will only know this absolute as a collective identity of the totalized *ego,* and thereby may never come into contact with the object that has been produced—yet then again the subject may. When coming into contact with this object, the content will remain within the Object, yet will have been somehow transformed by subjectivity as it *faces* the socio-cultural absolute. It is by these very means that rational objects are borne into the world—produced by human intellects—yet as they connect within the mind the socio-cultural absolute, the manner by which this absolute has come into being, is by way of its transmission from the unconditioned absolute determination that has fallen into a synthetic unity with natural governing principles of universality and collectivity.

## Phenomenality

*Phenomenality* is at the very apex of every constitutive manifold thought that is conjured by way of the concept—and its concurrent central status that coincides with the characteristics of empirical being. That human nature is formed by both the intelligible being and the empirical is coincident with the notion of disunity between the ontic and the ontological (empirical and intelligible) resulting in dichotomous formations of cognitive faculties as they engage the relational qualities that only adjure to normative behavior, while falling under the careful circumspection of those that seek the collective substance—never wishing to fall prey to this division between form and matter, subject and object, substance and representation. Though these divisions here always existed, they stand to divide community aspirations and partition them off into factions that only relativize the concomitant necessity for representational collectivity as a function of the participatory constitution that must be represented *a priori*. The "synthetic value" of every subject depends upon the quality of being that may result, and without question develops being into more than it is as an *apophantic* need, and into what it should be as a valuation for the subject within both its normative and constitutive status. There is no simple functionalism to the equation of how to render being as it equates with its own loss of substance however, but that the only solution to this *aporia* of consciousness is to recognize the Self within the Other as having its transcendental identity—without being aware of the proximity of the knowledge that should accompany it. The *phenomenality* that precedes transcendental identity is severe and can very well disable rational validity claims, yet this should never become the status of the subject should they wish to avoid analytic judgments that may lead into further falsity while in pursuit of the absolute knowledge that is attainable as a result of the identity of the subject meeting with its determinative qualities in response to what is the case, and what must in fact be the correct course of action in order to avoid a consequential loss of substance. Subjectivity itself must adjure to this in principle, as it helps to insure the possibility of the collective substance that may transform a divisional multiplicity into the collective totality of the subject—which ultimately accompanies the plurality of *monadological* existence for all subjects in the objective world—giving furtherance to the potentiality for *lifeworld* inter-subjectivity outside of the monad, and epistemic observations that come not only from self-same contingencies, but also the morality of the other that has the motive to preserve the collective substance. Only as strong as its weakest member, yet as with the *totalization* of the proximate *ego cogito*, the very formation of everything that may sustain its dialectical relation to the institutional forms and societal norms. The being that will result from this contingent dialectic between subject and system yields further contingent knowledge and epistemology, however the nature of the factual content is such that it has only the quality of having been posited—and no *temporological* basis is what has actually transpired within the objective world. The reason for this is that empirical verification is a strict and universal law of the *post-industrial* age—too much falsity is now possibly given the fictitious histories of popular iconoclasts and deceptive commercial enterprise. One can certainly isolate oneself from the ruse, but it seems more fitting to attain and acquire verifiable knowledge in order to further proceed. With every element of fact that does supersede consciousness of ontological matters however, the epistemology will of course grow and deliver the subject from all falsity into the realm of ontological understanding that has always been intended by every epistemic/ontological form of reasoning. Substance depends upon it, as does the facticity of the subject within the intentionality toward further objectifications of the Self and in pursuit of the capacity to produce the possibility of a self-generating representational intellect—now not only working *contemporaneously* upon the problematic judgments that excuse conceptual content, but bringing forth the concept as a function of the subject's contingent will—the functionalism of any intellect that is still in possession of its own otherness, that has long since passed as an absent object, but now is once again proximate and working for the good of the subject's collective identity. This will instead yield the *potentia* with which absolute subjectivity is assumed rather than earned by battling intersubjectively as a particular being—allowing for social being also to exist as an identical self that posits amidst its relations and cohorts. This would deter the legerdemain of the unidentifiable Other that conducts bad conscience and "gets away with murder". Any such otherness is within all practicality difficult to defeat, and does not fall within the interests of the collective substance, and must be removed from all conceptual content with acts of negation and *metacritique*. The deceptive element of this antagonistic Other is that it defies all rationality, temporality, and is bereft of the objective understanding—giving it no universality, but only the particular purpose to disturb and destroy the constructive positing of subjectivity. Yet, this Other is for the purpose of the subject's own necessary intentionality toward the objective world as one whom is within the capacity to discover social *problematics*, and to eradicate the inequality that may jeopardize both the subject's collective identity, and the possibility of a universally constitutive substance. While this remains conceivable, it is without its grounding before the *meta-logical* rudiment has been put in place as a function of the *phenomenality* that yields the subject's necessary status in the collective sphere. Only a priori synthetic judgments can fasten the potency with what may be universally and objectively posited, yet the analytic judgments are what establish an immediate course of action in preservation of substance and Objective essence.

## Causality and Reflexive Duality

The question of causality has a duality that sits between the dialectical relation between society and nature, and the relation between *noumena* and phenomena acting freely in connection with both. As society precedes the consciousness of the subject as a functionality of its universality and genus, so does nature both precede and interact with society and hence operates as the objective component of subjectivity as it sustains the *lifeworld* ontologically and empirical being *socio-naturalistically*. The essence of the origin of causality is found reflexively between the hylozoistic dynamical objectification of subjectivity by nature as a result of its societal counterpart, and the resulting social being that posits itself in accordance with which natural laws grant the subject the means by which rational agency may accommodate the *phenomenality* that results from *noumenal* activity—within the notion that both *noumenality* and *phenomenality* are equally capable of affecting the causal nexus—just as the *socio-naturalistic* restraints upon freedom are directly affected by social coercion and nature's proclivity for determining the activities of the parties that would wish to proceed with subjectivity without mediation. However in the *pantheistic* world-*in-itself*, Mother Nature responds to human activity as an equal and opposite force of the universe, just as human activity is engendered by the tumultuous activities of nature *and* the universe. One may wonder if a thought, or collective thoughts all engaged in a common purpose could yield an Earthquake, or if the Earthquake itself is what unites subjects with a common purpose as an event that signals the commonality between subjects as an objective natural event.

The revelation here being that the ontology of nature is such that it be a natural ontology—respective of both the empirical courses of the natural occurrence and the thoughts that result or interact dialectically with all of the events that follow the occurrence, and all of the events that preceded it. The *quod erat demonstrandum* is that truth is found as a function of the causality that ensues from humankind's socio-economic activity, just as it is found in the causality that limits economic activity to begin with. The subjective will cannot simply posit that it must engage economic activity at the cost of raping the planet of its resources, just as it is essential that life be transmitted from nature in an effort to sustain the *noumenal* and *phenomenal* activity that will allow us to sustain the natural environment to accommodate social infrastructure and economic stability. Though the *reductio ad absurdum* of *noumenally* causal activity, is the potency of the impact on certain institutions that resolve only to utilize collectivity as an avenue for economic growth—hence the transmission of *noumenal* freedom into an unbridled exploitation of resources. This as we all know has been going on for decades, and can only result in a raising of the necessary awareness that will become causal of greater collectivity—yet within the constant threat of an appropriation that yields further attempts to grow the economy. By fiat alone, there is no reason to gauge the social roles of subjects as an instrument of objectivity from the standpoint of subjectively induced causality, but it does stand to reveal that the objective, universally determined causality of the social order has been engaged by freedom—the free will to engage whichever higher causal purpose will yield the absolute that has the epistemic determination necessary to allow for all participants of the collectivity to resolve to the status of knowing *and* doing—not just responding as simpletons awaiting their orders from the boss upstairs. This of course means more democracy; a symbolic *totalization* of the ego; epistemic endowment that will most certainly yield a better capacity to choose, and a more moral universe—capable of transmitting its mutual essence right from the source of all being, directly to the understanding.

Furthermore, it will encourage a deification of rational subjectivity that will become dialectically interlaced with the objective realm of causality that emerges from the *socio-naturalistic* world-*in-itself*. Subjectivity has and will always have its objective counterpart—and therefrom should emerge the necessary understanding that our *noumenal* identity in its pathogenic form is as powerful a force to the objective world. Not only where concerns conceptual content, but also the actions and choices of others and ultimately the *in-itself* of the represented global community. All causality is both the source of the inception and impetus for notional agency and *noumenal* freedom, and the reflexive engagement of nature and all of its social and objectively understood encumbrances.

Though causality inevitably presents an Object at times without any active positing, judgment or concepts, it is not necessarily the object that is contemporaneous with the concurrent mode of thought that may have contingently produced the object. It is, in fact, a source of alien conceptual content in objective form that brings about the urgency to produce a work, or to reflect upon the meaning of objects as *things-in-themselves* for the purpose of arriving at deeper modes of reason so as to further one's thinking while it sits idle. Thought is causally reflexive where concerns the object—that there is always an effect; and in this case it may become that the end result of this alien object is the concept itself. Without any judgment, concepts proceed from objects to content in the *post-industrial* age—based upon the universality of forms that correspond to the transcendental subjectivity and collective substance that is well-preserved in the symbolic and *realiter* world-*in-itself*. The former presents images that may have no infinite *regressus* of space yet represent something of value, while the latter simply corresponds to the objectivity that determines every causal event as it interrelates with the nature of the active choices that determine the trajectory of the *lifeworld* as it engages otherness intersubjectively, and as contingent objects thrown from the causal subjective nexus out into the objective world. This dynamic will invariably produce an outcome that is determined by causality itself—in that the innumerable variables produce an output of conditions that all have an outcome respective of the various contingencies that all play a part in the selection of the agent making a judgment that corresponds to the given object. There is of course, the sense of the unknowable proportions and doubt that the freedom of the will is now under attack by its own causal limitations— but rather what is the case is that the object represents something of the world-*in-itself* that corresponds to truth and must be followed rather than destroyed or beaten. This *aporia* gives rise to a cause of action positing judgments that can only survive as functions of verifiable facts that are within the conclusions of speech acts, while the acts themselves may be propositions that elude to what may be the case—ultimately the object that presents itself and epistemologically will reveal what is in fact the case is in direct communion with the immediacy of being, entity, *Dasein* and essence. In fact, subjectivity itself will posit the *sublation* of the object by the very act of judging the foreseeable event through the speech act. Though this seemingly self-evident truth may preserve being, it also adjures to the further constitution of the self-identical in all *noumenal* presentations—giving freedom back to the subject who may feel constrained by the contingencies that stand to upbraid the metaphysical and *metapsychological* make-up of subjectivity. However, it does not change the reality that truth now vacillates—it is in dialectic between the subjective will, and the causality of the objective world that not only has contingent judgments for the subject, but also a determination that must be distinguished from the absolute determination of the *socio-naturalistic* world. The only way toward an establishment of this distinction is through the *phenomenality* that posits contingently as much as the subject strives to command the phenomenon as a thing-in-itself—regaining control in pursuit of the social totality that will preserve dialectical agency as a function of the transcendentally correlative subject that wishes only to preserve agency as a member of the *monadological* collective.

Thereby substance is preserved, the being of individuality is sustainable in its appropriation of objects, and dialectical relation to nature and society at large is never the culprit in this dangerous game of cause and effect that has been given the power to determine choices as though no agency were ever present with the subject to begin with. Agency is possible only through and by way of the "sustainable order" of rational *phenomenality* that never despairs to posit the very subjectivity constituted of conclusively verifiable speech acts, onto-epistemic truth as arrived at through objectively mediated *evental* occurrences, and the very essence of all the aforementioned that can only be realized through the notion of the concrete—the collective

## 76 The Dialectical Self-Concept of Symbolic Being

substance that survives the vicissitudes of philosophical *aporias* as doubts that remain within the economy of ontological currency and reified *lifeworlds*. Never but once has humankind taken falsity to be of the absolute determination and realized to much dismay that the objective world stands only to deceive—albeit the positing of subjectivity as an absolute suggests that one can be deceived by ontological events time and time again. With much credit to the *monadological* structure of consciousness, one finds these to be contingencies all the more, and for this reason, causality is better determined only by the rationality that results from *phenomenality* and a self-determined agency while in the absence of the absolute determination. The *transcendental identical* is the very epistemology that will deliver the necessity for cause of action to the subject, and thereby acts in harmony with the absolute determination. These are not only forms of knowledge but also modes of being—and by and large the quality of ontology that hypostatizes what the world-*in-itself* is to subjectivity within the vicissitudes of the pursuit of universal knowing.

# Chapter Three

## *The* Historicity *of* Vernunft

When considering the notions of what make the human subject responsive to all the multifarious and difficult to cope with forms of mental products that may be found throughout contemplation, reflection, and in consequence of all actions in the empirical realm, one hastens to imagine that these phenomena are not likely to be too easily thought away without a valiant effort. For all contents of the mind are indeed a product of experience and have been developed by the historicity of *vernunft* (reason) and can only be *sublated* with the genuine concern of one who practices thought as a daily regimen. The process is long and most certainly leads one to adapt reason as a function of the genus of where all truth is generated, and all understanding has the opportunity to grace thought with its *phenomenality* and justification of what makes us consistent in our observations, resilient in our thoughts and actions, and truthful in speech and the use of language—as they were within the epistemic content of what makes objectivity tolerable and *temporologically* accurate.

Though life in the objective world is most accurately a function of the active positing of the pure "I" through absolute subjectivity, the vicissitudes of the fallibility of human endeavor amount to a consistent and ever present possibility that we may descend into a mediated particularity—where intersubjective relations force the agreement to propositions that may result in the appropriation of the object and its content. This will always yield a particular subjectivity that dwells below otherness—the servant of a master that by no means should have control of the subject's phenomenal agency and *noumenal* freedoms. What is clear is that universality as exchange-value may be held accountable for this fall into particularity, and that the subject must once again regain freedom from the appropriation of use-value as a predicate of exchange-value by the public use of reason and collective substance—the mere concept of exchange-value may once again deify the subject into its universal status; making essence an abstract universality again that can inhabit the objective world as an agent of its own particularity rather than a slave of a system that considers *post-industrial* subjectivity indebted to the state a priori—a dialectical self-positing noumenal freedom negates this, yet the multitude of sophistical imperfections in the subject may yield this reflexive desire to return to the Platonic, oligarchic plutocracy that holds all subjectivity under the guise of objective controls that exclude many of the *noumenal* freedoms necessary for *phenomenality* and democratically rational agency.

What the subject will, however, always hold within its power, is the abstraction of the concept—which brings upon the scene the object of all rational positing, and the potency with which to make the objective world adaptive to subjectivity *in-itself*. The use of this will brings about an augmentation of the subject's relation to temporality as a function of the commensurate use of choice—with the hope of making synthetic unity a priori the sustainable status of the subject-object. This would make all further conceptions rich with conceptual content;—delivering the subject-object from the point of servitude and complacency into one of phenomenal agency; making speech acts more valuable and truthful.

## Conceptual Synthesis of the Self-Identical

One always has the means to employ the concept, and to synthesize objects—it is only a matter of starting from the positing of the self-identical: as here lies the unmediated particularity which is a *de facto* abstract universality with which nothing yet has been predicated but essence. And essence should be seen as an abstract universality and exchange-value that has not yet been posited into its object, which is a concept. Thereby, being itself is a concept of the existential universe that must meet with its own identity to the objective world before it may depart into the necessary judgments that produce further conceptual content and subjective truth that gives one the necessary understanding with which to proceed within reason. While this seems hazardous and quite precarious as a function of the public use of reason—that there may be intersubjective disputes over whom owns the conceptual content present to a "shared" *lifeworld*, it nonetheless belongs to the subject that has *monadologically* posited the self-identity into substance:—the objective world is only an observer to the products of any subject's mind, and there must be no oppressive constraints upon the mental activity of the subject insofar as it does not interfere or constrain the rational freedom of another subject. In this sense conceptual content that is universally apprehended is represented by the *originary* conceiving subject—that can do nothing with the possibility that the object may move freely through the objective world—taking on a variety of particular forms in others; the very notion of this is of course a case of what makes cultural anthropology a very intriguing field.

Yet the purposiveness of subjectivity is to produce its own being as a function of the actively positing "I"—and though *monadological,* there is no restriction upon its potential to be reproduced from its own representation as an object to another at a different point in time. Being that abstract universality itself as essence is what may have produced the framework of conceptual content that has been understood subjectively,—and as a function of the actively positing "I", it is seen as having the quality of being that could not transmit identical content to another subject, but that the form of content would be understood subjectively, based upon the subject's synthesis of subject and object a priori as it posits absolute identity.

## Essence Mediation and Abstract Subjectivity

Where concerns identity, the concept, substance and essence, subject and object, propositions and judgments are both the mediated particularity *and* the unmediated universality in terms of *ousia*. That essence could precede thought *antecedently*—as it does for Aristotle—raises the question of how it is possible for the notion that postulates essence as a function of abstraction, rather than simply coming to be from the essence that promotes both the positing of the Object and the thinking *ego* as it appears. In fact, this suggests that nothing has been totalized from the advancement from society and nature so as to the abstract essence of a subject—but that for all intents and purposes genus provides the subject with its essence before the subject has had any mental production, whether awake or asleep. What in fact lies as the fundamental contradiction to the principle, is that essence would ultimately be something purely active—though Aristotle's intention is to postulate the ontological genus of one's immediate essence, this is a *non sequitur*—the immediacy of the essence is a strict impossibility given the a priori characteristics of being that precede the identification of the abstraction that occurs when one engages consciousness with a conception. Therefore it could be affirmed that being is immediate, while essence is not that; in order to unlock to universality what is essence from genus, one must first become aware that one exists. The subject does not choose its essence, but wills it where the object that is its essence has been appropriated in connection with an *appresentation* of the objective world—how a subject must elicit the object in a sudden and *assertoric* fashion as in Hegel's master-slave dialectic motif that describes the emergent death that will result as two subjects risk losing their life for an essence that may belong to either one exclusively, but not a source that would drive the subjects simultaneously.

This grandiose *aporia* that confers upon subjectivity a certain corruption to the administered world unleashes the necessity of the subjective will acting even capriciously to renew its *energeia* with the Object, and the *Dasein* that drives being as an immediacy of the concept and self-identity. The question here should be asked, "Why not agree that essence is immediate, to avoid this calamity—seeing all other circumstances as a function of disease?". Well the answer is simple. If essence is indeed immediate before and preceding any conscious act, then all of the objects produced in the world are to be seen as the substance of the subject—while movable and the causality of what determines the content of the subject-object doing its thought and speech acts—but only as attributes;—the properties that determine the abilities of the subject. Aristotle knew that objects were movable, but he failed to see that this would mean that the essence of the subject would be mediated as well—adding to the object the quality of the abstract universality of subjectivity itself. In this case, perhaps from the standpoint of historicity the mediation of our essence is a characteristic of modernity and the industrial age, as for an object to be abstract universality to an immediate particularity and the absence of the object being an inter-subjective struggle of a mediated particularity suggests that more than simply rational constraints are still being placed upon subjects in pursuit of the content that the object may hold; and as follows that objective conceptual content acts as the *energeia*, the soul's filling of the subjects themselves.

In effect, a thinking being is a being that has an essence—while a being that has no consciousness is perchance a single celled organism. Where essence is abstracted most readily is as the social being of a societal collectivity with common directives that all aspire toward the collective totality of every acting subject as a member of this ideal of participatory democracy. As policies themselves cannot be administered universally yet are adhered to collectively by the intersubjective *lifeworld* as it is shared, greater degrees of agreement may be achieved and more complete universal liberties realized. As the social being is indefatigable in a dialectical union with its object and essence, appearances and representations are taken as counterfactual where no collective agreement has taken place from the standpoint of the objective world, and as problematic judgments that raise issues within the status of the subject and its epistemological *sociation* with the relations and other subjects of immediate concern. However, the process whereby a subject's essence is mediated is a prohibitive for the achievement of agreement to an assertion regarding the status of other subjects of concern, and is meritorious of the art of negation or the active positing of concepts that serve to defeat the purpose of the *violating* interloper or trickster engaging in acts of legerdemain to bring to life a moral and ethical wronging. As subjectivity is only constitutive of its own essence by way of *noumenal* and phenomenal activity, truth can only be obtained by way of the *being-in-itself*—all judgments that proceed from the causal nexus of a deceptive otherness are fictitious and only generative of the necessity for "negative dialectics".

## Otherness in the Post-Industrial Age

The inherent quality of Otherness is almost always to precipitate an unfavourable outcome for rational subjectivity in the *post-industrial age*—as propositional fallacies may produce speech acts that ultimately lead to the destruction of the status of a subject. Where the subject finds truth, a verifiable fact that has first come through an onto-epistemology, the rest is to be fulfilled with negotiations and resolved by the judicial branch of government. That a "prime mover"—the originary cause of the represented society as a totality to the subject may be by way of the unification provided by a common belief is not to be disputed but rather acknowledged. However, the citizenry are also all connected as a species with common goals—such as survival—and has taken the shape of the world-*in-itself*. All reality may be understood as a collective to the common identity of a people (genera) and never result in the separation or disunity of subject and objective world. Here, subjectivity finds all thought to yield a seemingly perpetual essence as it has been transmitted to the subject in recognition of the *causa sui* existence of subjectivity acting freely toward the collectivity that unites all subjects to their own *monadological* totality while minds produce the ideas that give acting subjects the content that is transmitted back to the subject correlatively from intelligible reality—creating an unified whole of thinking beings all in a collectivity that supports the public use of reason, and promotes the ethical substance of the social totality.

> Being as a totality is a function of the *apriority* of the world-*in-itself* in a reflexive relationship between the objective world and *being-in-itself*. Reality conjures the objective spirit as a function of its fundament of ineffable interconnectivity—that all objectivity appears to the multitude of subjects as a particular universality; never as a universal subjectivity. This would of course suggest that the subject were the absolute object, or the One.

Where objectivity disappears is upon the inception of the *metalogical* grounding of essence in the concept—reflection endows the subject with this eventuality, given the very nature of *aporetic* contemplation—subsequently, being has become a singularity within the notion. At the point of the epiphany that subjective *notionality* itself is the *being-in-itself* to the societal *in-itself*, is where subject and society co-mingle as counterparts of a much more elaborately constructed objective world. That this world apprehends the subject from the fundament of universal reason and the concepts of the understanding remains a great source of bewilderment, as being is ultimately charged with the responsibility of rational conduct where concerns all positing of the Self—should the world-*in-itself* be in need of any repairs from the standpoint of the collectivity and totality of being.

Yet, the source of all being *is* the world, and from this it must be derived that the positing of self is always constitutive of the pure "I", the thinking subject constructs its proximate identity throughout *phenomenality* as a function of the intellect—and also as a way of retrieving the truth that has been lost to problematic judgments. Being itself is better constituted by the subjective will—in both its *noumenal* and phenomenal states—though from *phenomenality* it is always concerned more with its *Dasein*, its selfhood to the bargaining collectivity. Free acts of consciousness are bestowed with *monadological* moments of factual discernment from the falsity of epistemological assertions that throw unanswerable doubt into the subject, devaluing objectivity as a mere legerdemain. *Noumenality* and *ontical* subjectivism will always resolve the issue in the absence of the objective counterpart, yet objectivity is still the conceptual essence of the subject and must be intuited as the grounding force of all rational and reasonable conduct. What this amounts to is the noetic side of consciousness in what establishes being as functional of its own subjectivity. The apprehension of representations as a counterpart to being is what begets the absolute identity of pure subjectivity that is always receptive to the objective essence that is providing subjectivity with its content to precipitate speech acts that resound of truth and establish objectivity as the prior component to what otherwise may be construed as the musings of a bungler—for whom no truth would ever exist had the representations not addressed the *being-in-itself* from the first point of understanding to begin with.

The objective world as a form of representational *transcendency* of the absolute subject produces the identity of beings that precede the understanding of subjectivity, yet are transcendent to the subjectivity of the individual, and are the only source of reason's own rational objectivity and the necessary datum for responsible choice and reciprocal conduct. Otherness is produced directly out of the understanding of any subject's thinking or facticity, and conjures most frequently the necessity of negation, or elicits pathic projection in an attempt to reconstitute the former condition of reflection that had produced the Object for otherness to begin with. Otherness is of course, the *being-for-itself* having only its own economic concerns in mind; harbouring resentment toward the very subject that has bestowed upon it its causality as an adjunct of the reflexive nature of intersubjective motifs that create conditions between subjects—eliciting the problematic for unprepared individuated beings. The response is, of course, always negative—especially where concerns the appropriation of surplus-value and the winning of fiat capital—and always results in civil disputes and litigation somewhere down the road.

## Collective Substance/Objective Essence

If only the being of consciousness as a *noesis* would remedy the eidetic claims of the disavowed individualists that precipitate harm and injustice upon collective substance would back-off the reified essence of others, then the prudential avails of the absolute Being of transcendental subjectivity could proceed with its many-splendored affair with a reasoned totality that gives thinking its just do in the face of all inequity and wrongful action. With this though, it is that society as an objective totality may find its own problematic—the very ills to be eradicated at the source; restoring the truth of all subjects that have lost both autonomy as thinking beings, and heteronomy as members of a collective multiplicity—thereby returning consciousness of the subject its much needed objectified and transcendent essence. As a function of dialectical abstraction, this would of course augment noumenal agency to plateaus of judgment that could *dirempt* the negation of hegemonic signifiers a priori that are acting as resolute beings with essence bestowed upon them with the intentionality to produce meaningful subjects—as opposed to *ontical* beings that had only to exist in order to sustain existence. Thought is generative of being where being is generative of thought; subsequently, the very beings that produce thoughts are correlatively enmeshed with the objectively intelligible world-*in-itself* for the landscape of meta-ethical policy implements that affect us all collectively. Being that these implements are not always rational ones, it is that *weltgeist* is to be taken very seriously as the source of many of the *problematics* that are now underway. It is not only geopolitical, it is also ontological—the severity of political institutions aside, there is no turning back from these philosophical *aporias* once they have come into being, and thereby the institution of dialectically rational collectives is needed, but only possible where the subject's identity has not been overtaken by a hijacked universality. It is essential that the forms be returned to beings that act in accordance with their objective essence. This will drive down *anomie*, and most certainly reduce the amount of societal ills that have always been the result of a mangled and disenfranchised subjectivity.

As such, the objective world as it recognizes the *being-in-itself* will always produce the necessary conditions for free acts of the subjective will as ontological events in pursuit of the reflexivity of truth, yet an oppressed being will ultimately wither and pass away—that its own subjective identity was never enough to produce a mind that could host its own objective identity as established by the understanding of the world-*in-itself* as it knows the *being-in-itself*. To compromise within the notion that the regional and the city-states are always first does not take into account the enlightened totality of *weltgeist* and the globalization of transcendental subjectivity that has been upon us for three-hundred years. The monads of Leibniz to the absolute knowing of Hegel have established the foundation for many *post-industrial* identitarian conclusions to transpire. The absence of the hegemonic state will ensure that the global community has a better stake and claim in the multiplicity that would wish only to reify the substance of a justly produced objective essence, and the value of a freely willed rational subjectivity.

The question now arises that when one wills the objective essence, does one also will the qualities, attributes, and properties of collective substance? Does the modality of substance affect the proximity of the property in this heteronomy? Properties themselves are qualities of being that are known to us as the representations that form both objects and self-same contingencies. In this sense, the quality of knowledge—the epistemology of the subject—has much to do with the properties of the subject: known as "synthetic value". Should the representational consciousness of the subject fade for all onto-epistemological truth, the knowing subject faces the immanence of not being aware of what the subject is: a being that is devoid of its own determinations. For this reason, *purpose* is the inherent quality and value of the objective essence, in that the subject has developed itself and been socialized into self-knowledge, and the awareness of which attributes are *in abstracto*, and which ones remain analytically for the subject as collective transmissions of immediate qualities of being.

The immediacy here is such that the subject is of course being determined, objectively by the genus *proximativa*;—and in fact is not without the objective being that should determine its epistemology for the positing of identity—which happens dialectically between subject and societal community. Without the necessary judgments—some epistemological basis for the positing of absolute subjectivity—one remains without a proper basis to practice its own encumbrances of the *meta-logical* rudiment with which to constitute an objective essence. It is transmitted via the objective world, and the subjects bereft of knowledge—both a priori and *a posteriori* are never in a binding situation with reason:—these beings devoid of any perceptual and epistemological truths are often doomed by circumstance and ultimately at a loss for insights or discourse that may assist in the developments of reason and the properties of substance. It is upon every member of the collective to do whatever is within their power to arrive at the objective truth that will fuel being with the necessary potency to posit subjectively with a valid claim—within the notion that the collective substance will be improved by the subjective will that has been properly and accurately informed as to what is in fact the case.

Contingently, propositions allow for reflective posits that would certainly yield objective truths; just as representations forward the thinking subject with the basis for the identification of properties that are or have been "sent" out to others—making the subject engage in further mental labours to constitute objective essence anew. Should this occur, being is flawed within all its speech acts and the predicate becomes a source of amusement for otherness—an unfortunate circumstance for the ethical pursuit of substance. The identity there may in fact descend into pure *ontical* being, leaving the subject with the necessity to work on regaining its own absolute.

Which is not to indicate that the self-identical is other than both *an absolute determination, and a contingent representation* of epistemological content at the same time. There is a correlation between the intelligibility of the contingent self-identical that corresponds to *ontical* being as to the transcendental identical. In fact, for all intents and purposes, without having willed beyond the constraints of rational subjectivity, it is the *de facto* being of the very same. What this amounts to in short is an earnest rapport with *temporal* epistemology that may bring to light facts that further connect the intelligible with the empirical. For all *transcendency* is "experienced" as ontological or onto-epistemological representations of *being-in-the-world*; and all empirical being is based upon what is predicated of the objective substance and what *ontical* conditions constitute the collective individuality of the subject. As social reality is represented to the subject ontologically, the *being-in-itself* is in direct correspondence with the empirical self as it relates to externality as such, and thereby its *potentia* for positing absolute subjectivity becomes engaged outside of the proximate limitations upon the *ego* by otherness that is (of course) either a *being-for-self* or a *being-for-another*. The former is always antagonistic and in pursuit of its own private interests, while the latter is more concerned with the collective substance as a synthetic unity—which leads toward the sense of reward for having posited concepts that benefited the collective—rather than only seeking the private interests of those that consistently triumph over others by fiat. The social being is better constituted by the recognition of how temporality acts as an integral component of the social infrastructure; and in line with the duties and obligations of every component of the collectivity, effective positing of concepts is an integral part of the assignment of just division of labour and substance. Though substance itself is of the collectivity as a whole, and a function of the objectivity of essence, it is by abstraction indivisibly granted the subject as an empirically given thing—while it is ontologically the "stuff" of objective reality, that the subject has posited its empirical identity as a *being-in-the-world*. Transcendental subjectivity as a correlate of the *ontical* realm is by-and-large the constellation of objects-in-representation from the objective world, and the *transcendental identical* that is both constitutive of objective essence as it is empirical being from the noetic side. The contingent self-identical representation of the transcendental identical is "summoned" as Fichte put it, by the positing of concepts that bring into being the necessary conditions of consciousness of which both the intelligible being and the empirical being are comprised. The yield of this is the ethos of the subject in relation to the collective—and subsequently the ethical constitution of all intersubjective beings of the *lifeworld* that constitute the objective essence of all subject-objects that are part of the concepts that have been posited. The objective world itself is open to all subjects equally through the public use of reason and as an indisputable *metapsychological* truth—thereby collectivity itself can only benefit from the positing of empirical being that elicits the necessary totalization of the subjective, pure "I"—the thinking cogito that is in pursuit of the proper objectivity that relates it *to* the objective world.

Without any self-determination from the empirical side, there can be no intelligible being that has already transcended the limits of the *ontical* quality of being that is antecedent to the representation of that which verifies the appearances of the natural and societal world to the subject ontologically—one must first possess an identity in order to find the intelligible being that corresponds with its *ontical* existence. There may be attacks here over the concept of what determines the human soul as a function of what has been given by the *ontical*—but it should be made clear that the reason of the subject is what is in fact transcendental and therefore eternal in quality as in quantity, while the essence is only identified by its unity with an *ontical* being. Which is to say—more or less—that what continues beyond the *ontical* may in fact be something other than what is determined by essence, but something that is determined by the absolute subjectivity:—which is both based upon the empirical identity, just as it is upon the ontological self-identical of the subject which has been determined more by the *being-in-the-world* that has transcended the *spatio-temporal* limitations of the empirical and become an independently acting, self-positing, representation of the self in its very own subjectivity—yet in correlation with what has been posited or neglected in contemplation.

This may reveal the possibility of a third substance—a connection between the empirical identity and the transcendental identity. In fact it is the beyond of it that makes this representationally possible—while indicating that universality, the world of forms is not only an institutional stricture of the objective world, but a quality of the conceptual realism that makes the *becoming* of absolute subjectivity an integral aspect of life's journey. Every subjective being that experiences an objective essence as a result of the positing of empirical identity has "become", is and will experience the "synthetic value" of being human and all of the benefits of the collective substance of an abstract and enduring universality. Particularization will occur only in conflicts with otherness that is self-seeking based upon the nature of the tasks (labour) of the subject. Should it become coercive, all subjectivity has within its power the resource of free will only limited by the restriction of the temporal conditions and facticity of other subjects within the constellation;—the collectivity is so constituted by these maverick acts of *being-for-self* as they eradicate the coercion for the *lifeworld* that is to be enjoyed and shared by all.

As follows there is more than enough substance to go around, and no private interest is more significant than the will of the collective in every case. This is not to suggest that all subjectivity is of mimetic quality from an abstract universality without any particular interests or activities, in short, a robot or chimp such as the case may be; but that the act of becoming will be subjectively endorsed in the use of natural properties that belong to the collective, and comprise its substance. With this, at the behest of the objective world, self-interest may also be an ethical pursuit should it benefit the collective will, or be a direct result of an absolute determination that has been recognized as such by the objective world. In this case, it has been universally endorsed and meets with all the conditions of rationality by ontologically perceiving subjects whom would wish for nothing more than a common good.

## The Triad of Being

Subjectivity is endowed with a triad of being that is constituted by the following: a transcendental representation of a universal identity; an objective identity only when it knows the *being-in-itself*; and an apodictic representation of otherness that stands before the social constitution. For the transcendental identity of any representational object is universal in its otherness, and the otherness of universality— that its identity has transcended space, time, causality, etc. And the objective identity of the *being-in-itself* confirms the *transcendency* of the subject—the absolute identity—while the apodictic representation of otherness is contiguous to the synthetic value of subjectivity itself. Which is to say and ultimately to posit that reason is endowed with the luxury of a world that already exists *sui generis*; in fact the world is represented to us through the triad as a form-in-itself of reality that adjures to the very *transcendency* of absolute subjectivity. In this subjectivity, one need not be possessed by the indefatigable requisite of the creation of the world out of nothingness through the positing of the "I think", but will also be anointed with the very *weltgeist* that gives preponderance to the object's inherent calling to pursue thought as an avocation that is meritorious of the world's trust. And in this trust will be found the production of the very conceptual content that may further thinking beings—pulling subjectivity away from its caprice in the will to create the world out of nothingness; and there the very reflective nature of compatibilist, *correlationist* being will propound to flourish. There is no need for subjectivity to produce all of its being out of the absence of notional concretion. In fact, certainty in the concept is what breeds the liaison between being and objective essence, which is the goal of every transformative contemplation. As within this notion of concrete being, one finds that all established truths are more likely to become acknowledged beyond the realm of epistemological certainty, into the realm of brute fact—by the very designation of which identity had been encumbered with its empirical realism—that the empirical being would find its own *transcendency* as a function of the thinking subject's representational consciousness. In no event, and by no means may the empirical identity achieve a transcendent representational status other than by way of pure objectivity—which being finds both its objective essence and its own transcendental subjectivity. These both lead to the promotion of the synthetic unity of the *ego cogito* with its objective essence, and the unity between objective world and the symbolic universal. That these coalesce is no surprise, as a disunity thereof would invariably result in the *diremption* of form and substance, which is known to be individual and collective respectively. That form is both universal as it is individual may evoke notions and speculative negation as the collective nature of substance—yet it is only with this that the absolute identity may exist. The form and identity of a subject is universal as it transcends the mediation of its particularization as a subject that is beneath the confines of the very universality that makes absolute identity possible. And substance itself is only collective where it responds positively to the collected identities of all transcendent subjects—reflexively this amounts to a correspondence between being and objectivity that is transformative to both the former and the latter.

For being as the absolute identity is *ensouled* by its objective essence, and there it may become the very *Dasein* or totalized ego that blends into the collective totality of *monadological* subjects that form the collectivity that makes the world-*in-itself* a knowable and tolerable place—both that it is universally accessible to the consciousness of the collectivity, but also as subjectivity must find its own being amidst the morass of particularities that have been universalized before the absolute identity has been attained. Once it has been, the inter-subjectivity of beings is well-constituted *monadologically* in its daily affairs, while the objective world only pays mind to the dialectical impasse between absolute identity and the political or economic resistance to emancipation from public identity; as it is known in its functional projection upon the world to all those representationally aware of the currency of the concept-at-hand—the notion of what is in thought an objectively conceptual content for a multiplicity of subjects concurrently. This event rarely does occur, as most subjects are undergoing determinations that result in the inescapable circumstance of a mediated particularity. But as it stands all subjects have it within them to attain the status of absolute subjectivity—where all concepts that are universal may become the content of the subject that is in pursuit of the constitution and empowerment of empirical being and a recognizable identity amidst the collective.

What abstracts from all transcendental representations that are in a manifold unity of authority, as it were, are realized within the phenomenal object as an epistemological self-identical of judgments. The triad is now formed of the objective/phenomenal self-identical and the particular non-identities all before the collective societal representation. That transcendental representations inhabit the pure "I" in a slew of judgments over the facticity of the subject may reveal that the *transcendental identical* has also achieved *phenomenality* as a function of the correlation between intelligible and empirical being. In short, rational agency is now possible—as the phenomenal objective "I" is responsible/causal for the speech acts of the subject in the effort to resolve the problematic *aporia* of *phenomenality* that is before the positing of the *noumenally* free "I"—in pursuit of new vistas of contemplation so as to further being as a mode of becoming, rather than simply a mode of survival of the vicissitudes of the societal framework:—being is more able to cope with abstract or empirical conclusions where it is issued free will from the collective;—a matter for its *ego* that should insure and ultimately guarantee the development of the being (*Dasein*) which we have established as the *phenomenality* of the transcendental representation itself.

## Assets of Reason

Yet as Kant had put it phenomena may also be mere empirical knowledge that stands to encumber exteriority with its necessary modality of augmentation, yet never fully delivers on the promise of this which develops the assets of reason so as to account for the progression of objective phenomena into representations that may then become manifold as the subject enters into dialectic with the objective world—a necessity of every dialectical negotiation where life is at stake—and a fundament to what constitutes "fair play" in affirmation of what remains valid in the judgments of the phenomenal object. That it is self-identical does confirm that the knowledge is both rationally and empirically sound—despite the apparent contingent nature of the judgments themselves. What it amounts to is what is likely a case of necessary validity claims and other actions of self defense so as to protect a subject from the inexorable consequences of not having acted upon what for all intents and purposes is simple epistemological truth. That this is known through subjective agency gives the actor the opportunity to either become dialectically opposed to the content of the object, or to find a passage toward a resolution of the problematic that is within the subject's means.

Most certainly, here, the face to objective truth becomes that of the authorities—with the duty left to the subject to validate the validity claims that are dialectically opposed to the will of the transcendental Other. What this does demonstrate, is that the phenomenal object of the pure "I" does abstract from the empirical other *a priori*. That is to say that the intentions of the other are known as posits within the phenomena, but the subject's object has for its contents the a priori synthetic knowledge of the other's "I" as constitutive of the subject in relation to an empirical subject that is of course, also an intelligible being. Things are, as such, this way to the degree that the abstract content of the intelligible "I" of an empirical subject has not yet been negated or dialectically addressed as the opponent to the purposiveness of the subject who's phenomenal identical has been overtaken. What this does reveal and indicate is that the subject's own Object, the essence, is being consumed by this Other, this opponent; and the subject must now take steps toward meta-claims that devalue the position of the Other—fully under the intention of eviscerating and disempowering the status of the Other for whom the phenomenal identical has fallen into service. The categorical imperative need not apply here as the subject's own Object has been virtually annexed by the Other, and most certainly the content has been reified; it would be more prudent for the subject to return to the self the agency that has been constituted by *noumenal* freedom and led toward rational speech acts that allow the subject to remain in control of their own content; and thereby their own essence—with the duty or obligation of the utilization of dialectical reasoning for a tool to attain a higher truth—rather than an abeyance to the whims and demands of an exclusionary hierarchical entity posing as a form of institutional authority. The "institutional order" as posited is a democratic empirical and intelligible sphere for the dissolution of established order for the sake of profit and private interest. This is why the abolition of the hierarchy will foster better global unity, and more creativity as a function of the collective output of democratically acting societies. The tyranny of the majority is not what we are mentioning here—this is a movement

## 96  The Dialectical Self-Concept of Symbolic Being

toward the establishment of an Order that cares for its collective members regardless of economic status.

With this, universality is a greater possibility, and the qualities of being as individuals collectively realized symbolically—not divisively. For the intention of coercive institutions is to rid the private needs of established power from the subjective concerns of those without the means to defend themselves *from* established power—the simple solution is to rid society from a coercion that can only lead to political upheaval and revolutionary tactics—yielding civil disputes and wars that will continue to go on as long as humankind inhabits this planet. It all starts with the proper connection between subject and object, collective substance and objective world, empirical identity with absolute subjectivity.  Objective truth never becomes of private interests for individuals or groups, but are collective interests for *monadologically* totalized subjects cohering with trans-subjective validity claims that have the potency to issue a change to the collective social spirit—reordering the distribution of wealth and power to the return of agency of a rational variety for those in pursuit of a more radical enlightenment.

# Chapter Four

## *The* Enlightenment *of* Objectivity

What comes toward objectivity where concerns truth is objective truth *sui generis*; though there remains the autonomy of reason where concerns how the representation of a self-positing, or contingently judging self-identical could be an appearance of what in particular comes to be the truth for a subject. Certainly the facticity of subjectivity is an object of the understanding that conjoins with the other—while the unconditioned has for its own universality propositions that engage the subject with the *de facto* claims worthy of reflection—as truth is both a contingent self-identical representation and a function of the self-positing "I" that may have the synthetic a priori on its side. Certainly, subjectivity must pay mind to the judgments that may have emerged from empirical being—as the judgments are posited into the intersubjective and reflective substance, the identities of all relevant parties are present within the judgments as they become a source of both abstract and empirical knowledge to the subject—leading to the necessary course of action and subsequent speech acts and verification.

*Actus prius* it is upon the subject however to never motion toward the ontological verification of any subjective claim that has emerged in the pursuit of ontological calamity over any empirical claim—this matter is left to the toils of epistemological realism, that the dialectic between substance and form, subject and object, concept and identity may verify the claims that are in appearance as contingent representations. One becomes a bungler should one act prematurely upon any of these claims in the same fashion as one is tortured throughout the attempts to gain certainty from the other intersubjectivity in pursuit of empirical claims from an onto-epistemological positing.

As is the case, being is not with its *aprioristic* concept through the identity of the other as a concomitant otherness to the self-identical positing of its own facticity. In other words, empirical verification resides within the other, should the contingent self-identical adopt the objective content of the intersubjective other a priori that is as a function of an abstraction that takes place while the other is at a failure to disclose factual being. The details upon which the epistemological objective other swims, are the same notions that are abstracted by the subject's own object—that is to say that though a subject is bereft of its own subjective content, the object is abroad performing abstractions that become objective representations for the subject to cling on to then approve. The denial of which essence should be mediated by this otherness, results in nothing other than the infinite struggle for retrieval of the object; it is far more productive to look upon the notion of the subject-object as having within the *being-in-itself*, and the *being-in-the-world*, the capacity to attain the status of what is given by every concept: the possibility for the *constituens* of an Objective Being that affirms its necessary content with truthful propositions based upon the contingency of the empirical being of the other.

Given this, it is that the Concept of the Other must of course be directed upon a negativity that it has toward the Object in question—this is a dialectic that is only concerned with its opposition in the other, and thereby the content of the judgments that face subjectivity are intrinsically negative and problematic. The other is a *being-for-self* having the capacity to abstract content and to reify the use-value of the subject, and therefore cancels the absolute identity—leveling-off being to a mere particularity which creates the *aporia* of a mediated essence which must go through the process of Hegel's identity, difference, and ground in order to even begin to abstract content and attain the dialectical impetus worthy of relevant validity claims.

Upon this note, it should be stated that no such *reductio ad absurdum* into particularity is here considered ethical, as the system itself is formed upon the very determinations that constitute rational identity—it is only where contingencies are present that *rational identity* should be in question—still though there remains a *being-for-self* that refuses to unmask its own identity for fear that the truth be known about the nature of its conduct. *However, now the mere concept of identity where concerns any identification of a representational other may bring to light the source of the deception or legerdemain to which the subject has been exposed.* More often than not, it is within Kant's manifold of relations; it is only that now these beings are remote in identity due to the technological conditions that determine collectivity and society as a whole.

Yet it is not wrong to hold that any abstraction has taken place where access has been granted a priori—the ontological verification of which is found in the concept and the identity of the intersubjective being within conception. The positing of the subject elicits the content of the other subject with a representational concept of the subject in question. What enables the former subject to engage the being of the latter subject is the process of the universality of absolute subjectivity. The unmasking of the concealed being there becomes coalescent in the sharing of the *lifeworld* that is unmistakably collective, yet selective to those that have been transformed by *this* mode of being.

It is one's experience of the world that gives rise to the subject's abstract universality, and the very nature of the empirical being that is presented by the objective essence. The absolute subject is the identity of the subject as both an analytically extended self out into the world as "projected", and a representational particularity as a contingency to the subject and others in a revelation that empirical being may be known simultaneously as an analytic *a posteriori* and a synthetic a priori.

That is to say that the subject-object is actually comprised of a unity between the universal subject and the particular object-in-representation to the objective world through its mediation of what has been projected or represented to another party from the *being-for-self*. The mere existence of this duality between a subject that is universal and an objective representation that is undergoing the process of mediation by the objective world through the collective substance, indicates that synthesis has already taken place between the subject and its particular opponent. What this means is that subjectivity may dwell upon the act of reflection without any disturbances from the other—while the other has not arrived at identity, or is under the limitations and reductions of the concept. What this may entail, is the hypostatization of the concept of the subject that is only in this moment of projection entering back into a unity with its own objective particularization—which is a certain road to the attainment of dialectical empirical knowledge, as subjectivity has taken precedence over the other's abstract a priori whereby the facticity and concomitant conditions necessary for the production of an epistemology are already in place for the continuation of the subjective pursuit of objective truth, in that the object *in-itself* is only a representation to the other—and thereby not the *disclosedness* of being that will lead to the covering up of facts to the perceiving subject.

As the subjective will is both a determination to the Self and to the Other, the instance where knowledge may be abstracted from the other is within the *being-in-itself*; for the other has no other choice than to posit its own intentionality in order to reflect upon what is true of the concept to the other; as it is its objective content. This methodology is practice that may lead to the legerdemain of the Other, or language games by a sick and twisted subjective individuality pursuing private aims—yet at the same time it may wrestle significant data from this opponent in the effort to advance the validity of the subject's future projections and representations. In addition, it will secure the concept for the subject, and objective content;—without which the intelligible being would be devoid of its substance, leaving the empirical being to reproduce its former actions in an effort to become a partner to the world-*in-itself* anew. Without any participation in *weltgeist*, rational dialectical subjectivity in pursuit of objective truths will consistently be constrained by the capricious will of the others in order to further responsible democratic practices—only the totality of the public use of reason will instill within subjects the applicable value so as to make dialectical abstraction possible, and objective reality feasible.

## Conceptual Understanding of Objective Beings

While particular judgments maintain the non-identity of the synthetic properties, synthetic value is dependent upon the unity of subject and object driving its constitutive pursuit of creative agency—that no idea may exist for any perceiving subject so long as the concept is not universal and working in direct liaison with the self-identity that is a function of the productive imagination of the subject, and the conceptual understanding of objective beings. These ideas are only alive in the minds of those that reproduce objective content thorough the projection of absolute subjectivity, and the validity of speech acts which have their grounding in the verifiability of empirical epistemological being. This would become a self-positing objectivity for the absolute subject. The positing of the other is also then to lead to the contingent self-identity which obfuscates the truth—yet in the abstraction of self-identity is constitutive of being.

The concept is metaphysically abstracted from a *temporal* source as it exists as a content—the very content of the concept of Being. Being as it has become endangered will always abstract the essence of the proximity from where the threat seems to originate, under the condition that its essence is constituted by the very threat itself; being cannot flee its own abstract essence, as thereby the object of a content is represented a priori as the essence of the subject in the pursuit of reason with which to resolve the difference or dispute that it may have with the opponent. The subject has only impressions of what may be the intentions of the other at this point—relying on an epiphenomenal consciousness with which to gather data as to the particular concerns of the current situation; with hopes of enabling being with the capacity to dialectically oppose the attacks of the Other with content of negation that will potentially stand to obfuscate all of the antagonism and coercion *of* the Other. With this though, there is also the off-handed possibility that a negotiation or agreement may be attained as a function of jurisprudence—but likely the subject will become enmeshed within the *aporia* of ontological discourse *ad absurdum* in an effort to relocate the truth to its former position of factual acuity, and essence actuality.

By this, it is meant that the reasonable owner of the essence at stake is recognized by the collective substance. The *noumenal* subject acquires its object as a free willing being; not only is the Object the essence of the subject, but it is the copula to the predicate of the subject's absolute identity to the objective world. Thereby, the subject attains *phenomenality* and dwells within a consciousness adorned with not only its Object, but the phenomenon which is the *being-in-itself* of subjectivity. This dual representation of subjective phenomenon and object provides the necessary fundament *in re* for all rational conduct in the objective world. The subject engages all *lifeworld* inter-subjectivity as a phenomenon, and generates its own object for the content of the rationally constituted objective world. Beyond this polarity of phenomenal subject and objective content is of course the Other as it represents the socially constituted *lifeworld* as both an obstacle but also an antagonist of all appropriation of the objective content of the rationally constituted *lifeworld*.

This "gatekeeper" of sorts is only the "watchdog" for the reification of the controlled content of all that this otherness serves—most notably the privilege of those that are capital "above the heads" of the collective substance that feeds universality its own developmental ideation insofar as productive minds are at work in the development of ideas that further human value *beyond* its most notably insidious quality of the universal exchange-value that drives and motivates human endeavor outside of the realm of rational conduct. As being is tendered only by its own *in-itself* rationality in pursuit of objective ends as an agent of the dialectically constituted *lifeworld*, subjectivity that proposes to maintain the status of collective substance is more endowed with the *potentia* of the *being-in-itself*—that is, it will become more of an entity or *Dasein* to the world, as objectivity grows out of the subjective determinations that have a priori knowledge more than it does the caprice of individuated *beings-for-self* that have no concepts for the amelioration of the objective content of the diacritical understanding.

## From the Knower to the Known

This motif is hedging upon the notion that the pure understanding is what gives life to judgments that are posited by the identical subject where it acquires verification of an empirical, *a posteriori* judgment. What in this movement from the knower to the known occurs is a judgment that has been constituted by the verification of the intentionality of the other—never simply experienced as contingent self-identical judgments, but contemporaneous posits of the other that have valid claims regarding an issue of the value that is a matter of the status of the subject where concerns the *ownness* of the phenomenal *lifeworld* as it represents the same value that is in question. Where one may err is where this valued phenomenal *lifeworld* is proximately understood as a function of a "truth event" (Badiou) or *weltanschauung* that has its currency in the collective; and with this it would only be the avarice of the subject to hold that this *lifeworld* were the subject's sole property—when in fact, it is the production of the collective of subjects that all identify with institutions that may have power over the forms themselves. While universality is a condition of emancipated subjectivity, and wholly objective in nature, it is also systemized by the institutionally collective use of pure reason—not to be confused with the public use of reason, and thereby adjures to the administered world as such; which is to take note of the unconditioned, the universally objective world and the subject's objective status. For where once the image consciousness was a noetic fact for all perceiving subjects, the image ban is primary to the control over the power machinery of where the key influencers are able to decide upon any subject's objective value based upon *ontical* or empirical facts—bringing forth certain very tangible discrepancies in class and physical appearance to this very world where we know the enlightened substance to be separate from form. In other words, collective substance is now not altogether equal in distribution of the forms and thereby the ideas. Herewith, there is a trend toward the nominalist approach to consciousness which universalizes material conditions and leads subjects toward further acts of reification—based upon the objective truth of their own perceived use-value. What this amounts to in the short term is class disparity; what it amounts to in the long term is the grounds upon which those that wish for a return to the age of reason would call cause for a revolution.

## Philosophizing of the Will a priori

While the positing of the *ego*, the pure "I" is the essence of empirical being, it is the collective representation of the objective world that constitutes subjectivity in its act of reflection. While the object is, in fact, no longer proximate to the subject, it is an actuality that is represented by collective society as an appearance of what facticity comprises social being, and what has been retained ontologically and epistemologically by the subject in daily affairs—inclusive of the world

The Enlightenment of Objectivity 105

affairs that temper consciousness with the *weltanschauung* of the age. Subjectivity, in this instance where the object is in absence resorts to the empirical a priori; that is knowledge about the world as it is without any awareness of what is being posited by the other(s) of this particular moment in time. Why, one may ask, "Does being possess a content that connects with the world without an onto-epistemology determining the views of the subject?" The clue is that the subject has impressions upon which the *being-in-itself* as an agent of the rational world-*in-itself* has always relied. For being is a determinate essence of the understanding that needs not necessarily identify with an objective entity that gives to the subject its content. Concepts are universal; and within the synthetic a priori abstraction of essence, so many concepts give objective content to the subject. Operating very similarly to an engine, the unconscious drives of the subject fill consciousness with the mere a priori understanding of the objective content that is the currency of the subject's "now present"(Mead). Though the moment where the content of the expression of what is to occur has not yet been posited, it is purely antecedent to the occurrence—thereby in direct correlation with the *progressus* of conditions as they have been set forward by the causality in the absence of the object; but also the former conditionality of subjectivity as it had engaged in free acts of the will whereby the positing of the *ego* took place within reason. No "I" that has not acted freely may gain this a priori knowledge without first positing the absolute "I", the pure being that identifies the status of subjectivity where concerns the Object. Without question Descartes' "cogito ergo sum" is always in play in consideration of the very process by which thoughts are realized, yet the content of those thoughts need not be posited after the initial act in pursuit of some degree of verification—as the verifiability of this conceptual content is better elucidated or referenced to other forms of content in pursuit of the truth of the object, which will lead toward a *being-in-itself* that has been anointed with the collective substance. This being is well-constituted and only bereft of the object for as long as the process of philosophizing "absence" is an act of the subjective will a priori —most substantively contingent and

Other to the opposing forces of the subjective will that had initiated the obstacle or predicative judgment at the outset absent of this judgment. Pure being, that may go on in elucidation until the matter has been entirely resolved as the object presents the subject with a comprehensive understanding wherever it is—and the dialectical subject pursues matters only for the length of time necessary to become renewed at the hands of an Object that has been educated and endowed with more content through the synthesis of the Other. Unmistakably, the absolute subject must again posit identity to regain the next phase of *apriority* that will lead to future elucidations;—but uncompromisingly Being is at the stage where it knows itself to be both an immediacy of content, just as it is an indirect transmission of conceptual content in another form to hopeful subjects—those whom appropriate the concepts most viable to their own facticity. The data is always available to subjects that utilize their own *being-for-self* as a modality that acquires a content, and thereby must abstract by positing concepts. Otherwise there will be no more dialectic between subjective and objective realms—reducing the potency of justice as it dwells deep within the hopes of the participatory subjects in this fledgling democracy. To further pursue the truth would be opening the flood gates beyond the *apriority* of the subject in absence of its Object. Yet the next endeavor is to principle the judgments that have been made to forge a new pathway for the motility of the universality of the Concept.

## The Otherness of Contingency

For Otherness, there is the quality of being a contingency to the Self from a past, present, or future facticity—standing before the objective world. It is identical with the subject, presenting truth as a function of both the preservation and the maintenance of the *ego*. This self-same other can be as antagonistic and misleading as the non-identical; yet preserves selfhood as a function of its adequacy as a *being-in-the-world*. To accept the pain of this Other is to recognize the *temporal successions* of consciousness, and to acknowledge the reality that being is encumbered with its very own self in the other—that otherness has been the representation of one's own Self into the world—and is to thereby reflect upon its own *being-in-the-world* as a contingent identity. The more personal the claims of this self-identical Otherness, the more potential it has to be constitutive of one's *being-in-the-world*; yet conversely it may also be in tune with a greater degree of falsity than would be acknowledged by a non-identical otherness that was exhibiting social praxis from the understanding. That the identity is cunning in its effort to gain power over subjectivity and produce the immediacy of action that could result in harsh consequents, may lead one to believe or hold that this is in fact a being that is cloaked in self-same identity—but is in reality a representation of another subject with designs toward the undoing of the social praxis of the absolute subject.

However, what comes more to the fore in this situation and circumstance is that the subject, in the dialectical effort to remain within the realm of objective truth as a *being-in-the-world*, takes contingency to be a function of the understanding as an element of necessity toward freedom; that the contingency limits freedom in that it imposes unnecessary demands upon subjectivity revealing the positing of the "I" that has become interrupted by intersubjective concerns over what is objectively true, and what is a mere function of the capricious will of those who's interest lies in the devaluation of the subject in question. As value is abstract universality that undergoes its particularization through the mediation of external interactions and circumstances, it can never truly become objective truth for either the empirical or transcendental identity of the subject unless the subject appropriates the *being-in-itself* as a *for-itself*—that it incorporates speech acts with posits and social praxis that make allowances for the absolute "I" to subsist amidst the collective substance that fuels all contemplation with its objective essence—making the emancipatory particular non-identity no longer a necessity of the individualization of the subject, but rather making the subjective will absolute and identical such that the freedom of the subject to express collective individuality is never questioned by a coercive Other.

    This all takes place *monadologically* for the absolute subject as a transcendental *ego,* and *collectivistically* for the empirical being that posits subjectivity based upon the situational concerns of any ontological inter-relation. Where this relation sparks the requisite negative dialectic, is precisely where the subject has been stripped of both its abstract empirical identity, and has been transcendentally reduced beyond where *performative* acts may be commensurate with the social praxis of the historical requirement. Should the collective individual gain more presence due to recognition of externality that corresponds with the contingent otherness, then verification has been attained—however, this is *in consequentia* of the contingent epistemology that produced the behavior or speech acts that precipitated the verification, and may dissolve the intersubjective relation once full disclosure has ensued. By and large, it is of greater abstract value to posit identity based upon *positive* inter-relations than to have to reflect upon outer negations. Negation is most effective as an ontological act of social praxis where being is undergoing determinations that have been interrupted by external forces. With this subjectivity may go out in the inner realm and procure conceptual content, universal forms, and representations and ideas that improve upon human reason so as to further knowledge rather than simply becoming immersed within the material concerns of short and long term fiscal existence. For this to become possible, knowledge—as it is in the *post-industrial* age—is shared with all those with the ambition to acquire it. It is in this manner that the socially collective substance is inured and imbued with manifold representations and collective knowledge:—a monumental improvement to the status of every subject with a conceptual understanding.

# Objective Truth and the Self-Positing "I"

That objective truth is phenomenological and self-identical is a fundament to the nature of the correlation between the objectively contingent *noumenal* identity and the *ego*'s own subjectivity. The objective world produces the transcendental identical just as the *ego* subjectively posits itself while taking on the epistemological quality of objectivity. The "I" posits itself as "I" yet is correlatively in sync with the objectivity of the contingent self-identical *transcendency*.

It may be thought that the "thrown" *noumenal* self is in unity with the phenomenal and proximate self where concerns the nature of the knowledge that is so understood. Taking on the quality of both a priori and *a posteriori* knowledge, subjectivity has arrived at a degree of transcendental determinations; indicating social activity that not only opposes but also affirms the status of being as *this* being both in thingness, and as a function of its analytic and synthetic relation to the world by which the absolute becomes an abstraction of the manifold a priori. The reason for this work being done on behalf of the subject is the concept that analytic and synthetic may stand on opposite sides of the poles of the subject-object; yet are connected as an objective totality. The process by which the subject attains this consciousness of the self-identical manifest in both phenomena and *noumena* simultaneously is the way by which universality has bestowed upon being the caliber of selfhood that is of this objective totality by mere individuated conceptions that supply it with the quality of agency over the subject as an active participant of their own thinking consciousness. This of course has been called "Godhead" by many, and remains what is to be called a consciousness of givens; but the question to ask is how is it possible that the mind produce these representations that have neither been "summoned" as Fichte puts it, but are rather appearances according to the others such as Schelling that simply *are*. What they indeed "are", is the production of a mind that has a priori conceptions that are both analytic and synthetic which subsequently "open" consciousness to the world of appearances as a function of the self-positing *ego*. Here both Fichte and Schelling were on to something—but where we find that simply all contents of Hegel's reason are easily *sublated* by active contemplation—in a suspension of the *noumena*, phenomena, representations and appearances of consciousness, somehow the objective totality is an existence, or rather, essential existence to the subject that is an appearance of the "rendered mind".

## Judgment and the Objective Totality

Whether or not the subject has become aware of it, the consciousness of being and the being of consciousness first begins with the concept and a judgment. These may even be the passive awareness of an idea or an event it merges with—entering into a synthesis with the objective totality as a rendering of the world of appearances and transcendental idealism. The *being-in-itself* in this instance does not employ *noumenal* freedom and posit the ego with the notion in mind to "conjure" its own *being-in-the-world*, but rather has produced its own identity by way of mere passing thoughts *being-in-themselves*. This reinforces the notion that the world-*in-itself* has for it the understanding of subjectivity and *being-in-itself*, and as such becomes an objective totality that is in a varied mode of consciousness from the positing of ego—as this modality presents the subject with contingent self-identical objective truth that reflects upon the *in-itself* notions of the subject, without the subject engaging substance *ontically* or ontologically. It is altogether the *transcendency* of Being in its most pure form; while not losing the quality of self-identical representation that is posited by way of the social totality. The society's collective apparatus and system of all production is balanced with praxis and mental labour in the *post-industrial* world. Yet, it is only balanced as such so long as philosophy never takes the modality of idealism before dialectical materialism that is in confrontation with the representations and essences of the *socio-naturalistic* world. Yet the modality of the objective totality sits more perfectly with the *being-in-itself* as a passive agent of the very determinations put forth by objective reality. The next motif of being that will alter this modality is the active positing of the phenomenal self that has its particular identity in the appearances. This is what will conjoin the objective totality with the *socio-naturalistic* world as it fuses in synthesis. Here the collective substance is everything to reason, and the notion of ontological being will be determined both by the efforts of dialectical *noumenal* freedoms, and by the *noumenally* and *phenomenologically* contingent objective truths that are carefully judged by the subjective *being-in-itself*.

## The Question of Freedom

The question of freedom arises most predominantly when we consider the self-positing of the determinate *ego* versus particular representations of the ontological societal realm; as if this modality of consciousness—the *noumenal* identity as absolute subject—has been *sublated* by both the experience of the Other, just as it is by the phenomenal *ego* as it posits contingently. That this is an indicator of self-knowledge in the face of a justifiable recognition of the *ego* as a positing being would be correct to assume here as a being that is in-the-world—it has been given its essence by the objective reality of existence. What remains unknown is how it is possible to then reconcile freedom with a phenomenal self-identical contingent positing that does not refer to the objective world alongside the concept of *being-in-itself*.

For this to occur *entity* must be in a modality of "absolute knowing" that renders the determinations of this self-positing *ego* to be in a connection of immediacy with something objective taking place in space and time; and something that begets the necessity for the activity of a self-positing—in this way of positing, the *ego* would be considered an objective determination that has been construed by the *temporalization* of this subjective *ego* as driven by its very own social determinations. These leave their mark upon the psyche of the individual, yet at some point become Objects of the understanding for other beings that stand in relation to the subject. Here the usage of dialectical reflection is most necessary as there is the possibility of false active positing that results in conclusions that will allow for further objective determinations based upon the active posits of the subject, with the resultant of a veritable slew of coercive and power driven attacks upon the rationality of the subject—forcing choices that only fulfill the incorrect positing that had occurred. The next move then, after objective truth has resulted in the self-positing of the *ego* in the form of determinations that limit the free will of the subject, is to identify the copula (Object) that stands between being and the predicate. The following action to be taken is to resource the phenomenal self and negate the determinations as have been posited by the copula or Object. This will allow for the employment of the Concept, and the rendering of a renewed consciousness that is both ontologically and *ontically* fueled with the possibility of free will only to be determined once the autonomous subject regains formal agency of the causal characteristics of nature—the environment in which subjectivity acquires its absolute identity as it posits as a *being-in-itself*. The identification of the Object copula will of course also precipitate *noumenal* self-positing that will determine subjectivity contingently—the work is all being done for being by its own contingent self-positing *noumenal* will; which does of course seem unfathomable but is to emerge as a function of any subject's genus and qualities that are in use. The absolute identity is related to its Otherness as a self-mediating particularity to the abstract universality *of* the Other. The structure of

Being remains *monadological* as the identity of the subject and as non-identity of a particularity for the other in its own monadic status. The inter-subjectivity of multiple non-identities to an absolute subject are also all independently monads to the social object of the subject's own *monadological* being—which is absolute subject and ontological Object with non-identical manifold representations which in effect is a *de facto* dyad. Yet the dyad itself *is* its own monad, in that the absolute subject and ontological Object are to the objective world a totality of a *monadological* dyad that only represents multiplicity as non-identical entities that refer to the same social object within a subjective totality of their own absolute identity. Thereby the multiplicity of the One, the social object is inherent of the *monadological* dyad—all subjectivity adjures to the continuous magnitude of the objective world in its ontological Object while identifying it as its own totality.

> Here the subject posits its self-determination as a function of what should effect the economic laws of social mobility; in that chance has become the causal determination of the subject's ability to apply the conceptual understanding to what is being disclosed as particularity and non-identity to all others in perception of the social object within their own abstract universality:—that the positing of the self-determinations themselves are to be understood as non-identical particularity within the multiplicity to another perceiving subject; and the social object is more indicative of a collective universality of ontological objects and a function of the unity of subjective and objective totalities.

Given that the object is one for many subjects, the objective counterpart to the epistemic representations of the subject are found to be more a function of the multitude of particular non-identities rather than a phenomenal epistemology—that the dynamic of this mode of consciousness is more existentially bound by self-determination as a totality of the multitude rather than a causality of the totality of the subjective understanding of objective truth. What is however clearly a function of causality is the advance of the social totality that may yield the very prospect of a self-determined totality. Here, no violence or damage is done to subjectivity; rather the ontological Object acts as a unification of the dialectical relation between subject and social totality—or society. This prompts the collective substance to the disclosure of being of a mediated universality and forwards the epistemological status of the objective totality for future causal conditions to be administered through policy initiatives. However, as self-determination has set the stage for democratic action, only the oppression of the multitude would reduce further actions of free will—limiting concepts and the objects that go with them.

The objects of which—shall we say—are more fruitfully employed as social totalities that make way for the absolute subject to pursue all initial determinations before encountering the ones that emerge from nature. Then, and only then may the subject connect with its collective identity to all the conditions of universal Being and the totality of the understanding.

# Chapter Five

## *Conceptual* Signifiers *and* Symbolic

## *Representations*

As we undertake to comprehend the ontological relation between essential phenomena and things—those entities that exist yet present no valid epistemological content, one is encumbered with what may in fact signify a departure toward thought beyond reflections concerned with essence and phenomena, or the object, and recognize the ontological process of thinking as an endeavor that could return us to the more conceptual components of philosophy; most notably those still concerned with the image as a representation of what is present in the mind, and relevant to all acts of collective social praxis whereby being is never confined to the mere observation of inner phenomena in pursuit of essence, but what is in fact opened to the horizontal plane of thought that receives both what is conceptually real through the image, and the social totality that is produced by our objective being as it is posited in relation to the horizons of consciousness with which we are faced.

We shall term these images "conceptual signifiers" or "conceptual identification", as with this we are bound to situate ourselves more comfortably on the world stage as subjects with both the powers of praxis, but also observation, reflection, *techne*, and *poeisis,* etc. Language as a "semiosis" of what is represented to the mind is found within all aspects that have been hypostatized and reified in the empirical world, and as such, so should consciousness possess the same powers of perception that are available to the sight. The mind is in-itself the very instrument that interprets what we see, and *sui generis* it should also be the case that the ontology of which we speak possesses the qualities of existence that are greater than mere physical/material experiences purvey. However, still we may insist that the origins of all contemplation begin within the subjective positing of what it is in fact we undertake to accomplish, though here we may also say that we invariably will end up without a comprehension of why, or how the social totality is for us this represented world within the mind.

## The Tetrad

We acknowledge that it is, as such, the immediate result of reproductive forces that are always already at work; and from there we may ascertain that the world is the very totality of both our subjective and objective essence—that these co-presences are in fact synthesized on both planes of the horizontal systemization of thought, and therewith the very human reason associated with the capacity to abstract mental images of conceptual content that signify something that exists in the world. We should also recognize that our subjective understanding of diachronic and synchronic relations of production that are represented epistemologically to us as judgments are there in order to propose the necessary pre-suppositions so as to abstract mental images as *noematic* universals from the temporal horizon that is the social totality in an other mode of perception.

Cause always plays a definitive role in the inclusive nature of this formal universal ideation—it does fall to some degree to what is by way of chance or mathematical possibility what occurs within the mind where concerns conceptual realism, and the co-presence of mental images, objects, representations, the social totality, etc. Here we endeavor to design a model of consciousness whereby the ontology is imbued with the inner-world "tetrad" of conceptual identity(image), object, Otherness and contingent representation(the thing-in-itself), and social totality.

This develops our ontological undertaking even further, since the existence of phenomenal entities is becoming infrequent where we have reduced being to the signification of each relevant notion that will produce the necessary signification for us as subjects to all the aforementioned categories of the "tetrad", which is of course inextricably entwined with classical semiotics, and now shares the terrain with post-Marxism more readily.

As such, the transcendental signifier is considered to be more of an *Other* than conceptual identification, since what is there reproduced is being posited and represented to the mind by the very relations of existence throughout the world totality. In fact, we will call this "co-planar", as appearances are present both within the mental image, just as they are represented by the presence of the world as a social totality. Notwithstanding this, everything is inured with the organization of the mind into what epistemic truths may be attained through thinking alone—that all considerations of what social productions are, are ontologizations of the social forms themselves—as comprehended and understood to be a formal universality, whereby all particularizations of the self are posited into the object by the subject as a representation, a signification of identity.

Given this grounding, we hold the knowledge of the self as it is signified to the whole, and grasp the possibility that what may be known is available to us should we articulate a conceptual understanding of how we may be universally represented.

## Diachrony and Synchrony

Intellectual production and reproduction is key to the process of ontology concerned with the conclusions that may be divested from the diachrony and synchrony available to us, and thereby consciousness finds its place in the world as a complete being-in-and-for-itself and for

Others. As the ontology is conclusively one of inclusion and openness, the intersubjective knowledge that may be attained through concepts is only limited by the frequency with which we engage random concepts that have no correspondence with the manner in which the mind has been ordered. This of course will always yield a concomitant randomization of objects, phenomena, contingent representations, and prospectively conceptual sequencing.

But for the most part, by and large, our thoughts will better respond to the mode of being associated with conceptualization and ontological praxis that corresponds with the objectivization/ontologization/universalization of our ideas, significations and representations.

Here, there will be an effort to determine the objective of knowledge, or economic phenomena as it relates to the social totality and goes on to precipitate the ontology that is in question. We abstract from the Other as a presence of phenomenal representation something that persists as a determinative force of what epistemology may be obtained from economic relations themselves, then conclude that this precipitates within us the content of an economic determination that has, in effect, produced our own essence as an alienated being that is immediate to us as essence, and thereby an obfuscation of the conclusive philosophical notion that our dialectic is resigned to a correlation between concept, object, contingency, and social totality.

## The "Post-Industrial Dialectic"

Yet here, we find as functionary of the epistemology of the "objective universal" what appeals as a verifiable statement respective of its understanding of how we relate to other subjects through both philosophy and economics. This may be key, but yet becomes something problematic to the abstraction of synthetic concepts which may further our project. That being said, it is for us simply to never utterly reject the notion of alienated labour, but rather to perceive it as a road to realizing a profound understanding of economic relations where they become forms of knowledge to us that suit our dialectical reasoning toward the establishment of a more secure footing in the post-industrial dialectic.

Without this sense, even though it overtakes the clear pathway which leads to the necessary ontological communication associated with the higher forms of reason, we will still acknowledge that relations of production have for them a historical context that broadens our self-knowledge. This we should call "philosophical baggage"— but for our purposes we will call it the "diachronic synthesis of historical materialism". For where the objective is a universal that falls into any formal relation of production inclusive of the "species being" as a *value in-itself*, the social totality will recognize what dialectical grounding is commensurable to the ontology where subject-totality dialectics form an elucidating synthesis between object and social totality that reproduces subjective identity as a conceptual image to be abstracted by the agent of production, or is a representation of thought that correlates with the existential unification of concepts. What is intended here, is to further the modality of the objective knowledge that may through thinking alone again become associated with totality to reproduce identity from the in-itself to the for-itself and back.

> Given the aforementioned, it is here posited that what we may have on our hands through the ontological "tetrad" is the very formation of what is in-itself also a monad, a dyad, certainly a triad (where the object is in essence in part apportioned to the social totality). The *de-coupling* of essence and social totality then will become a "tetrad"— what is *in situ* an outer and an inner subject-object dyad that collapses into the tetrad during ontological reflection.

With every allowance made, what is effectively sought out in this particular elucidation is the status of the subject where concerns the modes of being and the levels of administered reality that come along with the former—respective of all reality projected by the social totality as a socio-economic, political, cultural, and temporal horizon of subjective consciousness. We will admit that the objective universal is in conflict with our dialectical process, since there is nothing that may be projected upon the whole by one who's subjectivity has been annexed by alienated subjectivity; however though, what is here being determined is the potency of our dialectical argument toward all *universalization* that is represented by the social totality—for this may be ineffective in the establishment of how collective relations determine the project of insuring that class disparities do not determine knowledge or capability through the hypostatization of dialectical universalizability.

With this, there we shall forward the way by which we are signified beyond the stratification of our being as one who is purely determined by historical facts, but also has the dialectical knowledge so as to preserve the universal identity that we know to be just as possible as the social totality. This is based more upon the "source" of experience, and the dedication to the appropriation of knowledge as a guarantee that our pursuit of truth, justice, equality, etc. is not to be discarded, but rather the affirmation on the universal value possible of ontology that is inured with an ethical boundary that prohibits discrimination and cancellation of one's natural properties. We will of course have to explain ourselves in this regard, as attributes may be "shared" under certain circumstances, and if we posit that what is possible for one is equally possible for another, we must thereby suggest that the subjects' histories (biographies) be taken into account for which attributes are appropriated by others who have spent much less time at labour on those objects of use-value produced and reproduced by subjects engaged in their quotidian practices.

This is of course a tautology, or self-evident, but must be stated within an open system of ontology, where the goal of universality must not compel the subject to afford all that exists without limitation; if for instance exchange-value made it permissible, but otherwise we should feel that no one by the very same argument should be excluded from the properties should they participate equally as both producers and recipients of the collective social whole. We by no means intend to suggest that content is anything other than this which falls under the rubric of a semiotic representation, rather than a *being-in-itself* projecting an entire work upon another reader of the collective ontology; but certainly may conceive of the ontological realism associated with how being is posited/projected by the subject or others, could very well be the representation of a content to another subject.

## Open System

This is the negotiation that we have to make with a representationally "open" system of ontology—yet by this we mean not to suggest that those that have not done their homework deserve to abstract at will. Here we suggest that if one is within the ontology as an active subject, the content may become known to others through what is abstracted or projected by the subject. Certainly no individual would wish to have ideas abstracted directly from the *being-in-itself,* but where the manifold collective is concerned we believe that the content is intersubjective at the very least, and sometimes reproduces ontologically. There is no purpose in battling this possibility other than to possess the sense of trust that if we compose the ontology as a "tetrad", conceptual beings are within our grasp related by their self-awareness a part of the distribution of the cultural plane of consciousness "inter-objectively". No one content will be openly distributed to other parties without consent, and the same rights to the value inherent of works are retained, yet there is no escaping representations as semiotic content whereby they appear. We should however, state that this is rare, and the self-knowledge of the ontology generally produces more representational knowledge than abstract content.

However, with the "tetrad" we will formalize relations of production into an ontology that enables the internal dialectical conflicts over content with commensurable exchange-value judgments that will not reduce any subjects' creative powers, but rather add to them—whereby all community relations are not merely subject to hostile qualitative/quantitative judgments or preferences—but rather directed more toward a sense of the Utopian possibilities of any such existence.

Yet with this, we know that of opposition there is always our dialectical projection and all those that fight for freedom of expression will never be alone when it comes right down to it. So in essence, we have both at this point the "object of knowledge" that has yet to become the "real" object, then our return to the objective being of the self in relation to the Other and the social totality, and finally a synthesis and reflexive *de-coupling* of object and totality.

In fact, it is the productive social totality that gives to us our conceptual signification/identity since it is the universal source of what becomes the synthesis of our subjectivity with its essence. The abstraction of the conceptual identity of the Other may very well constitute the essence of the subject as well. Both as an exchange-value commodity-relations of production, and moreover as a universalization of the dialectical concepts put forward through the subjects' projections and representations.

# Contingency

Thusly, where the identity forms itself as the universal, or "Contingent master-signifier" to nothing other than the subject's own self-representation, being is notably engaged once more by the necessity for emancipatory measures to reclaim the ontological terrain whereby subjectivity had first become established as a value component of the social totality, and an agent over the inter-objective concerns that inhabit consciousness while the subject is in pursuit of its independence from the master signifier. Invariably due to this occasional presence, the subject becomes disconnected from the ontological awareness that would bring forward the presentations available for the subject's involvement with reality as an active participant. That here, dwelling upon the horizon as a signified to the participants of all active social strata—institutions, objects of the universalized world, and relational beings correspondent with the rationalism posited by all intellectual subjects, the represented content of what has been posited and engages the social totality from the standpoint of "thought production" elicits a becoming of the social agent as a being that is not necessarily phenomenologically engaged outside of exchange-value relations.

The subject is, on the other hand, only encumbered with any such relation whereby the economic phenomena have posited being in an exchange-value relation of production to the subject—therewith, subjectivity merits not from phenomena that has excluded the subject from binding agreements. This exists as an emancipatory measure for the subject where essence is at stake, and confines all economic phenomena to its rightful place of abstraction based upon the content of its own substance and value. To posit here, however, that this is a discrete substance that in-itself has been emancipated is to conquer within the forces of superstructure as an ontological edifice prone to suppress the subject's engagement with the *tetralogical* conceptual identification that allows for signification to the social totality. Hereby, there would be no inter-objectivity or "co-planar" existential awareness of the consumption of the subject's substance by others seeking their own signification—and therewith reproductive conceptualization of "the real"—respective of all those compelled to "self-realize" a subject-object relation within the social totality and become active within the nominal praxis. This would "contain" the subject, and by way of which all social actors proliferate consciousness to the others' ontological "senses", it would thereby be utterly perfidious to deny social actors this right and privilege whereby freedom of thought has been justly administered.

## Nominal Signification

Given this, it is never to suggest that one oppose representations that determine activity where it's an objective universalization of the subject's relation to the collective ontology; but here we suggest that there is knowledge that is not acutely in accordance with an emancipated subject's agency—it only encumbers the subject with a necessary process of verifiability. As such, things such as "rhetoric" are more infused within this conceptual ontology where they are merged with dialectic. Whereby we suffuse ourselves with the "idea", it is that "universals" certainly co-exist with their ontical counterparts. And at times, these two poles do not co-exist within the ontology that depicts the subject as a signified being—yet ignores the nominal signifier entirely in the process of scrutiny and evaluation.

The follow-through of the process, is to summon the social totality as the very horizon upon which all subjective praxis and objective universality will co-mingle, in order to restore the conceptual signification of the nominal identity inter-objectively. As such, the concept exists to the subject upon its own abstract universality at the *ontical* pole; and *noematically* is abstracted from the social totality as a concept that is within its "social existence" the "image" of the Other, that is being represented by the social totality where concerns inter-objectivity, and the image of the concept whereby the praxis of the subject has actively abstracted from totality a synchronic conceptual representation that has been copied ontologically and universalized for the subject as a "perceiving" consciousness.

This is a given, yet the economic phenomena persevere to resist this act of rational ontology whereby it questions the subjects/objects as social actors comprising autonomous activities of the emancipated subject. Yet, it is within this ideation that we conclude that this is an integral component to conceptual realism, and allows for the awakening of a content and a universalization of the nominal signification that is posited by reason itself.

## Symbolic Representation

The following will be an examination of the symbolic representation as it is here also called conceptual signification—an image content that is abstracted by the subject from the social totality and likewise also projected upon the subject by the world where there is a confluence of inter-objective ideas associated with the identity of the image and how it may correspond with its object. To here suggest that—as Hegel, Marx, and Sartre had—that an inter-objective exchange is *ex parte* to ontological encumbrances should then be a dynamic readily associated with the ontology with which we are concerned. This being the case, the positing of essence as a function of totality would express the conceptual context in which all symbolic representations are experienced, and thereby the way by which the social totality is upon the horizon rather than a superstructure dividing the subject from its essence. We see here that subjectivity becomes meritorious of everything inter-objective, in effect the causal chain of the ontological domain is affixed to the very co-presence of concept and object, and we are well-refined where the image/appearance is *semiotically* represented to us while active in the reproduced spheres of the ontology at hand—namely this that is never alien or suppressed of purpose whereby collective aims are socially recognized—valued.

In fact, far from it—the open ontology of this realism surpasses the sense of alienation that has historically been a large part of the subject-object dichotomy, whereby the objective essence has been commodified for private/public usage by the power machinery that once stood over the subject's *autonomized* being. In fact, historically, identity was in effect the result of a synthesis between objective power and subjective autonomy in order to position subjectivity in a place of servitude and obedience. We believe that the goal of rational agency is to become emancipated from this psychologism, and re-connected to the ontology of universality and collectivity. The intersubjective hegemony of the Other is only a negation of the ontology where it has become dynamic to the social totality as an objective referent for being within the totality, and for the positing of subjective observation in pursuit of the constancy of the remote conditions of abstraction from the objective horizon. Dialectic here finds a home with existence as a proper measure of the extended subject that must project its presuppositions upon the world with the intention of grasping hold of the subject-world synthesis—should one pursue causal *universalization* as both a particular subject and as objective agent. Any dialectical process that is undergone however, invariably results in the return to the self, and in this instance the potency of abstraction for the other as well. So tolerance is meta-ethically of the ontology in order to preserve the conceptual reality represented to the subject as what is "the case".

## The "Post-Industrial Aesthetic"

Where in fact the alienation from the world returns, may be in the process of the positing of a universality that is not within variable conditions of a produced awareness, such as in the case of capital inhering through the Other that is merely managing the use-value of all social components of the ontological dwelling itself. These "groups"—the social beings that manoeuvre with legerdemain to bring value to themselves in pursuit of a reification of ontological use-value—remain the parties that have not yet undertaken to posit the same universality or social totality that enriches the post-industrial aesthetic.

Given this, one questions the possibility or impossibility of any such ontological universalization, that for all intents and purposes is for us a positing of alethic truth, and never falsehoods and misgivings. In its stead, we find the road to our "solidarity" through the ontological formations concerned with the general principles of what is good, rather than the manufactures of any particular self-interested party. This falls entirely into another domain, whereby relations of production and competition battle dialectically from world spirit (*weltgeist*). In so doing, these parties promote division, exclusion, and ultimately alienation from the widely, considerably authentic inclusivity of any open ontological terrain. As being presupposes essence, and essence appearance, we see our reason as an "equivalential chain"—a universalized "tetrad" that forms symbolic representation/conceptual signification/nominal identification through abstraction from a social totality. Herefrom, it is also that it would be inter-objective and not concomitantly present to two subjects synchronically. It is an either/or dynamic—and where one subject objectively perceives the other through symbolic representation/conceptual signification, the Other does not and vice versa.

Yet if we suggest a co-presence of image and noumena, or a "noumenal image", thereby we could afford the possible ontological dynamic of co-present images as well (with the thing-in-itself). But it stands to argument that this would be an impossible world of inter-objectivity. In fact, we conclude that without a re-structuring of the "administered world" that it may never happen. Which questions our very notions of what universality is for "the real", and what "the real" is for universality. In this sense, with the givens of consciousness—the concept, the object, Otherness, totality—we are as such, here negotiating with something beyond our grasp. Although, this very positing of the subject is a sublation (*aufheben*) of the object itself, and a return to the prospects of a void universality, rather than the engagement with other social beings.

Within the aforementioned, it is that the for-itself is the ontological instantiation involved with dialectical reproductions and abstractions of the concept, and acts in accordance with the synthesis of the object with the reproduced whole. Where the object is still an essence for the subject, is where dialectical reasoning has met with an abstraction of essence and a regression into the alienation that we negatively endorse. To be positioned as a subject without object or social totality is to have been "cut-off" from the ontology that has become such a large part of the subject's lifeworld.

## Social Abstraction of the Concept

Here we passage toward the notion of the social abstraction of the concept, or "*noematic* referent" from the social totality, to the conceptual determination of subjective praxis that enters into dialectical ontology with the nominal signifier that has been abstracted from the nexus of the totality in-itself. The projected noumenal identity of the subject benefits from the materialist dialectic in this certain instance, and therewith, garners favourable attentions from the collective—that subjectivity is in preservation of identity as a for-itself and for-another. This ontological interpellation of material and ontological formal *universalization* expresses the *hic et nunc* of the situation particular to both subjectivity *en masse* and also the objectification of the essential properties of the collective—whereby the phenomena of "state essence" is in fact not the universalization of the subject's apprehension of all collective aims, but in fact a subordination of the emancipatory praxis so concerned with this ontology as an abstraction of concepts, as it is a praxis concerned with the conceptual determination of nominal signifiers that have been represented to a subject.

In this way, the subject presupposes not an "idealist" ideology, but one that is entirely not only the synthetic a priori, but also the encumbrances of how being is conceptually related by way of its universal formality—as is for instance found in all reproduced forms of technological media and "thought" cultural objects and representations. That these must be explicitly under the overdeterminations, or of the political economy to the degree that they are "state formations" is entirely without grounding—whereby we have already dismissed the economic phenomena-as-essence of state capital never to be what has produced or reproduced this collective essence—but rather the universal consciousness of an emancipatory and ontologically collected will of the population, where social interest exists not in place of the Other, but rather all social relations exist because of the Other.

In effect, the multiplicity of the ontologized being is combinatory where it is explicit to its own nature and ontological encumbrances—produced from the source as being of an inter-relation that can only be known by those responsible for the collective consciousness itself; and the conceptual determination originating at the subjective pole of being. In effect, the combined influence of every particular subject toward a rational ontological goal is the very consciousness that is needed in order to form a social totality that will eventuate possible relations of reproduced Energeia and productive activity. Through the concept as a reflexive subject-object component, the "real object" can only be the object that has been posited by the experiences of the subject and the currency of its relation to universal social forms.

However, this decries the need for investigation into the narrative that will support the subjects' involvement with the economic, political, social, cultural, etc. We see here that normative time as a form of knowledge operates in close unity with the behavioural mechanisms that ground and center all subjective relations to the objective realm in which they may receive conceptual determinations from others. Yet still we subsist in the ideation of the subject as the concept by way of which nominal signification may become a distraction for members of the objective plane, and thereby acknowledge that a determination is required by the subject in order to formally universalize identity whereby it is undergoing its own process of being determined by others to never be in conflict or contradictory to what has been set out by the individualized being of the subject.

Given this, there is nothing but the positing of the subject's own being in relation to its objective counterparts, and the social totality is or has become an economic presence for established wealth. However, the conceptual reality of this strata of "bourgeois consciousness" is limited by its mere obsessions with accumulation , while we are mostly ensconced with our pursuit of the ontology of concepts, ideas, representations, and "silent revolutions" that will be authored on the world stage by way of our ontological praxis and dialectical projections upon those with the resources and access thereof to change the political economy from its nascent state of exclusion—toward the possibility of a formal universalization of all nominal signifiers into conceptual abstractions for the reproduced totality. We will in turn also become co-present conceptual beings with those that propose an ethical pursuit of the reproduction of collective essence that is ordered by subjective praxis and not solely by organized power.

## Self-identification

Alongside the conceptual signification, is of course the posited self-identification—the eidetic and retention. As a correlate of the property relation between two intersubjective un-identified beings, the synthetic a priori of the memory component of the subject's own metalogical praxis is copied by way of the signification of another such object as would the property relation signify. In this instance, the self-identical projects upon the property relation another signification that is related to a particular ontological component that represents itself as memory, and the subject is without the requisite "abstraction-negation-concrete" of Hegel in pursuit of retention, but more retaining the content in-itself as an immediately composed subject—a being-in-itself. Whereby the for-itself is instantiated only in order to reproduce symbolic identity and ontological signification, subjectivity finds the essence beyond any phenomenological representations thereof, and is *de facto* only displaced by the very transformation of ontological subjective identification into an ontological being of retention. Therewith, all eidetic prospects are in the becoming of ontological representations as temporal *noematic* symbolizations—*noema*—yet also as the very representations of those property relations that may interest the subject in pursuit of self-identification. That they are also projected upon the social totality engages the object as a formal universalization of what has been retained by the subject, whereby public (social) enterprise has been elicited by formal *universalization* of the property relation instantiated by the eidetic properties within the concept that has so been signified.

That this may lead to further ontological significations through projection upon the subject-object in question is open for investigation, but we think that this would reduce the objective phenomenon to a mere representation of social production, rather than encouraging the conceptual formations that have become part of the property relations in-themselves—such as the object of thought (being/essence), memory (retention), *noema* (image), social totality—all universalized forms of collective thought and consciousness. Herewith, perhaps we must distantiate ourselves from objectivity, should all acts of retention be the modality of our representational self-identification. Yet, in the case of the preservation of the projected identity upon the social strata (totality), we fully acknowledge the merits of the "tetradic" formations of the ontology with the intention to direct ourselves toward the objective from the vantage point of an actor and a participant.

With this in mind, all social relations involving "eidetic" retention are to be addressed as a pure form of modal consciousness affiliated with the inter-objective relations of production recognized and socially preserved. However, where these are immediate property relations to the subject by way of which the reproduction and preservation of identity is at stake, there should be no prohibition over any act of ontological property relation that has been found within an ethical process of dialectical reasoning. Therefore, the abstraction, whereby the concept is copied into consciousness from its object, may be universalized in order to produce a property relation that will reproduce one's own conceptual signification to the social totality—where the property has been valued to the subject's own social praxis and object of thought *vis-à-vis* the social totality.

> This merits temporal inter-objectivities of modes of reproduced conceptual signification and relations of production, but also may confer with an ontological status of a social praxis that is of "intellectual beings"—entwined ontologically with diachronic and synchronic meaning.

When we say "conceptual formation" we mean to say this that conceptually appears by whatever means possible and enters into a property relation with the subject, is abstracted, or has thereby been posited/projected upon symbolic/real identities as beings-in-themselves.

## Objective Self-Identification and the Emancipatory Social Being

When the subject presupposes any identification with the representational consciousness associated with post-industrial capitalism, the diachrony/synchrony of what appears posits its own object—the subject in relation to the ontological exchange-value relations. In this instance, we find the subjective positing of the "Cartesian Ego" a starting point for the reestablishment of the objective reflexivity endemic of the "bourgeois" phenomena of Kant; therewith it is suggestable that one must again synthesize self-identification with the synchronic representations proposing use-value "commodifications" as a mode of the reappropriation of the same conditions that had produced the initial division with the subject's "objective self-identification" toward a possible horizontal totality.

That these are "regions" of "intentional objective totalities", or in any event the originary displacement of this "objective self-identification", proposes a Marxist social praxis that is imbued with the deification of the subject through the abstract negation of its "totalized" capital relations. Where this resembles overdetermination, is precisely where the provisional abstraction of the subject's ontological substance had been divided and appropriated from another regional (economic) social totality.

That it would be compromised inwardly or externally throughout empirical "commercial drives" is here revealed, whereby the ontological/ontical reflexivity of the subject's own rapport with its own conceptual *transcendency* through the nominal signifier and the "understanding social praxis" of the Other suggests the potentiality of a social undertaking that supersedes bourgeois representations and allows for a socialist positing of the "real"—keeping in line with the originary project of the positivists; yet well within the space of something that has been more formally determined temporally.

> It must be noted that between "objective self-identification" and subjective praxis, there is no dialectical reasoning that confers the positing of identity with its counterpart in the social forms as they are—as such, it is an expression of the sense that the subject must identify with what has been signified conceptually by the cultural ideation affiliated with the aesthetics operating from a synchronic involvement with the potential currencies of thought—promulgated throughout its ontological terrain.

Therewith, the strata of diachronic impressions/representations to the subject become enmeshed with the cultural leitmotif affiliated with its "character identification" in absence of any formal representations that are imbued with the dialectical reasoning of the subject. The "political subject" as it were, has been identified by regional totalities a priori as a "this" or a "they", and subsequently finds the expression of subjectivity engrossed in certain a priori determinations that would perhaps be considered "residual artefacts" of the subject's own identification within the world as a "this" or a "they"—that in fact, we are both,—whereby "objective self-identification" has become part of the particularized social identity of any acting subject in pursuit of a subjective social praxis that may exist in correspondence with the Other, and in fact become represented by a collective identity that becomes the social identity of subjectivity in the form of the "synthetic a priori".

The proximate determinations of subjective social praxis themselves are never "residual artefacts" of the interobjective status of the collectivized/stratified beings as such, but are the *non sequitur* of the social existence of regional totalities that are intentional toward the production of a social identity that exists in conflict with the "conceptually signified" or "symbolically represented" social beings that persist in the quest for social identification within a verifiable use-value adherent.

In this circumstance, the in-itself and the for-itself are nugatory without conceptual grounding insofar as it identifies with a special interest—usually that of a group or particularized substance that holds subjectivity for "ransom". Here, the totality and its collective correspondence with the social horizon of consciousness, is never binding in its pursuit of the emancipatory concept of self-identity in its ontological relation to the Other; that this is the "puissance" of state or corporate representation that is not in correspondence with the emancipatory elucidary dialectical reasoning of the much more erudite subjective praxis in pursuit of a reality that never exists within the confines of superficial market-value induced beings that possess only capricious standards where regard more well-founded ontological claims.

That these "existents" or artificial "homo sapiens" must become inverted into the dialectical reasoning of the *"homo faber"* exudes the objective understanding in confluence with more powerful resources of the human enterprise. In this respect, subjectivity produces the in-itself as a for-itself—yet only by way of which subjective social praxis has negated the obsequious regions of consciousness that have not developed self-identity beyond its delimited potentiality to socially produce a subjective praxis through "objective self- identification". The positing of the concept is bereft the very notion of its rapport with the totality as a collective "we-subject", and here the visionary images of social beings fade into the blackness of antiquated policies that stand in opposition to the emancipatory social praxis affiliated with "being" as an instrument of reason—the logical plenum of dialectical projection intentional toward its consummation with the affirmations reflexive of administered negations of the possibilities confluent within the subject's own identity; this being the formal universalization of the abstract possibilities produced by subjective social praxis beyond caprice, yet ensconced within the ideation of a choice that had only been determined by the reflexive process of emancipatory self-identification reasoning dialectically with the abstraction/positing of the

Other as a being for-itself or for the subject. That it would only become for the subject's understanding reflects the notion that the subjects have produced a social praxis throughout their own dialectical reasoning as a "process". Therewith, as an opponent that represents administered reality projected upon the *objectivated* "being-in-itself", the very concept of being is appropriated by the Other for exchange-value reification—the for-itself.

> To remark that in this particular instance one must portray subjectivity as something in-itself—a higher minded being in apprehension of the epistemic content available—is not the provisional affordability of reified substance upon the objective pole, but rather the dialectical context that has been produced by the subject's ontological praxis—seen as "work" more than "play".

Stationed within this very notion however, is the idea that social praxis would also be "at play", whereby the conceptual social praxis of its ontological terrain would be within the collective as an acceptable projection upon common purpose—collective aims. How to distinguish between the mode whereby the ontology is entirely controlled by an institutional for-itself, and a subjective-collective "we-subject" is thought of a priori within the concepts that are posited ontologically by the subject. This is how one differentiates between what is "evil" and what is "good"—what will become *de facto* emancipatory possibilities for ontological subjects within the collective in-itself as a "we-object".

The prospects of the subject are not limited by a pure, empirically reified value exponent, but rather "being" as a "this" and thing-in-itself within a substance worthy of engaging forms of social and ontological production that will not necessarily identify with the synchronic exchange-value interests merely consumed by privilege, and unilaterally given a position in society because of their compliance with the administrative-determinative powers *in-themselves*. That these would ever become renewed as only exchange-value components of a reified social reality is an oppressive concept; yet that these would become social perversions protected by reified state power seems ever more in collusion with the social praxis of any subject's becoming available or substantiated as *beings-in-themselves* a priori.

Here, the denaturalization of the social being fights dialectically for something projected by their own alienation from themselves as a comprehensively social ontological existent of the identified social reality that has become subjective—thereby the "*plateau du conscience*"; the necessary possibility of being confiding in the Other as a "being-in-itself", but also having to negotiate with representations/signifiers that oppose the subject's individuation from obfuscated social forms.

## The Other as Contingent Possibility of the Self-Identical

As a synchronic signification of universal identity is the intentional projection of the ontico-ontological being-in-itself, the potency of an absence in mediation of the being-in-itself as a particular identity by its Other is attributable to the preservation of universal identity while the latter is thought of as a *stricto sensu* of ideology and the state apparatus.

The very concept of the self as an "identity" is here dialectical with its absolute *subjectivization* in an ontological terrain as an emancipated, *significatory* universal identity, that it becomes "co-present" with the signifying image without any contextualization to objective being—the phenomenon as it were. Rather, it is instead purely the reflexive co-existent of the image with which it becomes an *in abstracto* nominal signification; yet only insofar as it preserves the identical within the signifying chain of the universal apparatus whereby images (conceptual signifiers) are appearances posited before the projected self-identical. To posit here that there is dialectic between the self-identical and the image seems a lofty claim, but none the less it is still within the signifying chain as such—a concept—represented to nothing particular to the totality that seems under the conditions of a "void universality", but to the subject is the contingent thing-in-itself. In this particular instance the contingent possibilities (truth) posited resist the totality, and identity is able to become universal only in relation to what is signified by the conceptual image that is here a synchronic appearance that responds to the contingent possibilities of the self as subject throughout the signifying chain.

The for-itself in this instance is posited as identical and contingent to the perceiving subject as a represented Other than the self, yet an object of reason whereby it is of the pure understanding as a thing-in-itself, and therewith to my estimation the "Real"—or something relative to what is Absolute to the subject where concerns reality, or the circumstances and determinations diachronically ontologized in order to produce the representation, and arguably a considerable projection of the exchange-value component affiliated with the subject's own empirically ontologized temporal value as an *interobjective* being. The middle ground between the universal subject and the particular subject is this very *historicization* of the substance/value attribution that confers with the signifying chain its own singular appeal to the self-concept as a being within the ontology proper, as both contingent possibility and self-identical projection behind the appearance itself. The identical here is universally singular as it is still part of the signifying chain, yet is only *semiotically* represented as an abstraction to the Other through the synchronic projection of the self-identical as a dialectical move operating in correlation with the presence of a dialectical abstraction posited by another subject/object that has become Absolute through the objectivization of their summoned *significatory* status.

Where subjectivity posits its Other as a self-identical contingent possibility, one is prone to identify with the proposition should it become a corollary of the Other as a contingent in-itself *in abstracto* of the dialectical reasoning produced upon the subjective pole as

Conceptual Signifiers and Symbolic Representations 139

projections a priori, intentional toward what has been signified by the image. Here, the image could be anything that's been depicted by the *techne* or *phronesis* of contemporary "medial forms", or as ontological representations of the thing-in-itself as a synchronically posited "semiotic image" available for abstraction; or to be posited contingent to the actual determinations of the pictured subject *in situ* of another domain, yet still a *de facto* conceptual identity of the ontological terrain wherein the subject has been signified, as such. Therewith, one must observe the *interobjectivity* as an existent of the exchange of self-identical contingencies, somewhat outside of the particular agency of the subject, yet still within the ordinance of the universal *significatory* status of the agent as an actor that produces thought from the standpoint of an absolute subject where concerns the preservation of identity, while only acting as a non-identical particularity where concerns a universalized totality.

To suggest that the signifying chain leaks self-identical particularity to the universal becomes more of a dialectic between subject and "invisible" social institutions, yet to posit the subject as a universal self-identical projection upon the social totality presupposes division between being and essence—in that the object becomes of the totality as a social object representing the "mass psychology" in which the subject may become involved at the outset of universal self-identification. Should this last, the dialectical reasoning as projected by the for-itself must congregate a collective ideation within the ontological terrain and produce a negation that will become the *sine qua non* of the institutional Other's reified exchange-value.

<small>In absence of this, the "singular universal" is more prone to become engaged within the productive social praxis of an agent in possession of no recognizable claims—such that reified substance upon the objective pole had not displaced the use-value of the subject's own process of social integration.</small>

It becomes something of a balancing act to measure totality upon the objective horizon as a being-in-itself, that one universal identity should possess the reified exchange-value of the socially (socio-economically) produced horizon that gathers subjective social praxis as both an emancipatory project, as well as a "semiotic signifier" to the ontological terrain that persists throughout its journeyed quest for conceptual symbolization to a horizontal totality—beings-in-themselves as such, within the preponderance of an objectifying synthesis between contingent self-identity as an *interobjective* substratum, and the subjective synthesis with an ontological counterpart in the Other as its exchange-value component within the signifying chain. These are the regions of confluence and appraisal of the socially produced being, and therewith, the *interobjective* signifiers that have represented themselves as "co-planar" things-in-themselves in the process of an ontological inter-relation that posits the Other as a contingent self-identical representation within the certitude of a reality that is both a relative proposition to the self as subject, but also an absolute subject; in that through the contingency as an in-itself, reason has become posited of the former.

## The Detachable Subject through its Ontological State of Corporeal Supersession Toward a Representational Other

It is here suggested that the body and the mind are two independently produced co-existences, that where matter and form combine, there has been a synthesis that is outside of the realm where possible horizons of thought become detachable ontological representations in signification of being as identical to itself—yet herewith, it is argued that *co-presence* does in fact involve the naturalized *potentia* of the corporeal substance as a signified existent to the necessary ontological terrain that orders *Dasein* toward its more natural impetus as a thing-in-itself that comprehends the causal chain. In this sense, something possessing the necessary conditions forming a temporal *noesis* that adheres toward its representational Other as a "being" that inhabits conceptual thinking.

That this most notably originary point of contact between the self and its ontological Other becomes a positing of the "Real" for the noetic subject, presumes that in fact a synthetic a priori evaluation of the conditional status of the ontico-ontological consciousness has become involved upon the primordial substrate as an intersubjective, *bio-economic* "labour value", but is here to engage the positing of being as a detachable objective essence with the necessary properties in exchange amounting to the onto-genesis of what becomes more resigned to an *ontical* status than an ontological projection of the conceptual determination embodied in the subject as a being of acting social praxis. The terms by which subjectivity adheres to its naturalized ontological state, presupposes the necessary dialectic between *ontical* subject and ontological existent, thereby becoming apportioned to the subject as a naturalization of being and a detachable signifier to be represented to the social totality outside of the inherent qualities of being that presuppose *ontical* possession of the qualities *in-themselves*.

Although here, the projected co-existent that emerges from the noetic understanding confers identity more with its *noematic* counterpart, yet only insofar as "pairing" is never reified upon the primordial substrate and exists only through its detachable form. Therewith, the subject presupposes dialectical notions on the noetic pole toward the abstraction of the conceptual image, in lieu of its formal ontological detachability, wherein the counterpart of an *interobjective* hypostatization is an objective positing of what imbues subjectivity with an apotheosis of the primordial substrate and has been *sublated in toto*.

That the primordial substrate is not in conflict with its ontological component is clearly the case, as one does posit from the subjective pole as a being-in-the-world, yet becomes conceptually signified to the totality as a substrate to the conceptual content as a representational object. But what is in dispute, is whether or not the subject posits *as* a substance to the Other ontologized beings that perceive the essence of any subjects as "commodity forms"—primordial magnitudes that fill a void universality with a reified exchange-value component endemic of any institutional forms that presuppose the "image ban" on subjective beings; whereby the obfuscation of the very material forms that are being posited enter into conflict with the ontological existents that are a priori possibilities for the transcendental subject.

Here it becomes quite necessary that the subjects presuppose an abstraction of a conditional reality from the social totality that would only become available through dialectical reasoning as detachable beings-in-the-world. This projection is never a variable of the social praxis with which subjectivity hypostatizes the very being that would have the necessary *potentia* to enact a dialectical move, yet here, by way of which one has become a conceptual identity, none the less the projection of the being-in-and-for-itself is entirely produced by an *ontical* being-in-itself able to become conceptually signified through the projection toward the totalized substance. Perhaps there becoming involved through the homologous state of primordial substrates and particularized ontological self-identifications—whereby the subject's own core being is in full possession of the aim to recover the naturalized *potentia* of productive social praxis—ontologized through its projection to the totality as a value component of the collective identities within the same process of hypostatized social being. These are thereby abstracted and become conceptually determined, whereby the causally ontologized social praxis is projected through its temporal/conceptual identification—throughout the synthetic proportions of diachrony and synchrony. That this would presume "being" as a detachable component of the virtual/binary self that is for the Other as an existent of a detachable conceptual content that may be reified, becomes its own condition for the "post-industrial dialectic"—whereby temporal determinations have already positioned this which may be posited ontologically by subjects toward an ontological Other—

that to be signified is the *de facto* status of any being as part of the cultural anthropology of what it is to be human, but also that where we consider the aforementioned, perhaps the substratum comes to the forefront of our sense of ontico-ontological self-evaluation.

Thereby, one might construe the self as "identical to itself" as Hegel had, and verify all ontological projections within what we should now ponder as "detachable proximities"—that the object is our essence but also what posits conceptual self-identification to the Other as a horizon that has recognized the process by which conceptual identities come into being as images.

## Conceptual Universalism: Ontological Impossibility, or Ontico-Ontological Preservation of Reflexive Universal Self-Identity?

Where we presuppose that there is an objectifying synthesis between the subject and the objective social totality that posits a phenomenal object—a magnitude as such—the ontical pole is rendered as ontological throughout this synthesis, and there we recognize the possibility of an a priori connection to the object as an object of epistemology as much as we do the essence or ontological *being qua being* of the subject. To recognize the "Real" as this object—that being is comprised of its *ontico-empirical* status as much as the ontological identity posited by the objective pole of consciousness of the object in synthesis with the subject's own "identity thinking"—presupposes a logical connection to the "Real" and the natural attributes that compose the subject's essence and identity through its object.

That things would enact the "inner difference" of Hegel, or to suggest that the subject has no value in *being qua being*, would be to reify the concept that human life is not something other than a mere property to be "moved" as an object-in-itself for Others' financial prosperity, or to posit being-in-itself as a concept that presupposes the politico-ideological wars and dialectical contradictions inherent of global capitalism. While we are able to project that the object fills the lacuna with the epistemic content synthesized of the ontic—whereby the ontological presupposes the preservation of identity—we conclude that the ontological space of representation is the "free substance" of any subject in preservation of its axiological being while in full possession of "rational agency". Yet therein, we acknowledge the "administered world" may appear once again in the hands of those that reify objectivity through an objective synthesis with social production—the means by which use-value becomes this object for the subject's discovery of the "Real".

Let us here elucidate that this object is a *de facto* representational phenomenon of the object's own social enterprise as a being of "substance" in the Kantian sense, while closer to Marx—whereby the object is identifiable as a Cartesian or Husserlian "ego cogito" directed toward its natural state of contemplation in apprehension of its "Real" connection to the strata of social production upon the horizon. To decenter the subject from its own "natural form" as an *ontico-ontological* being of essence of use-value propriety, is to commit a social wronging—whereby it is dismissed as something conclusively delusionary of the social being of the subject whom has become conceptually represented to the social whole, or society. We acknowledge the psycho-analytic principle of transference here, as we notice that the dialectical reasoning of the subject's objectifying synthesis has become the ontology of the analyst rather than the labour value of the *analysand*.

Here we simply must dialectically introduce the positing of a negation of the appropriation of the subject's use-value in order to reveal the dialectical contradiction that has positioned subjectivity in an impossible state of a lacking of self-awareness. The subject in fact has been "un-invested-in" by the Other that has been empowered by the negation of the substance the subject once had possessed as an *ontico-ontological* being-in-and-for-itself. That this affordability of state/institutional power would be a regulated practice seems to be a contradiction endemic of the capitalist system—sometimes marked as compassion or the "welfare state", but upon inspection seems to be an appropriation and cancellation of the subject's identity. This binds together Marx with Laclau, and also presupposes the inclusion of a Hegelian totality—that state power would not necessarily be in agreement with any such action in this way, other than to protect exposure from whichever arrangements might be made by the subjects to resolve the dialectical contradictions as an irrational for-itself. It occurs to this writer that *being qua being* for Hegel was the unmediated essence of the ontological identity of a subject in *Phenomenology of Spirit*, yet where it is purely an epiphenomenon, is the reflexive objective synthesis imposing upon a subject the a priori negation of identity and use-value—herewith, an ideology more affiliated with Fascism than Liberal Democracy or Post-Industrial Socialism.

Whereby the socialization of the subjects is presupposed to have mental representations that are to be identified as a form of "illness", is where the representations themselves have taken on the qualities of the subjects—while projecting negations of the proper essence of the subjects as beings-in-themselves; a *de facto* "Evil" of the strata in pursuit of the very dialectical contradictions that have instantiated the inefficiency to posit the "Real" as an a priori presupposition. This self-positing aspect of the objective synthesis between subject and self-identification has now been jeopardized by the Other that is clearly in pursuit of the down fall of the subject. This would be what has been identified as "paranoid schizophrenia", but here it is also that the commercial drives of the Other may in fact be projecting something antagonistic toward the subjects within the ontological space of representation—an internal conflict usually affiliated with these "psychotic representations" that are in pursuit of social capital, reified use-value and profit. To posit that this is a *de facto* act of ideology, whereby one considers representational content to be generated by state authority, is to present an argument that subjectivity may be presented with an a priori conflict with the state that has instigated an internal contradiction. In this particular instance we would have something resembling a hegemonic or rogue state—usually the city state rather than what falls under nation-state jurisdiction. One might also present an argument that the space of representation in this instance is occupied by a dialectical conflict between hegemonic subjects pursuing the same concept—which could be the positing of an effect that is produced by empirical conditions that have not been met, or that there has been a perceived "civil wronging" that has instantiated the dialectical contradiction. But nevertheless, the subjects' being and *ousia* had been damaged by the space of representation—as Rancière suggests, "divided from essence" under the capitalist system.

This of course in the Freudian sense is often the super-ego of the representation of state authority, or the "father figure". We discover here revealed by Rancière and Freud a dialectical contradiction anew where subject and object presuppose an ontological relation in ideological conflict with exchange-value/use-value and unconscious lifeworld ontological strata, since a subject that is a "father", super-ego before the social totality, and the gate-keeper of the Energeia of community substance appropriates social production in order to fund the very institutions that have *sublated* the subjects' own use-value toward the state social production in its social totality. Here the "welfare state" will not hold the opportunity for subjects to develop through public education any process whereby they may reify their rational use-value, and as beings will only become the recipients of failing social programmes. Therefore, the system must be represented as a thing-in-itself more than its paternal authority, and operate legally and ethically in order to administer a state where "the real is the rational"—going back to Hegel's ideal state in *Philosophy of Right*, where the subjects' essence depends upon their inclusion into the substance of the nation-state at a neurological level, in that *being qua being* would be sacrificed by smaller governments, less regulation, and more privatized competition.

We see here how Canada may in fact resemble to some degree the Constitutional Monarchy of Hegel's work and that our concept of identity must be both particular and universal—whereby universality is an identity for the citizens—that we are all treated equally under the law, etc. Given this, what is hereby introduced is the notion of the "conceptual universal".

The "universal concept" is an idea that we shall here address in Adorno's sense, where he suggests that the concept is "anything but particular". The "conceptual universal" is something that has been ontologized from the particular and become of the universal. This idea brings forth a notion that is being posited by matter, ontically, but is reproduced as a concept universally where the particular properties of the object are posited in relation to a social totality that recognizes the conceptual identity of what had been ontologized from the particular into the universal. I hold this to be possible without redefining particularity as "Real" and I will argue that since the qualities of a particular subject or object belong to that subject or object in particular, that the conceptual components of the particular are synthesized in the form of matter to then take on a conceptual universal form. In the case of the "nominal signifier", I have already elucidated that it is not universal, but I am here arguing that the concepts affiliated/attached to both subjects and objects are.

Firstly, to make things quite simple, this pen is "blue", "metal", it is a "writing instrument", etc. All of these qualities of the pen are universal concepts. As pedestrian as this may appear, it reveals that the tautology stands to expose the pen as a particular object that may also be *noematically* reconstituted ontologically through its reproduction to the totality—that what is being written may be equally universal as generated by consciousness and the pen and paper, but also what is conceptual to the Other ontologically is not just any pen—it is this one, because the qualities of the pen are universal concepts—hence the "conceptual universal". This reasoning also works from an ontology in advance of the ontic—whereby every quality of the pen is reflexively co-existing between the ontic and the ontological. Therewith, as something is written, it is ontologized just as the pen is as a thing-in-itself. In as much, it has been conceptually determined.

Therefore the nominal identity of a subject is also conceptually universalized as a symbolized thing-in-itself—posited as the Other *intersubjectively* and there reproduced by the "total subject". In general, we will present this argument as an identification of a particular subject *as* a conceptual universal; respective of the qualities related to the thing-in-itself of its nominal signification—yet *sublate* the thing-in-itself as a particular Other at the precise moment of synchrony where the subject has become a universal object as well. In this sense as a concept, the subject's ontological properties may be abstracted at will by the Other—coming back to the dialectical contradiction inherent of commercial drives that propel the economy for some, while cancelling possibilities for others. The principle that Western Democracies are comprised of "winners" and "losers" is an inadequate determination of those seeking greater social and economic equality and justice. Since the *elucidary* notion that the objective synthesis will sometimes, under given conditions produce the ontic, I resolve that all dialectical contradictions be eradicated in order to administer rational agency to the subjects as beings-in-themselves.

This would further the project of self-awareness and *interobjectivity* as a conceptual universality for those whom wish to posit a horizon of inclusivity based upon choice and free will, and would also give regulatory status to the "administered world"—the state as an institution that does not present the subject with dialectical contradictions a priori. The process by which one would fasten reality outside of "Socialist Strategy" or "Capitalist Hegemony" would be based within the rational agency of the subjects that had not found that any contradictory ontology were stripping subjectivity of rational agency in-itself. With this, the subject may choose to reproduce identity with universal access, or decide to remain stationed within anonymity as a practical "political subject"—pursuing dialectical reasoning with the intention of developing the world in such a way that it becomes comprehensible to *ontico-ontological* reflexivity in order to determine the causal nexus of the *significatory* chain and administer a social reality that is functional to those that have clearly become rational agents.

To suggest that a greater presence of the regulatory body, higher taxation, and less personal freedom would render this feasible has been the historical solution, yet to regulate freedom of choice is of course a more conceivable representational determination of an ontological proposition that will not reproduce the identities affiliated with the dialectical contradictions administered by the free market system. Ideas, as ontological representations are in essence "free", but the reified value to which they stand in relation in terms of market share is in possession of economic power, and therewith the hegemonic subject persists in today's world. The economic powers monopolizing a nation's resources and wealth will always fall prey to the hegemonic subject, yet these subjects must also apprehend that, as beings-in-themselves, we are developing an ontology in order to reproduce a more rationally administered "freedom of choice".

In that quest, we will also find that universality contains within it a dialectical contradiction of its own—inherently where concerns the *ontico-ontological* being as a "conceptual universal". All particular identities subject to ontological signification and representation with opposing social, political, economic, and cultural views clearly have a stake in the terrain of consciousness available in order to practice ontology that relates to the aforementioned claims from the vantage-point of a community substance or universalized ontological terrain where the identities as things-in-themselves are preserved. In order to pursue the matter further, let us turn to Plato for a moment and proceed onward from there.

Philosophy at its foundational level presents Plato's system as one where "realism" posits the independent existence of forms and ideas before the material object, and reality's "knowable existence" independently of the senses. In the present day, the ontic would be entirely driven by the ontological—all experienced knowable facts would be the "Real" within mind as ideas. As a universal, thought would precede being under all circumstances—rational agency would be a nullity without a Guardian. All political, economic, cultural, and ethical notions would be without the justification of the material reality—the ontic. To this day, though we still may experience "reality" independently of our senses reflexively, a particular self-identification is required in order to address its corresponding universal form or idea—otherwise universality is a flagrant impossibility for contemporary living. This falls into the territory of the relativists, while the former is clearly an Absolutist concept. Where it foils itself is through the dialectical contradiction that accompanies its very concept. Where we look more closely at *Aristotle's* matter-producing detachable forms, we conclude that perhaps there may be some middle ground between Plato's idealism and Aristotle's materialism whereby the particular is also universal on both the subjective and objective poles. With Kant, the universal is also paired with the concept of reality as in Plato, while the particular is paired with negation, and through the qualitative judgments yet another dialectical contradiction exists where particularity and negation are fused.

So far, we are not making great head-way in pursuit of the categories of reality and negation where the Other presupposes these alongside a possible limitation. But we will leave limitation alone for the time being. It is only through the phenomena of Kant that we discover the subject as a "magnitude" through the ontological self-identification of the reflexive subject that we may find the "Real" between subject and object as an *ontico-ontological* being-in-itself—where the *noumenon* is particular and self-identical and the phenomenon universal and identical. Since the substance of the subject in Kant is simple, again every subject will be in conflict over the distribution of "objects for consciousness" and thereby no universality will necessarily become possible for the multitude of particular social/political/economic/cultural identities.

Onward to Hegel, with what he had adopted from Kant in order to realize a subject-object synthesis that presupposes an a priori relation between particular and universal—yet it all comes down to the state *in toto*. We might propose that in the present age a justly administered society would eliminate the dialectical contradiction due to this, given Hegel's influence, yet it had been clearly observed the instances where this has not been the case.

But since Hegel's "essence" is something given to the subject objectively by the universal (God and State), the ontological contradictions are many. We see how this developed in Marx as a way of giving particular subjects *being qua being* as a use-value, promoting the concept that religion and state power were robbing subjects of their identities in terms of labour value and the means of production, but also the particular agency over the ability to "choose" something that has not been administered by the master-slave dialectic—in brief Hegel's dialectical contradiction for Marx.

> The manner in which he stood to eliminate this base-superstructure "vertical" ontology was by replacing it with a horizontal political-economic system. That this political philosophy found its way into the State is what I call an "inversion of the inversion" of Hegel. But of course we can readily acknowledge the dialectical contradictions never eliminated by state communism throughout the 20$^{th}$ Century.

In that Century, the philosopher of note that had perceived those dialectical contradictions most vividly was Adorno—in particular the book *Negative Dialectics*. It is here suggested that this work is a "reflexive inversion of the inversion", whereby society (production)—not the state—precedes the positing of subjectivity, and the subject will "produce" themselves as either a "universal identity" or a particular "non-identity". What he means by this, is the ontological "self-identical" while universal, is just that, yet a non-identical to the subject is particular. To point out the benefits of this, we elucidate that the free will of the subject to produce reflexive self-identity is an ontological possibility while unmediated, yet subject to judgments before the concept, but that a Marxist monism would be found in a dialectical contradiction with other particular subjects—coercively and antagonistically never allowing the particular to produce a universal self-identical. Therewith, in Adorno exists a dualism that allows the subject to "consume" the phenomenal object in apprehension of self-identity. Yet where society precedes the subject, the dialectical contradictions mediating the universal by another particularity are ever-present.

Forthwith, in order for "conceptual universalism" to be possible with all of the aforementioned philosophies in mind, the "concept" must precede a judgment. This would necessitate an overhaul of a universalized administration, but also brings into our command agency over rational choices that coalesce with a process of collective self-identification through those forms that exist in the present day and age. Perhaps there is a project underway should ontology precede the ontic—where it will also become reflexively engrossed with a symbolic language acting as a *tool* in order to produce concepts as universals that won't end-up in the battles inherent of exchange-value reification for the purposes of progressive accumulation of capital, thereto standing to propel social/political/economic/cultural antagonism forward—while cancelling the universal as a 21$^{st}$ Century likelihood.

## Metapsychological Coherence and the Socio-Symbolic Identity

Where we identify any individual as a "person", we are asserting of them or positing certain rights, qualities, thoughts, expressions of the self, etc. that we assume to be natural and also administered by their inclusion into the stratification of the social whole. In this general sense, an individual is not only in possession of their value as a being, but also part of the processual production of society whether it is by wish or by choice. From the top (i.e. governments, financial institutions, etc.) to the bottom (helpless homeless people), our society acts either in concert with the ontology of the foregoing disparity, or fights it within—that the under-classed and desperate would either cave-in or fight economic power in some way by resorting to crime and acts of public disruption—intentionally disturbing the order in society for other more fortunate individuals. But what is necessary to observe, is that from an ontological perspective, we find the latter class of social being has not lost all agency over social and economic concerns, while the former is clearly without the capacity to function without the formal universalization of these subjects as a class of social dependents into a cooperative, objectively driven platform of publicly stratified socio-symbolic identities.

This falls into the Kantian split of "agent" and "patient" in reference to the latter and the former respectively, or for Marx the bourgeoisie and the proletariat; but from another perspective, simply the inter-relation between the subject and the object. To clarify this point I will cite those that fall between established society and the forsaken by considering a class of social beings that are either in too deep to dig themselves out of their problems and end up destroying themselves, and those that simply commit criminal acts because of their dissociation from the notions of responsibility, morality, action and consequence, etc.

When we think of established society, we identify a class of people with employment, property, education, recreation, access to visible health care, etc. That often these are the groups that fund governments with tax revenue and so forth, when we think of the marginalized, we imagine that some of these conditions may not be met at all. For example, social and economic delinquency, the mentally ill and disabled, the sick, visible minorities, refugees or low income citizens that rely on the system for help. But what I intend to fully demonstrate is the ontological perspective of what may have led to these strata of the populous being seen as those that "choose to be a victim", rather than disclosing the fact that perhaps in most instances, falling into the margins of society does oftentimes result from problems within the system's ontological difficulty with the realization of a more coherent social totality that is not prohibitive of the possible universal appeal that may be put forward by an altruism within the administered social forms themselves.

The former situation is one where the metaphysic or social psychology is of a society lacking equality that actually develops those social problems through the division of the "object" from the "subject". So we look to Marx's notion concerning the ownership of the means of production and adapt it somewhat to what is the "means of essence"— the use-value of the subject. We can also identify that the subject's separation from property and land would send away the essence if it had been part of the livelihood of the subject, such as were the case for First Nations people. Furthermore, as in Marx, a worker may be paid below the standard of living in Western Democracies and does not "own" their product as it is the object of the business owner or the consumer; and the worker struggles to possess enough Energeia to labour the length of hours required to earn a living, and subsequently may choose or wish not to pay taxes, for instance, as they have already been institutionally marginalized, and the only essence or objective being available is through the exchange-value possible of a uncoupled lifeworld and system.

So here, I think in both instances—from the autochthonous person, to the proletariat in the margins—potential outcomes are legal issues for governments and political problems for law enforcement, whereby objectivity as a form of rational agency has put subjects in a position of "false truth", wherein self-destruction and the possibility of crime developing out of what is *not* being instituted is outside of a universally objective ontology that is never in any way fully willing to endorse social equality, and thusly creates inhumane conditions for the aforementioned identified social beings as *ontical* particularities. Not only will it become a virtual impossibility for these subjects to find their footing as a subject-object in full possession of rational agency, but they may actually go in the other direction and end up completely destroyed, etc. To posit that those that control the distribution of exchange-value were responsible for the ontological punishments inflicted upon a defenseless subject while never taking responsibility for the dialectical contradictions that may have caused the social ills, is a flaw in the system that must be repaired. And as I have already presented in a previous argument, where the ontological post-industrial world precedes the ontic, it is my judgment that we endeavor to repair things from within. This contrasts Marx's notion that the ontic precedes the ontological, but I believe that this, as a form of "post-industrial socialism", may be the answer. It would be a an ontological objectivity that is a public forum for social existents that creates subjective perspectives that are never driven by the irrationalism of those who are already dialectically battling something that were thought or perceived to be unjust to begin with, but rather those that are dialectical opponents of social injustices in-themselves.

For out there, problems do exist, but to say that it's purely a genetic defect that makes someone "evil" from the systems' perspective is an incomplete evaluation. We are not doing enough with ontology to make society a more livable domain for those acquainted with the social psychology that produces the conditions in which some subjects find themselves where exchange-value is in a dispute right alongside social discrimination and human rights infractions. That most consider the free market system (the free world) to be a place where it's "dog eat dog", and that there will be many casualties while the aforementioned pay the bills, indicates an absence of responsibility for one's fellow man—caused of a reflexive degeneration of objective social forms within for those subjects—and things such as urban decay, poverty, addiction, crime, etc. If for a moment we collectively were to acknowledge all subjects as also objects, and that identity would be preserved subjectively after it had already been produced objectively, then we are closer to a universalization of social being as an a priori ontology that would greatly reduce the sense of need for money by any means necessary, inclusive of the foregoing.

We can readily identify the fact that governments and financial institutions see ontology as their "market totality"—e.g., their contributors, producers, shareholders, etc. But seldom do we undertake to reason that *being* at its outset was a collective public enterprise from the origins of social organization and the development of institutions through Socrates, Plato, Aristotle, etc.—thought of in effect as nothing else than how we all relate within an ontology *as* beings; and I think that the active development of Western Reason has been for the purposes of evolving our world society for the better. This must exist in order to develop conditions of living that are acceptable not just to the privileged, but also to those left-out from the way things could be if so many weren't possessed by the capricious over-standardization of the need to produce wealth in order to bolster the economy. This sort of "kill or be killed" dynamic that some subjects have in order to put food on the table, pay the mortgage, shop, take vacations, pay taxes, etc. is clearly more of a detriment to the ambition to develop society to a state whereby most can live without losing everything or going to prison, becoming ill, etc. It is here claimed that most social ills start from within, usually identified as "mental illnesses" or problems with "addiction", but it must be elucidated that these problems are ontological actions taken by established society to continue to produce wealth and expand ownership and control over the determinations that keep them "on top" and the rest "underneath". I cannot say enough about the potential beauty possible of a horizontal ontology. It seems as though it's not until one has lost the war with economic security that this becomes the "Real", but as a starting point for access to world consciousness and public/private agency and control over one's personal affairs, there has been no better ontology in which to subsist.

What is the matter at hand however, is that those whom perceive the Western world to be made-up of different income classes due to inheritance, education, life choices, etc. that have developed a higher economic status, would not want to be considered an equal to someone who had not been given or accomplished the same. But if we acknowledge ontic subjects as the effect of whichever ontology exists—and the nature thereof—we must admit that Western democratic economies are not really democracies. They are discriminatory. So again, philosophy comes back to its ground state of dialectically opposing the way things are, and the power machinery sees it as a threat to their economic security. The vicious cycle begins anew.

For instance, those who fantasize about fame, wealth, and popularity will either achieve it, or they will go entirely in the opposite direction—another example of the how culture is affected by the corporate machinery that has been put in place historically to produce the aforementioned "casualties". We should now ask ourselves, if each subject has a very particular vision of the way they want their life to be, then how would universality be possible, without the same difficulties arising over and over again? There is no easy answer, as society is comprised of a multiplicity of conditions that are regional more often than not, especially in the West. This doesn't give a lot of detail as to what we might do to eliminate socio-economic disparities that bring happiness to some, and misery to enough that we can readily identify it as a problem deeply rooted in the causal mechanisms of ontology as a institutive formalization of the governance of the ontic subject's existential possibilities. In order for subjects to possess social, public, human and civil rights, inclusivity is said to be the goal of the State, but upon closer inspection we can certainly see that it's not being carried-out to the degree that it could be if we expanded public resources to a level whereby the ontic was never being "hammered" by the ontological machinery in possession of the social capital required in order to appropriate the social and ontological praxis of an emancipatory subject; where a rich ontological existence would be a universal prospect for all those engaged in social activity through self-identification. Herewith, where identity has been *sublated* by those in control of public resources, indeed a civil wronging has occurred.

As collectives we are not just a "market" or "stocks and bonds" but persons for whom thought and being, being and thought is where we derive a starting point for our sense of personal value. And as the sense of an a priori inalienable value is posited, it is through this self-identification that we are symbolized and epistemologically determined as subjects for the Other. Thereto, through this conceptual symbolization in reflexive self-identification with the Other, it is necessary that there already be in place an ontology that precludes discriminatory overdeterminations that may interact with the ontico-ontological subject's public use of reason, ego, super-ego, and id, embroiling subjectivity in something effectual of what would be the positing of causes intersubjective for others belonging to the same social ontology and public spheres that adhere to the meta-ethical processes by which ontological determinations may interfere with rational agency. The transcendental subject, as it were, sees beyond the aforementioned, but without the publicly administered objective and juridical conditionality in place—where free will meets rational agency and elicits dialectical contradictions—the constellations of social being in confluence with the metapsychological presence posited and projected by the subject become those very institutional forces acting as social prohibitions to the subject's self-identification with primary needs, etc. That this convolutes the ontological determinations causal of the very same through the institutive discrepancies and contradictions embodied through socially administered forms, identity runs the risk of losing everything to the social, political, and economic machinery—driving a sense of division between subject and object further—until finally the subject has become part of the statistical datum that has already ontologically determined the activity that would result in such an outcome; passing responsibility over to the subject having already been stripped of an ontological landscape worthy of "supplied substance" that has been produced by the praxis of the social subject that is positing awareness of the produced regional totality that could politically deliver subjectivity from its state of psychophysical and bio-economic reduction to being within its capacity to overcome the strata that reproduces empirical being as something of objective value at its outset.

In the process, self-identification would not be reduced to an object that had been destroyed from within—that being's possibilities were in confluence with a horizon that presented an ontology of ontical self-awareness and metapsychological coherence, synthetically in concert with an objectivity that has been meta-ethically founded by the elucidations touched upon by the foregoing.

## Representative Collective Identification and the Ontology of the Real

Whereby the notions of the self co-exist within the ontological presences *in situ* of a horizon representing the social totality, the conscious mind of any subject has the opportunity to project what I will here call "absolute identity". This is a self that is identical to itself, acting as an ontologization of the ontic properties of the subject as a being-in-itself. As a detachment of the subject's own ontical being, it is a co-existent of the actuality that is projected by the ontical self upon an inner space of the subject's *realiter* experience.

This begs the question, "Will this self-identity project universally to all subjects of the totality in representation of the subject's ontical pole of noetic consciousness?". I would say that the short answer to this is *no*, even though the transmission of ideas is verifiable under certain conditions, which means that it is understood by others synchronically. But whether or not one can actually project something self-identical upon the social totality *universally* is something that only a dictator of a totalitarian regime would hold to be the "Real".

Certainly, we can hypothesize that since the representations of any individual may be manifold, that this would express itself intersubjectively, or even inter-regionally/internationally under given conditions between heads of state or leading minds of a nation. One must however address this "absolute self-identity" universally at some point where we concern ourselves with the transmission of content available on the "World-Wide-Web"—that the ontology of the technological apparatus presents objectivity as something of a *deus ex machina*. Any time someone posts something to the web, it becomes public and available, and whether or not it is found *first hand* does not necessarily determine the corresponding ontological formulations that come into the subject's experience. Just as television before it, and radio before television, the signifiers are on the screen or *heard,* and act as the point of contact to the social totality from the subjective pole as a point of departure for the collectivization of ontological thinking. But here what we experience is non-identical rather than *identical*.

Perhaps to the subject's perceptual experience in-itself, experience may also become intersubjective with other subjects as self-identical or non-identical particularities depending upon the potency of the *interobjective* thought-projections. But I wish to make a distinction between the self-identical and "identity". The former, throughout the history of philosophy has usually had to do with self-representation that is ontologically "identical" to the subject, while the latter is more concerned with the ontical qualities that the subject may or may not possess. That is, while ontic speech is non-identical to the mental representation that is projected, the ontological projection of the self-identical is objectively identical to the ontical self. However, the phenomenal subject represents the subject with the self-identical as either a contingent object to the Other non-identically, or as a noumenal thing-in-itself contingently to the subject or synchronically to the Other identically. As were certainly the case with Kant, Hegel, Heidegger, and Adorno, the subject's self-representation is both an object-in-itself, and the projection of the subject's ontical pole of consciousness as a detachable ontological positing of self-identity. In this particular instance, the universal *is* the particular as a universal possibility in that it may exist in the world.

Since our present day definition of universality is quite different than before the advances of science and technology over the past century—where communications were often ontological transmissions rather than a technological communiqué—self-identity was the ground state of any subject's essence. While it led to the development of human reason throughout the 19$^{th}$ Century in particular, then becoming more of a political-economic movement in the 20$^{th}$, the human race's self-identity was, in fact, the manner by which ontology could produce things such as Kant's "pure conceptions of the understanding" or Hegel's "absolute knowing". This was what provided Marx with his initial pretext for a realization that led to the concept of a "dictatorship of the proletariat", whereby any such absolutes were the "property" of the bourgeois class and not the objects associated with use-value.

There was, in fact, no definitive sense that level of education was the reason for this classification of the proletariat, it was just the idea that economic privilege took priority over the value of beings-in-themselves as more than simple commodities to be exploited. So the notions of "possibility" come into play quite actively—whereby self-identity may indeed be available to those that are without bourgeois mediation of ontico-ontological projection of the for-itself; which thickens the waters where concerns our notions of post-industrial collective universality, as such. For the bourgeoisie as a ruling class, once thought of as the "universal class", seemed always to be fully in possession of self-identity—and the proletariat battling over their identities as devalued subjects. It is certain the same situation is still in existence in the present day and age, though perhaps we should insist that level of education be considered, given the cultural advantages made affordable to those without a higher level of knowledge—a university degree or its equivalent.

However, "identity" as it stands has now become more of an issue over gender and race equality, gender identity, cultural self-identification, etc., in so far as the projection of the self as a "political subject" with a voice to change the world around the being-in-itself would never wish to be oppressed by hegemonic factions or oppressive institutional forces. That being said, where problems develop is where the ontological space of representation of the subject-object that is being projected upon is replete with a multiplicity of hegemonic subjects in response to any such disturbance—reproduced in-themselves through policies that continue to further oppress those very identities. So a paradox exists whereby "collectivity" is required in order to reproduce identities as particular subjects of identity that go unmediated by an institutional universality. Again, what society would require in this instance, is a representative of the people that were capable of producing self-identity on behalf of the collective, rather than breathing life into what would for all intents and purposes become social anarchy.

What this presupposes, is that the self-identity that represents the collective particularities that are in full possession of ontic self-identification rather than ontological self-identity attain "universal collectivity", as projecting particular subjects with a social representation of self-identity. This gives what Sartre considered "direct democracy" a chance—that the philosopher or the writer in possession of ontological self-identity's raison-d'être, is to represent the collective thereto, but also may put them under attack by the public or the institutions motivated purely by pecuniary interests, rather than the content that is possible of collectives that all share in preservation of the representations of subjects throughout a consciousness that is productive of the conceptualized thinking associated with collectivized consciousness—re-doubled upon a representative of the collective, as it were. The problem of course, is "What motivates the decision?"—election, populism, economic status, social recognition, ontological conceptualizations or a creative oeuvre, etc.

Conceptual Signifiers and Symbolic Representations 163

There is also the possibility that factions or cultural sects develop, leaving someone that has been a representative for a length of time without the necessary ontological strata necessary to continue being so—replaced by another due to ontic or empirical status, social activism, performative activities, etc. That "popular spirits" would in fact be replaced by the brutes, would represent the downfall of reason in the *post-industrial* world. These are the subjects that "give the people what they want", and that's all that counts to them; not the development of the very resources of the human ontological collectives that would otherwise preserve the species beings as a productively creative social totality of subjective and objective agents of identity. In other words, ontology is not immune to the superficiality of certain social subjects.

However, in order for collectivity to be reproduced, there must be a "common good" for the collective as total subjects and universal beings-in-themselves—ontico-ontological subject-objects. It's only as matter of establishing of what that is comprised where concerns the *idea* as a source of what this involves—concerning political subjects where the concept is the collective self-identification of the whole—but also in Plato's sense, the hegemonic subjects not willing to commit to the "common good" that fancied themselves Philosophers Kings and wished never to be relegated to a life of mediocrity and would thereby be oppressed in some way. Thereto, the issue of happiness would come down to the *idea* as a common good to the collective and not the subject in possession of universal self-identification—whereby the "objective of the collective" consisted of contrite or trivial superficiality and passing fancies—rather that the ontological concepts affiliated with the preservation of collective universality from those very things that are emancipatory to the subjects resisting the conditions that are necessary in order to produce any such sense of liberty, wherein the absence of an oppressed identity may sometimes never come about lightly.

As for those collectives that only pursue certain capricious activities, or are entirely consumed by the enjoyment possible of what are suspiciously called "free societies" who are not really "political subjects" moving ontology forward to the state where all ontical performances of the social collective are properly represented within, the representative collectivization of ontological strata may be capable of synthesizing identity with its self-identical counterpart from the horizons of social totality. And any "universal collective" is only made possible by the participation thereof, just as it has been since the beginning of the Western *res publica*. But then again, it sounds as though we are discussing the sort of democracy that would make hegemony the manner by which political subjects operate within the collective. I will say that this is only possible between opposing collectives, not within them. The issue there again becoming of the question a representative may be asked, "Who died and made you King?"— (And the answer: the one that was appropriating my identity along with yours!).

## The Projection of the particular Ontic identity and the Reflexive universal positing of its Ontological object

Where there is a re-appropriation of the object and projection of the ontological non-identity (particular) into the outer space of representation through the object while subjectively grounded in the ontico-ontological identity, let us assume that the possession of the object as an exclusionary phenomenon presupposes ontological identity, while the outer space of representation projects the particular. For us the object *is* identity where it may be identical through the inner space, yet entirely ontically mediated as a particular representation to the universal (collective) understanding. As such, the object presupposes particular noumenal ontological projection, while conceiving of the self-identical as occupying noumenal representation from pure ontological projection as a being-in-itself.

The antinomy is between the Kantian universal as noumenal identity, and the Marxo-Hegelian conception of a reified objective phenomenal identity—mediated through the Other as confined to its particularized, non-objectified status. Where we may consider the ontico-ontological universalization of the subject, the absolute is projected *in situ* of the ontological in-itself as a noumenal being-in-itself—without a conceptual datum other than this which presents subjectivity with its own identical ontological being-in-itself in the gap between particularity and the ontological totality or collective.

The quest that is raised in this instantiation of the objective toward particular self-identification, is for a universalized self-identical. We know from the aforementioned through the foregoing that mediation of identity exists upon the objective pole of consciousness—the social totality. Therefore, we can see four essential possibilities for the ontological space of representation for the being-in-itself:—

An objectified inner-outer particularity; an intersubjective self-identification toward the others of a noematic collectivity; the self-identical of a noumenal ontico-ontological being-in-and-for-itself; and a contingent thing-in-itself of the noumenal self-identical within the inner space of representation to the being-in-itself.

As this *ding an sich* replaces the appearances of the Supersensible reality to the subject, the Hegelian totality is absent this form of knowledge. It is suggestable the Heideggerian *throwness* of being is upon the world from its absence of objectivated reasoning under these conditions. Yet ontical being presupposes an outer attachment to the claims of the contingent thing-in-itself—and therewith, "opens" the space of representation upon the objective plane as a self-identical; though under these conditions the subject will be projecting without a phenomenon *in situ* of the inner space of representation. Even in fact, without the Feuerbachian object before the social totality.

Herewith, it is not constitutive to presume an objective absolute noumenal projection—rather if anything this is something that is abstracted by the knowing subject from the Other as a being-in-itself that has already been represented in other ways and by other means. Certainly, one observes Heidegger's claim to identity as a "jump" into the essence that is there upon the outer interior space. But here in order for this to become of philosophy, it is that dialectic must be introduced to form the object upon the outer (objective) pole of being—as the thing-in-itself has already replaced both the appearances and all abstract conceptual data, as well as the objectivated *Dasein*. Ontical being has not been noumenally represented other than through the ontologization or universalization of the speech act—the *res corporea* extending throughout the outer space of representation (to a collective or totality).

Though from this we observe the object as a self, the produced *potentia* of the being-in-itself as an ontological existent—therewith the projection toward its ontological counterpart in the Other as an intersubjective/interobjective being-in-itself as precisely this which identifies within it its own ontological particularization. Yet there, the unmediated self finds its attribution through the abstraction of its noumenal Other—throughout the conceptual identification with the being upon the objective pole that has been represented otherwise.

> Functionary to this, the ontico-ontological positing as a contingent *ding an sich* or objectivated phenomenal existent to the subject's apprehension of the horizons with which subjectivity instantiated the dialectical noumenal projection upon an abstracted conceptual Other, is "being" in possession of its own self-identification with the Other as a thing-in-itself, and an objectively projected ontical existent that transfers self-identity at precisely the same moment that the Other's abstraction has formed within the subject's consciousness throughout its conceptual signification.

What this breeds, is the interobjective abstraction-negation-concrete as a conceptual abstraction that has become concrete through a *hic et nunc* inter-conceptual transmission of ontical-phenomenal data that reproduces itself to the totality through the subject's own process of reflexive contingent self-identification. There is no short fall where come the judgments as presuppositions of what has been objectively self-identified. Rather, the existent has reproduced the conceptual datum in furtherance to the abstraction that had transferred self-identity upon the object that would reflexively posit as self-identification with its ontical (ontico-empirical) communiqué with the in-itself that has procured others from within determinations attributable to normative speech acts in production of the abstracted noumenal identity in co-presence with the being-in-itself.

# Grammatology, Semiotics, Ontological Dialectic and its Symbolic Nominal Significations

The ego cogito (Being) is not a dominant force but a proximate determination of the autonomous self. A phenomenal will exacts as both a noumenally positing thing-in-itself to the objective totality, and the proximity of essence through the onticality of being as both an ontologization of the psycho-physical, but also the actualization of the noumenally positing identical self. Thereby, *domination* is never an act of a positing of ego from the subjective pole (noesis), but a dialectical process of the established order that confers with a proximate *de facto* actuality or empirical reality of the subject. The post-industrial technological rationality is here in fact a synthesis between established order and ego cogito with its conditioned determinations that may once again act as the clay to be sculpted and shaped by noumenal positing and projection.

The question arises whether or not this process in fact enacts a dichotomy between the technological stratification of the ego and its objective counterpart, or hosts the reality that we are dialectically entwined by way of the stratification of the collective network of subjective substrates all engaged with the same regional determinations involving their labours and selections of content in connection to social production and the abstract nominal significations that we have in thought, speech and creative acts such as writing—hereby to be considered the form of *semiotic representational production*.

As the consistent positing of collective identity sublates the objective rationalization of the *techne, praxis*, or technologically driven self-same objects within the ontological directives of conceptual reality, one resumes all phenomenal and noumenal ontological activity within the lifeworld with the same extensions of being as any autonomous individualized subject would have in pursuit of identity and an unmediated universality, replete with the world-in-itself upon a horizontal totality, while symbolic nominal signifiers are represented to the mind as both transcendental and conceptually signified beings of appearance. This gives the post-industrial aesthetic a purpose toward the designing of fruitful posits that birth more content—moving beyond the limits of Adorno's administered world, into a social network of freely positing individuals that are not *dominated* by, but united by the collectivity of the systems of thought that are comprehensible to the subjects as possibilities for positive reification of the object, significatory abstract content, and productive social experience—a dichotomy to the advanced industrial consumerism of the "Darwinian subject", presumably phallocentric *in toto* and within a growing and natural fusion between subject and object, ego and thing-in-itself, being and nature, essence and society. The inherent dialectic between subject and objective thing-in-itself never disappears (resuming its representation contingently upon the positing of the subjective will) or abstraction of the objects dialectically opposed to the will, while creating a fusion of subject and object based upon the freedom of the subject from the chains of traditional forms of reasoning that have only ever resulted in the eventual occurrences of military action that put into action the downfall of reason from its former heights of collective autonomy and eventual productivity, creativity, and labour power over

Conceptual Signifiers and Symbolic Representations 169

coercive forces responsible for the inequitable capitalist divisions between exchange-value and use-value.

The question of being here implies the differentiation between the signifier and the signified—or the being-in-the-world and the being-in-itself. From this our representations are only in fact that which is related to the contingently represented, yet does in fact affirm and entail the certain existence of the Other as concomitant to the being-in-itself as a being-in-the-world.

Of course the concept of interobjectivity suggests that this is the very "sous entendu" or "retinue" of the ontological expression of what dialectic is at its outset as an essence to the subject. The epistemological dynamic here is where the propositions of the interobjective Other are only concerned with the predicate "world" rather than a particular attribute of substance. This establishes and affirms the co-presence of substance and world as a percept to the ontological experience of being-in-the-world, yet does not necessarily suggest the proximity or non-locality of the cogito as a signifier co-extensive non-locally to the interobjective Other's cogito; but it does in fact re-submit as fact the notion that the ego has been totalized and the existence of the world as a percept is a fact posited in lieu of the reflective ego from the being-in-itself, proximate to the subject, and *thrown* as a particular noumenal thing-in-itself to the locality of the interobjective Other, which suggests the Other is conceptually attuned to the temporalization of substance (collective substance) that has installed the objective totality as a contiguous representation upon the horizon.

Where argument for a concomitant *realiter* representation of represented subjects becomes affirmed, is where the sublated components of the lifeworld in fact become synthesized with the attributes, and as such the subject regains the status of autonomous being (merely ontic) with an a priori sense of its own natural counterpart in the being-in-the-world as a symbolic or conceptual signifier to the Other. This affirms the suggestion that non-locality is endemic of being—that as a dialectical interlocutor the ontological status of the subject is conclusively held in its *realiter* temporal form as a "this", rather than a "what" to the cognitively aware Other being that both signifies and represents either contingent or concomitant notions of a specialized interest and impetus toward the attainment of a particular goal—the "matter at hand" as it were.

For us to hold that this is entirely contingently signified as Derrida does in *Of Grammatology,* we lose the phenomenological existentialism of being-in-the-world as signified and being-in-itself as signified where concerns the epistemological psychoanalytic components of the consciousness that would yield a judgment as to the fact of the matter—but we regain the dialectical means with which to negotiate and posit propositions that conjoin with a greater yield of the world/collective substance as an asset of all ontological endeavor so as to net greater profits for truth and the real in order to secure a better position for rational subjectivity in the objective totality *in actu.*

In other words, there is no short fall that determines subjectivity by the psychoanalytic properties of the Other that impose unnecessary limitations upon the process of self-determination and free will with the eschatological goal in mind being the transcendence of causal limitations and negations that may threaten the being of the subject as a being-in-the-world. As this being-in-the-world may in fact be more than the noematic copy or signifier to the subject and its *Dasein*, or ontico-dialectical compositional projection toward the subject. It is in fact the very objective essence of subjectivity, and thereby responsible for the ultimate hypostatization of the subject's essence and manifold properties.

Once subjectivity understands the magnitude of the problematic, then the pure "I" may return as an *eidos,* an *ousia,* and the *nous* of subjectivity—rendering reflective capabilities free from this "not I" that imposes the exhaustive measures of an temporal dialectic. Of course we would not have it that there be no Other—this is entirely acceptable to the qualities of being inherent of beings-in-the-world—however the totality is encumbered with its own substance in the representations of thinking, speaking, reading, and writing. Both the symbolization of the Other and its mental representation are present within these acts, and ultimately summoned by dialectical positing and projections. As *Grammatology* is the transcription of ontological dialectical experience of the Other, so must speech or logocentrism be more dialectical and immediate—intentional toward the symbolic nominal significations as exposed by elucidary means alone.

Therefore it is here held that writing precede the speech act where concerns thought, ideas, notes, etc., and that thinking *dialectically* before one speaks operates as a negation of the being of the very objective determinations of what the speech act entails—whereby one relies primarily on the representation or signifier to form words that confer with the external discourse underway. To adumbrate this conclusion would be to unpack the necessary objective totality for further investigations that would be better found on the page before they encounter others interobjectively.

Here we find that essence once again has become an asset to its own socio-cultural determination, and thereby the production of the *nous* all over again, as the being-in-itself anticipates the attentions of those that question the propositions asserted within an ongoing dialectic. Where it departs, it once again will find a home in negation and limit this which propels another round of ontological positing for the procurement of further insights into what is the real—how do we go about learning the truth?; and where language and fact acts (*tathandlung*) are signifiers or representations, how are they also a priori concepts that benefit from *Grammatology* and its ontological positing of pure reflection and the process of reading or positing the written notions posited by being and its objectivated collectivization?

## Self-Consciousness as an Interobjective Experience of the World Totality Throughout Our Dialectical Presuppositions

The stipulation that a macro consciousness or universalized Being as a collective substance is comprised purely of exchange-value relations, presupposes a motility of ontological objects—where what in fact should be the case is that the noumenal will determines the quantum reality of the subjects based upon the universality present within the subject's positing of its legal identity at the point of contact where the conceptual status of subjects within the signifying chain achieve ontological self-awareness. This identity is based upon the unmediated empirical being of the subject as it posits the self to the general proximity where the object may be constituted (the inner space), and in connection with the substance of the subject as a member of a collective that aspires toward the same rational freedoms where concerns the necessary application of use-value. The particularization of this absolute subject will happen through its own work, yet it should remain unmediated where it first appears as a noumenal identity to the collective subjects' own phenomenal magnitudes or Objective Being.

The speech act and ontological projections of the Other do mediate the noumenal identity of the subject as it becomes non-identical, and thus neither fully constituted through its universalization as a social interobjectivity, or resolute as an ontical and empirical conditionality. However the conceptual signification of Otherness becomes a remote possibility for subjective abstraction and collective self-identification. The intelligibility of the ego is no longer in its mode of self-positing within the understanding, but exists more as a contingent being-for-self as either a representation, or a conscious impression. The representation as a conceptual datum triggers interobjectivity, whereas the impression triggers ontological projections and outer expressions of the self. The truth content of the expression has its basis in the judgments present within the representation and the sense of nature present within the impression.

The judgments of the Other where negations are determinable of objective being *in abstracto* persist while the object becomes present through its universal identity from a return to the ego for which a certain length of time is purely driven empirically by outer experience and not the ontological terrain within consciousness. Once the abstract universality meets with the concept it reengages the object as a thing-in-itself—both as an intelligible being of the subject and the empirical objective essence of Being qua Being. The notions of the understanding are then posited into the being-in-itself of otherness, while the self-mediating reflective object of subjectivity has become ensconced with a slew of concepts lost only to objective essence—for the object has for it the content of the concept of the essence of being. Any randomization or constellation of concepts would be the result of an indirect transmission of essence from the object to the subject. For the conceptual content of the object is both the essence of the subject just as it is the understanding of what may be relevant and applicable ontico-ontological *praxis* appropriate to the conditions of the situation present-at-hand.

The read a subject *may* have toward what we are permitted to convey is a choice between the real, or what is for the understanding a truth that has been disclosed to Being. As an object of experience, Otherness posits its own presuppositions arrived at through a posteriori conclusions and will only reveal what is necessary for the preservation of its own substance. In correspondence with assertions that appropriate the object in order to render it false to the subject, the manoeuvre of Otherness has been posited as such. The consciousness of the Other is now epiphenomenal and intentional toward the subject as the Otherness of a negative determination. This restricts the noumenal identity of the subject bereft its own object—eliciting a necessary and free act of the will in order to regain its own determinable self-identity. The loss in-itself is not permanent, yet leaves subjectivity to produce its own mental work without the completion of its substantive Being.

As the subject wills into Being its own ego, it is that the apriority of world consciousness posits an Otherness particular to the perceptual understanding of the subject as it pursues its own self-awareness through judgments and presuppositions that are concomitantly posited. Though subjectivity posits contingently into the sphere of the Other, it is that this Otherness provides a "mode of understanding" as such to subjectivity in pursuit of an emancipation from the empirical limitations upon identity. The particular non-identity of the otherness acts as a mirror to the reflective Being of the subject's presupposed contingency as may have been posited for otherness, real within its necessary potency to project a dialectical enhancement of the ontological representations that move beyond Otherness toward a world-consciousness present to the subjective understanding with an epistemological break from its status of subservience and compliance.

This process is to a large degree a self-affirmation of the being-in-itself as a contingent dialectical for-itself—under certain conditions also affirming the existence of the Other as a being-for-another which is reciprocated once the universal concepts of the positing subject arrive upon the scene. There is no abstract motif to which negative judgments have been presupposed by the perceptual understanding of the Other, in that it has provided subjectivity with its own outlet of reflection once summoned a priori by the perceiving subject that has been engaged as such.

> The consciousness of the subject has thereby conjoined with a world-consciousness a priori through a union with its own object that is the productive force of its experience, labour and mental representations—yet the *episteme* of the ego object only happens to the perceiving subject once it has judged the conceptual content with which it has been presented. At this juncture, the positing of judgments is necessary as a function of the ego, yet more a percept of the being-in-itself before it has engaged its proximate substance and subjectivity and is merely a being-in-itself that is simple to the representation of the Other that has not yet posited interobjectively.

What is born from this is the self-positing contingent thing-in-itself in the lacuna, where subjectivity and its Other were first absent from the space of representation, only to be filled by presuppositions that are also contingent to the identity of the subject and the non-identity of the Other. To resolve this dichotomous presentation of self-consciousness, the process begins anew, as the subject reflects upon no object in Otherness, and remains in-itself and singular to the causal relation of Otherness or Objective Being. However the process of thinking away objectivity and reducing Being to a mere singularity is an a priori *reductio ad absurdum* to the subject's substance—what will one do without its Other?

Now, that we may observe that the Other is no more, Being has found its dialectical stance whereby the social totality appears upon the horizon and subjectivity has attained the self-consciousness of Hegel—for the unity of subject and object is really the unity of subject and world-consciousness. The object was merely the vessel through which subjectivity would come to experience the world as a totality and thereby a complete entity posited by Being itself. Therefore the subject's being is the being-of-the-world and in this sense a *relational* absolute of the perceiving mind. In this sense as well, the subject has negated Being only to render being in-itself *the world.*

By way of this, subjectivity finds reflection to be its own non-being that its being has become the world. This motif survives the law of contradiction in that it is now that Objective Being has sublated the ego and unified it with its objectivated dialectical self. Where the subject now will find identity is in the world, not in a proximate ego as it relates dialectically to the perceptual understanding of Otherness "before the world". With this, the subject submits to the loss of ego in place of a unification and sociation with an identical noumenality as part of a collective manifold of representations all held under the same conceptual determinations. This as a "form" of reality is of course idealistic, yet is very much based upon the real—in that the primacy of world consciousness has first presented this as a plausible horizon to being-in-and-for-itself-and-for-others.

The subject has attained a universality that allows for rationality to supervene without Being caught up in language games or contingencies based upon subjective problematics with the aim of throwing subjectivity into a state of panic—ensuring that reflexive behavior is equally productive under the unification of subject and object just as it were until things were dichotomously posited and dialectically contradictory. The difficulty is to contain the essence of the subject (which is the object) as a function of its world-consciousness without the necessary empirical conditions already in place so as to render this a fully viable alternative to the presence of an ego object that confirms the proximate substance of any subject. The route to the maintenance of this substance is through the positing and affirmation of identity as a freely projected noumenal subject approaching the horizon of objectivity through creative and productive acts, and the creation and positing of concepts that synthesize or fuse identity with its dialectical position intentional toward the social totality (production).

As I posit my self in this objective consciousness truthfully and responsibly—that I am purely rational in my undertaking of what I am to be, indeed I am something. I have achieved rational identity amongst other phenomena that have no universal claim to my Being and therefore my essence—in that I have lawfully appropriated the very phenomenality that is presented to ontic Being as a causal attribute of the world mind that precedes the positing of my being-in-the-world. By this it is not only that ego and phenomena provide subjectivity with its essence, but yet it is a representation of one's conceptual and significatory status to the totality that reifies the subject's substance. In fact, it is through this enlightened totality that the modality of the transcendental subject attains its Being toward the rational understanding of its dialectical conduct, and the conscious social activity that confers the negative status of the Other upon subjectivity.

In the same sense, it is by way of the *sublation* of a negative totality that the self is to realize its identity as a signified being to others ontologically—and as such mediation is only viable by way of the ethical limitation placed upon the phenomenological identical as it posits itself as a "something", where it is sublated by the collective in pursuit of its collective identity. This eliminates from bondage the particular where a synthesis has occurred between the particular non-identity and its own self-identity throughout the signifying chain, thusly engaging a fusion between universal Being and particular noumenal freedom. As such the essence is not simply a reification of the produced value of others, but the very productive activity of the thinking mind that is existentially fueled by the world mind. On the other side, consciousness is of a mass or collective that apprehended the world-in-itself, yet singular to the monadic status of the reflecting subject that has posited Being.

## The Self-Concept and its Dialectical Limitations Upon the Otherness of Contingency

Epistemology is an act of experience and an experience of the act, where of course proportions of conceptual universalized forms express existence as a self in relation to its Other through reified forms that have been represented throughout the context of an ontological projection of its signification, and what has been signified to the Other as a dialectical transmission or positing of objects in flux that have become determinable interobjectively. Where noematic components of the ontical existence sparks the world mind, the subject engages it through its abstract semiotic reflections and significations. In post-industrial times, this determines the cultural mass of representations, or the cultural signifier that bears a striking resemblance to the universal consciousness of Kant, Hegel or Marx. As a totality it has been founded by the representational Other that imposes the limitations upon Being that render sublation an abstract necessity, yet through a universal consciousness in-itself can act toward the sublated negation of the being-in-itself where it has been detached from its own subjectivity into a concretion of essence.

In such terms, appearance is constitutive of essence toward a nature that has been founded by its own dialectical address throughout our history, and humankind has essentially found itself divided with its own historical identity—suggesting that Being has an innate connection to the Other dialectically where an act of universalized self-concretion has been denied the right of passage, determined mostly by the act of synthesis which is only attainable reflexively throughout nature as the other Being that has been posited in immediate opposition to the essence of subjectivity that must here propose negative terms for the Other toward a reprieve from the barricades presupposed by the projected Otherness. The notion that Being may never become dialectical with nature or essence would obfuscate the determinative aspects of Being's necessary abstraction of essence from nature, yet persists within the acceptance of the fact that it comes along and is accompanied by a determination that arises from the Other. This acceptance of division between self and Other as a natural determination of essence posits Being in a dialectical synthesis with essence-as-appearance, functionary of Being as it is both essence and nature. A dialectical universalization of subjectivity comports itself toward its appearances as a being-in-itself, and gathers universal consciousness for its own determinable abstraction of a concrete universality.

Thereto, language is a copula to the maintenance of essence as its concrete abstraction—as thought and the positing of philosophic notions present consciousness with a yield of formalized content in order to stratify the necessity within its reified objectivity; which is constitutive of both Being and the epistemologically projected presuppositions of the Other. The propositions therein must be

Conceptual Signifiers and Symbolic Representations 179

dialectically reduced as obstacles before the essence while in the absence of appearance, yet are non-identical and contemporaneous or contingent acts of legerdemain to the subject that engages in dialectical opposition to the very same with a soldier's vigour. Notwithstanding this, the reified consciousness may propose its own negations in reprieve of the master-slave dialectic—now posited as a devalued comportment of a disenfranchised hierarchy that has been sublated by social production as a horizontal totality. As universal consciousness is an act of a collective that has not been negated by the whole, but rather provides a basis for the unification of a totality that gives birth to greater reflective capacities and rationality—a more reasonable grip upon the horizon of the unconditioned, and the necessary synthesis between subject and object that renders Being a complete experience of the mind, rather than a pure limitation put forward by the not-I. The ideation of a consciousness that has been emancipated from this is one that exists within the social forms that comprise post-industrial living as a dialectical position more than simply a state of submission to the instituted norms of universalized exchange-value relations.

However, the contingent self-identical upon a dialectical positing of the ego is a negation of the potentiality of the subject and signified of the contingent self-identical as its *Other*. The identity of the signified is only disclosed through the content of the propositions being posited as such. The effect that this has, is that it negates the dialectical component of reason, as the essence is inherently being posited by the contentions of the Other as a being-in-itself; rendering no other option than a dialectical negation of the signifier through a process of sublation of what had first been posited. This process is an act of self-mediation of the essence, and is the Real of matter and form, counter-posed within its stance of opposition to the abstract exchange-value in negation of reified objects a priori. Here the Real is essential to the determinations of the Other as they are negative and problematic, and propose to put into play necessary abstractions of the subjective will in-itself, as though it were a component of the self that had only previously been disclosed through reflexive observation. It is in effect the super-ego intertwined with the essence of the subject—rendering the posits of the other necessary determinations of an essence that is in the absence of appearance; yet also making the subject necessarily bring into action the will with the intuition of a reversal of negative determinations that have developed out of dialectical relations with exchange-value. The subject's use-value is temporally destroyed by the Other which leaves only external conduct intact—distracting from the subject's own positing and self-determinations that *will* into Being greater use-value than may be achieved by way of a negative determination in-itself. Ultimately this only becomes the actuality of the subject should it fall into the trap laid out by a super-ego or Other that has been reified in contingency.

Furthermore, this reveals alethic truth vis-à-vis the Other to subjectivity, and forecloses the necessary signification of knowledge and understanding to an abstract positing of the ego within the intention of furthering thought and being into a place of absolute knowledge—where dialectical materialism is synthesized with the ideas as a function of a more distributive exchange-value abstraction, negating the self-referential negativity and replacing it with a concrete universality that may synthesize objects for the purposes of a collectivized abstraction of the social whole as a dialectical projection upon counter-posed authoritarian ideals. This renders the subject more homologous with its Other, and analogical to itself as a contingent self-identity that progresses past the negation of dialectical reasoning into the aforementioned pursuit of the ideas that shape conceptualized Being.

The question is then, how would the self-concept always be a positing identity, or is it socially constituted by totality acting as a form of mediation to the subject as either the self-concept or a noumenal projection of the being-in-itself? The short answer is, of course where the mediating particularity occurs within the social substance, while proximate subjectivity experiences its own identity as a self toward an actualization of the concept, that it would then abstract and reify its own objectivity through a subjective ontologization of the very objectivated Being that presupposed that there must be a process of self-identification. Therewith, the social totality presupposes a simulacrum of subjective objectivated reflexivity, overthrowing the despotic signifier and bringing it down into its own conceptual significations within the pretext of what has been established through a priori negations of the Other. As follows, the self-concept has yielded its maximal output of social Being as both an identical phenomenal object, and thrown noumenal identity. The simulacrum has been attained, and a constitutively classless horizontal ontology has been formed throughout its dialectical oppositions to the bondage offered by a reflexive social self-identification with the Other, that has constituted its status as a contingent identity that stands with the totality of society in order to reduce collective social substance. Herewith, subjectivity merits from its own Being as an essence that is objectively constituted on both polarities of the ontological terrain.

While it may be said that Being here as self-concept is purely ontical and predicable of its ontological counterpart in the concept, it is here claimed that the concept is the *pure* concept or transcendentally constituted "I" that has in fact advanced beyond the limitations of the self-positing of the Other, therefore while we have totality in the equation, we also have entity, in that the only other representation is either a particular noumenal subject as is posited contemporaneously by the subject, or a contingent identical that reflects the apodictic judgments of the subject while positing both its self-concept and the Objective Being that represents the proximate phenomenality of the ego's conceptions in the social substance. As a consequence of this totalized unity between self and Other, a separate region of consciousness becomes the essence through an abstraction of the self at the point of departure from its own self-identification and conceptual reification of the objectivized Being—the conceptions of the Other that have now undergone their determinations in pursuit of the same social

## 182  The Dialectical Self-Concept of Symbolic Being

substance as had been apprehended by subjectivity as a dialectical exponent of the totalized unity in-itself at the horizon. Here of course, it brings one back to the theoretical notion that arborescence through its environmental structural form, is only possible of humans where duality of consciousness is entirely removed from Being in order to achieve the aforementioned unity.

But in fact the synthesis is real and therefore a new vision for reflexive interobjectivity where subjects remain uncompromised by the Other and devoid a significatory status proposed through the dialectical opposition of the Other. With this emancipatory resolution of the self-concept comes a positing of the actuality presupposed by the a priori abstractions composing subjective dialectical negation of the contradictions in-themselves, and reconnects the transcendency of abstract universality with its social praxis through the grounding of its concrete essentiality. While the subject acts in accordance with externalized judgments through a taxonomy of abstract Objective Being, the self-actualized existence of the reified emancipated subject becomes localized through their public universalization. Lawful Being is within its own capacity to posit the self-concept and identity where concerns society and the social substance, despite institutions sometimes inherently available for the oppression of the subject's conceptual self-identification as a being-in-itself.

> This gathers much ontological territory for the subject and is a *de facto* "reterritorialization" of the subject as a productive *machine* of consciousness. In other words, with a selective autonomy that presupposes a heteronomy at times (the contingent self-identity), it is only proportional language games that would deter the subject from making acquisition of its own reified consciousness to the objective totality—thereby regaining footing through a prosperity amidst the demands of the post-industrial world society. Where this falls short abstract determinability is over claims of solipsism—but these are negated by the dialectical affirmations made by contingent identity should they coalesce with the positing of judgments and reasoning of the subject's own self-concept.

There essence is an immediate outcome of the positing of the object in communion with the horizon where dialectical abstractions become presuppositions of the transcendentally motivated social subject, and the social substance wherein conscious acts may be experienced in a collective totalization of the individual into a reification of the self-concept and its abstract compositional dialectical positioning.

# The Hypostatized Universality of the Existential Being Otherwise Known as Artist

Insofar as universality is exchange-value and existence, particularity is use-value and thereby essence. The attributes of substance are of use-value predicable of exchange-value, and the properties of the identitarian subject where it has fully abstracted and realized its universalized subjectivity as an objectified being to the ontological stratification of the world society. The transcendental actuality of subjectivity is an object of exchange-value that is intelligible to rational subjectivity where an ontologized society precedes ontical Being, yet the relations of production are mediated by universality as objective being by the essence of the subject through its particular symbolizations and representations reified through ontological use-value qualities of the existentialized ontological landscape. The mediated particularities are apportioned to abstract quantities within a universalization of predicable particular use-value essences that compose subjectivity as a being-in-and-for-itself.

Where existence precedes the concretion of essentialized Being, an unmediated abstract universality corresponds to the exchange-value quantity of substance and attribution that grounds subjectivity in an unmediated use-value particularity.

Where the development of reason is "public", substance and attributes are inherent modes of Being to the subject-object as both use and exchange-value—essence and existence—where it is "private", substance and attribute are withheld from the subject and subjectivity has been ontologized without its constitutively reified objectivity, and thereby is reluctant to adjure to a substitute for its own objectivizated substance toward the actualization of its well-reasoned dialectical presuppositions. The ontological exchange-value relations as such are both exponential to the posits of subjectivized social praxis, and concurrent with a substantive division between the reified objectivity of the social being's attribution toward a fortified dialectical projection as an ontological other—yet erstwhile, reason is within a process of the development of collective distantiation from its sublated economic whims; and the universalization of a hypostatized subject's own reflexive identity with its ontological counterpart in the Other as an invisible abstract entity has been compromised within the necessity of a realized particularity unmediated by its own abstract universality. Where exchange-value is collective through its particularization of the subject's own ontological self-identification, the attribution of ontical particularity finds an unmediated universality within its concrete existentiality.

Concerning the social expression of "surplus consciousness" and abstract labour, it arrives as an alienation of the *ego*, while positing the very same through its determinable interobjective dialectical relations to the social totality, and expounds upon its own dialectical standpoint toward civil society and the state as what becomes a determinable capacity that sublates its own reflexive objectivity to become functionary in the aforementioned—yet the representation of established order and all commercialized economic activity never become fully actualized to the public spheres where concern the appropriation of objects, their content, and relational attributes. In this instance the rational, free thinking subject resists an abstract exchange-value component that replaces subjective substantiality, and dialectically opposes its Other where it presupposes the a priori abstraction of use-value precluding subjective collectivization as a reified emancipatory objectivity.

With this comes the demise of the hierarchical superstructure that had held public rationalism hostage for time immemorial—subjected to punishments for which constitutional rights are in place in order to protect subjects from violations and oppressions of such things as freedom of thought, expression, etc. In effect, the reality principle has become a distortion of rational subjectivity in that the alienated substance of artistic expression has been imprisoned by what would otherwise be invisible administrative powers—those existences that limit and prohibit creative endeavors. For it is through aesthetics that all content is fully realized as both Being qua Being and as either a thing-in-itself or a totality—undergoing its particularized activities through the manifold language of expression that reifies its object. The conceptual symbolization of the subject here plays an integral role in the process a hypostatized subjective formal expression of the abstract and the concrete. As subjectivity through its social praxis first identifies the object, it is then that it is able to determine the nature of its content, and if it will indeed undergo any constitutive determinations so as to become a reified work of art.

The artist then, is in full actuality of the sublimation of the alienated substance appropriating the object or image, as it is hypostatized into a living, breathing mode of Being that gives birth to the necessary ordering of ideas that constitute any mode of productive creativity. The subject remains grounded in the concept through each moment of the creative process as an eidetic consciousness in pursuit of a dialectical unification with the object and its content—subjugating the reality principle to its institutional counterpart in the hypostatization of all predicable ideas that are manifold to the concept.

The abstract relationhood to the objective world is both a form of engagement *and* endangerment to the aesthetic and existential noumenal freedoms of the subject, yet in the process of self-realization, the risk proves to be worth the taxonomy of the undertaking—that it is a work that hosts a sophistication of the conceptual content that may be based in a realism that transcends fictitious boundaries and false hypostatizations of the ontological terrain in which subject-objects, the world, and history dwells. In this may be realized an objectively powerful attribution to the public spheres from whence it originated as a reification of the hypostatized universality of the existential Being engaged by the process—otherwise known as the *Artist*.

Whereby this individual is collective throughout the creative process, and an integral essence to the ontological spheres that encompass post-industrial living, it is without bounds that aesthetics merit from what has been posited by the reified object of the former, and that collective Being will remain fully grounded at the subjective and the objective pole of consciousness as we utilize a formal universalization of contextualized social progress and ontological endeavor so as to hypostatize our collective ontological determinability as subject-objects all in conference with the constellation of existences formed around a particular reification of the conceptual whole. Should this reduce subjective *praxis* to a passive state of awareness and abidance with something that does not represent the constellated entities as an emancipated particularized totalization of the conceptual posits elicited by subjects that have already reified free expressions of the real, the abstract has been sublated by a comportment of social perversions that transcend the projection of actuality as an ontological component to the objective unification, where subjectivity realizes itself as a free conceptualized component of the aesthetical domain that one's significatory status may become an abstraction. Thereby becoming a reified object to its Other in apprehension of ontological drives produced where subjects have been ensnared by habitual practices that compromise ethical social *praxis* toward the real conceptual significatory conditionality of a subject—that is reduced to a mere obfuscation of self, yet exposed to universalization that unwinds the revelations proposed by truth that has now been subordinated by capricious wills, and will only disclose its being to the necessary dialectical opposition to follow.

## The Real as a Fusion of Transcendental Subjectivity and Social Production and the Transcendental Social Subject

As pure consciousness never acts in prohibition to the experience of mental phenomena, symbolic appearances, noumenal projections, or the positing of the object as both a Cartesian *ego cogito* and an abstract objective self from the transcendental horizon, we find an essential contradiction wherein we concern ourselves with the forms of production that rest before the transcendental subject. Therewith, the bio-genetic substrate of ontical being is addressed within a "scientism" before it has the opportunity to possess its own transcendency. But here, while the possibility of a synthesis between the social totality and the transcendental subject seems an ontico-ontological impossibility, one discovers the renewal of the image through its symbolization of the real throughout the fusion of transcendental subject and social production.

That the horizon represents an ontic subject with an ontology that proposes transcendental subjectivity in a formal engagement with the very ontological horizon where the subject dwells interobjectively—and with its presuppositions dialectically abstracts a transcendental subjectivity through its transmission of a priori conceptions in order to fuse ontical being with its own ontological abstract self—the inner space of the ontological manifold posits an image of the abstract concept to the Other from the ontical pole towards its own transcendency; yet it is also transubjective with the other ontical pole upon the horizon of production that has been symbolized. Thereto, the aesthetic becomes an *ethic*, in that the forms of production posited upon the horizon between both transcendent beings have an "opening" rather than a "closing"—in effect a quantum reality that could intervene with the interobjectivity of transcendental subjects, rendered one or the Other a damaged being upon the ontical pole of consciousness.

Yet an ontic subject is precisely this, before its ontologization has posited subjectivity as a cogitative being toward its own transcendency as an abstract possibility; but where the horizon has temporalized both the infinite and finitude, subjectivity performs as a transcendental Being simply by its ordered existence within the infinite possibility of abstraction from the other side of production as a universal self-concept. In other words, the produced *realiter* existential possibility of social or public engagement has an equal potentiality toward an abstraction of its symbolized identity to the Other that is within the totality of its own conception as a "self"—producing its own ontic conceptualizations at the causal nexus where ontical subject and transcendent being may collide through an ethical genesis upon the horizon of production in the very negation of this as an abstract possibility.

Where the subject as an ontico-ontological transcendental subject posits the "virtual" totality from a dialectical abstraction, subjectivity confers between the ontical and the transcendental as an abstraction upon the objective pole of consciousness as is exposed to ontical transmissions—from one corporeal quantum artifice to the other. Yet what this is in effect, is the determining agent of how social production would potentially strike the transcendental subject perishing as an ontological possibility of transcendency to the being-in-itself.

The concept that diachronic contingency could possibly protect subjectivity from the dialectical contradictions between capitalist social production and socialist transcendental subjectivity, is clearly defined by the ontological dynamics of those that pursue bourgeois subjectivity as an material reality that posits its *potentia* outside the transcendental ontology of the socialist enterprise. Further to this, the inversion of the abstract possibility of ontological transcendency beyond the socially produced horizon should impose a limitation upon what generates capitalist consumption between the abstract transcendental subject and its meta-ethical dialectical position upon the horizon.

Where the subject falls to antiquated notions of the base-superstructure model of consciousness—vertical hypostatizations of the ontical process of a de-transcendentalized being-in-itself—transcendency as a social possibility of the abstract Beyond of horizontal social production has been in effect *ethically* wronged. It *has* been, in so far as the social transcendency of a subject is determined by its ontological projections toward the social horizon, before the abstraction of transcendental social identity may be dynamical to synthetic experience within the post-industrial aesthetic. That pure exchange-value commodifications would obfuscate the transcendental universalization of social subjects into ontico-ontological interobjective "conceptual" or "symbolic" beings, is a delimitation of human potential through ordered class consciousness—procuring a devolution of the transcendency possible of $21^{st}$ Century ontological becoming. It is, as such the prohibition of our own evolutionary possibilities as a species projecting upon the edge of an awakening that will allow us to advance well into the next century and beyond.

That our ontological concerns remain part of human potential and the dialectical universalization of a transcendental social reality, is not an obstacle to the other concerns facing the planet—in that a social horizon that has been fused upon the ontical pole with its transcendental abstract self-concept, and reflexively coordinated with the social totality at the interstice between the ontic and the abstract self-concept, will produce identity through contingency and noumenal apodictic certainty—toward the social aims presupposed by ontological self-awareness in synthesis with the ontic social production dialectically constellated upon the social horizon through its ontological transcendency as a Being, and an abstract socially produced self-concept within the public space of representation.

As such, ontic considerations may become equally manifold of ontological presuppositions, and the conceptually signified abstract self-concept a mere objectification of the transcendental subject's prospective rational agency as a socially acting transcendent agent of production and ontological self-positing of claims that are presupposed by the social totality in order to rest within the spheres represented to the subject as a natural agent of social change. In effect, the transcendental subject is an appearance that produces an understanding of the causal terrain for which the subject may be engaged *as* a transcendental social subject.

Therewith social change is enacted by the dialectical projection of Being upon the social horizon that has been informed by the representation of the transcendent Other as an interobjective participant of the same objectifications of the rational need to produce the social engagement necessary to occupy the ontological horizon with a projection of what will effectuate a natural process—whereby ontology is activated as the originary point of contact for the dialectical opposition to what produces the contradictions hypostatized by those that are in social positions that promise to "close" a space of representation off from its natural conditionality of representing the ontological possibilities that may be formed through the synthesis proposed of the foregoing.

# Chapter Six

## Monadic Symbolization and the *Aesthetics of* Transcendental Signification

## Introduction: Symbolic Rigidification *of* a Transcendental Signifier

Insofar as cultural significance has a world of its own—a component that drives the economy of Being as a form of social production that inheres in the subject—opposing factions propose the cancellation of what may be posited as an image-sign, relying primarily upon the focal point where horizons of *realiter* experience merge with an aspect of the social imaginary as signified entities. The transcendental "I" of consciousness—for which ontology presupposes the mental representation as a copula to the produced social totality as an objectified whole of naturalized cultural existences—delivers inner space its formal stratification as an embodied Being with purpose that is therein contained within a monadic symbolization. The ontological field of view is inherently part of the signifying chain and is harnessed through its reflexive self-identification, and it is succinctly consummated as a mirror to the reflections of what has been universalized by the constructs of social becoming; yet transposes its normative condition into a plateau of existentiality that projects its a priori conditional framing upon the horizons as a sustained reification of the objective counterpoint to the objectification that has been abstracted through proprietary ontological relations.

As the substantiation of regional becoming to the invisible universe is edificial to the symbolization of its monadic reification, the positing of the imagined object of thought is posited as a motif to the subsidiary promises laid-out by social horizontality—a *superstructuration* of collective value is composed upon the edge of its stratified ontological structuration as a residual artefact of ontical co-presence, while the liaison to symbolized Being is its own verification of the veridical context in which the representationally posited Being is repelled—yet willingly compelled by the production of the stratified whole that natures social existentiality with its conceptual positionality as an aesthetic context whereby the image-sign is posited through its Kanto-Husserlian *projectional* becoming. The transcendentally composed "I" acts as a subjugate to the abstraction of the contextualized image-object as though Sartre had commanded Descartes to compose a symphonic movement with his mind that would never have been experienced by the world as a totality, but rather as a reification of social relations that were co-existents of the conceptual collective self-identification that would be borne wisdom's truest and most empathic soul—if only for the purposes of what would propose to reify a solicitude that resisted the totalization of conceptual notions. That these would be ossified within subsidiary social production as an inclusive conceptualization of formal intersubjective activities, is within the confines of what perhaps the Cartesian positing of actuality as an ontological verifiability would denote for another equal verifiability through its objective counterpart that is projected by Objective Being.

Should this epistemological nuance become of transcendental subjectification from the *Transcendence of the Ego*, outside the social formalizations that posit the social horizon as a totalization of economic activity, the reification of this transcendental being will as such be one that may only sustain Being as a *positing* object before the stratified objectification of the world, as it stands in relation to the contingent possibilities that have been sublated by active self-identification. Kant's synthetic a priori is at work here, whereby the subject's possible finite experience with existential realism is merely a projection of the ontological inter-relations—thereto the supply of value must comport collective substance as a subjective reification of its objectively totalized social relations. These all reside in the conceptual universalization that is first posited as objective self-identification, then projected toward horizontal Being as the potential abstractions of lifeworld experience that confer with the temporalized ontological becoming of subjective experience from within its roots in the natural aesthetic that posits substance as a collective reality to social activities throughout the inner space of representation.

Where this verifies the objective unification between subjective positing and the abstraction of the Other's projected self-identification, it bestows upon subjectivity a unification with the social production that is counter-posited to what is reified by the subjectification of the image-sign as a residual object that has form and content, but is yet without positionality as an ontic existent, other than by way of which it is a shared experience throughout the signifying chain of ontological co-presences that inhabit the same ontological stratification or positionality within the capacity to produce objects of conceptual content that have material form. This in-itself is an act of a Transcendence of the Ego, as it proposes to reify what is transcendental to a subject from its objective horizon, and reduces subjective self-identification to the monadic symbolization of which we are in the process of evaluating.

That this monad is existential in some manner, a manner by which the present elucidation is subject to profound criticism, is without doubt. Yet that its symbolization may be monadic is without question, since we can purely see how Leibniz contained human existence through a pre-established harmony that still identified with the ontological inner space from its presupposed universalization. Kant, having considered Leibniz carefully, adjusted this vision of universality, and gave it the same dualistic component that had been denied Descartes by Leibniz—but surely we can endure the presupposition that form and content are most notably separate conceptions, and that in order to see beyond an existential monadic symbolization, we are merely proposing to project beyond as Kant had with his Transcendental Aesthetic. Yet here what is presupposed is that the commitments to world perception from the subjective pole of consciousness is never in conflict with its monadic symbolization, given that the objects of the image-sign are posited by dialectical abstraction and grounded in the substance of a reified collective of conceptualized subjective Beings. The not-all of subjective totality is hereby verified, yet the social totality is stratified into its signifying universal composition as ontologically produced existents of a determinability of particular socio-ontological relations. These are composed of a synthetic symbolization of presupposed ontological monads that are posited a priori and are subject to conceptual abstraction as an active positing of the abstract transcendental ego that has become so once Sartre's vision has returned to Husserl's.

We may here consider a duality on both poles of the inner space of representation as this which *transcends*, and this which is *transcendental*. One must repudiate a synthesis of these two conceptions of symbolic Being in order to sustain the representational ideation possible of monadic symbolization. Though for Leibniz, we can see the *Universe* outside of the monad, but not another monad's inner soul. However, in *Cartesian Mediations*, Husserl were unafraid of the concept of a community of monads. In fact, for Husserl, in the *The Crisis of European Sciences*, the positing of a multitude of "Is" is consistent throughout its attempt at an amalgamation of metaphysics and (philosophical) science. Therewith, we resist an *ontification* possible of universalized ontological co-presences that have been projected as ontical components of the psychological socio-economic stratification of Beings that are subsidiaries to the projectional *realiter* experiences of something such as the *aesthetic seeing* posited by Bakhtin. In fact, though the basis of monadic symbolization presupposes residual "Is" and other egos, these are projections that act in sublation of the process of symbolic objective self-identification and its residual *symbolic rigidification* of a transcendental signifier. That I may turn myself into an object or posit myself as an image, I may abstract and posit the conception of the Other through nominal signification—most certainly where an individuated totalization is *in-itself* also an a priori abstraction of the subject that has perceived Being in relation to a universal possibility that were necessarily reified as a particular reality from its existential originations of Being.

## 1 The Distantiation *of* World-Society *for* the Instantiation of Identical Singularity

Human intellection has never prospered from its glimpse inward without a symbolic unification composed of identifiable concepts that are arranged in proportion to the Self as a signifying Being. In this sense and in such terms, relations with the Other are not naturalized to their identifying characteristics where identical Being is a presupposition of the positing ego as a self-relating ontological representation. That the outside of consciousness is there upon its horizontal counterpart, identifies Being as a *suchness* to compose subjectivity as the very instantiation of the likelihood of its identical relational counter-positionality. In forward motion, identical singularity is a presupposition for its horizontal aspirations, where it would be participatory to the social totality from the standpoint of a presupposed identical singularity. The world, in-as-much as it is for all a presupposed ontological universal concept, is not to be thought of as a totalization of the subjective *perceptuality* unless its judiciary substantiation is posited as a totalization of the presupposed notion that the world is posited in relative proportion to its identical limitations of noumenal personhood. It is bound by these identical limitations insofar as its positing stands in relative proportion to subjective Being, and identical to the horizon whereupon the world is posited in unison with its subjective transcendentality—albeit the negative consequence of objective reason presupposes subjective participation in the enterprise of the Communal Self, as we exist as subsidiary Beings throughout the projection of our identical natures that have sublated the totalization of the ontical social collective that ascribes a negative totality to the subjects' own personhood—thereto, presupposing a potentiality for reification of the capital that is instantiated—notwithstanding the identical limitations presupposed by the subjects' own reflexive objective self-identification.

With this, where we supersede the limits throughout our noumenal projections of personhood upon the identical flux of ontological boundaries presupposed by the Other, we distantiate the positing of world society as a totalization of the formal ego that has posited its subjective presupposition as an object for identical reification toward the horizon as an signifying exponent of ontological self-realization. Whereby we accede the throne of expectations, we render the identifying properties of ontic existentiality as a presupposition of the formal organization of symbolic significations that fall into the hands of the non-identical opposing forces of human nature bound by the impetus to subvert possibility with an identical qualification of Being that supervenes the dialectical output of ontic relativity. De facto subjects may posit an absolute within the presupposition that all relative non-identities are *noematic* components that bear no significance on subjective reasoning, yet the instantiation of propositional subjectivity is a formal negation of its ontological reflexivity from the *noetic* stratum that determines its possibility as a noematic referent. This is the dialectical ontological stratification of symbolized experiences into a stratum of consciousness that determines the visual semiosis of what is identifiable to the mind as a "this", or a "that". We as human subjects have it within our faculties of cognition to apprehend the objects from the phenomenal components that are posited *a priori,* and in fact become the perceivers of these "happenings", just as though they were the tree in the yard, or the house on the street, or the car on the road. Human perception is not locked into an eternal mode of darkness and shadowed

## Monadic Symbolization and Transcendental Signification

Being that is outside of propositional reality, only looking out as transcendental subjects that may receive the objects as they are in the world—there within perception, within our grasp and involved with how we compose our inner space as subjects of fruitful endeavor.

Where we succeed as Beings apprehending this essential quality of natural world-substance is how we become self-realized, and how in fact we convene as ontological signifiers reasoning toward the horizon that is "out there" rather than a totalization of reflexive self-identification—oftentimes the delusive thoughts of the minds that justify reification more than its distantiation from an ontological composition attuned to self-identification. A global reunification is its totalization, and for this reason one must presuppose a subtraction of polarizing ideological vantage points, toward the synthesis requisite of a process by which world society may persist as an existential possibility within reason. The ontological instantiation of a synthetic totalization of non-identical Beings is to be repudiated and replaced with the conceptual reification of a self-identical symbolic singularity that posits its object as a unifying composition of self-realization—within the presupposition that synthetic representations are deceptive as totalizations of the existential realism necessary, wherein the world may posit itself as a disconnected experience absent the furtive claims of an embodied mass-culture that refuses the symbolization of a dialectical exposition of an ontology that had fused identities from within its negation of their ontological self-reflexivity; and within the grasp and hold of such negativity, had substantiated *en masse* the relativization of hegemonic substructures in proposition of an antithetic superposition and its qualifying signification. Thereto, reason supersedes as an obligatory self-positing of its transcendental subjectivization and subsequent objective distantiation from the world-society in totalization of the Self.

## 2 The Return to Subjectivity: Socio-Ontological Existentiality

While objective phenomena has its place in the world of Being, it is simply that it only serves its purpose insofar as knowledge may be acquired outside of its rational limitations throughout the logic of capitalism. That one is to regard an Object as contingent to the Self—or that subjects should find themselves in servitude of phenomenal objects of consciousness, is to recede into Hegel's master-slave dialectic—that Being is merely the state of one's Self and is accountable to Objective agency a priori, and thereto an apprentice or an underling to rational thought. In most instances, the vertical use of reason becomes merely a form of compliance that abstracts true forms of rational agency from subjects that have already established normative patterns of behaviour—though these may be perceived as out of order with the *status quo*. Creative activities are altogether driven by another more radical form of subjective reasoning, and leave the platitudes of sober no-nonsense limitation with some tractable ideas that shape post-industrial living with vital concepts that conjure and invite the passions of human life that are not mere reductions to critical thinking.

One's rationality should never be beneath the formal sophisms that ultimately act in mere solipsism to the soul. We are not condemned to accept these notions as givens of civil justice, just as we are not to identify with hegemonic strains of ontological becoming that motivate pernicious activity with the same thought control. For this reason alone, one must resist the master signifier and actively posit one's Object—and with this be in possession of dialectical presuppositions that are incumbent upon subjectivity by their socio-psychological center of Being. Though if we look back to the days of Aquinas, we may perceive how a formalization of human conduct is normative to those involved in capital relations, and that their binding agreements are entirely based upon the conduct associated with said normativity.

However, from Locke to Hume, Descartes to Kant, we surmise that the impetus to resolve our objective concerns rests not with only with the phenomenal object as a leading force of determinability, but as the ontological component of the empirical act of subjective rationalization. For the aforementioned—as for us—it is to drive away forms of freedom that propel radical thinking toward the nexus of reason's own dialectical imputation, that its existence is one of subjective agency that is not posited as a normative Being that subsists only insofar as it follows the judgments laid out by an Object as a self-identical constraint upon philosophical endeavor. We never produce what is there always already available for consumption at the levels of Being that reproduce content with vigorous intention. Should we perceive this impervious rational object to be of our sophistical Self, we are at a loss for what may become of productive creative activities that provide more salient ideas that propel critical thinking *forward* in this world. Peace is only a possibility where the outer context where we reproduce ourselves in public discourse is based upon a level playing field.

Dialectical reasoning is the moral imperative for subjectivity in order to compel Being toward its identical presuppositions in radical pursuit of an abstraction of the universal as an induction of horizontal thinking, and a departure from the vertical, medieval objectivation intrinsic to medieval philosophers such as Aquinas. The world is there for a purpose, and as subjects we must presuppose our place in it as Descartes had, and therewith, dialectically participate as though in forward motion necessary of civil undertaking—pushing the frontiers of what throughout the distant past had limited philosophy to theocratic subservience and compliance. Now, these are economic barriers superimposed by institutions—not aesthetic boundaries closing transcendental subjects off from their ontological becoming—where the only place to hide is in the shadow of the prosperity of those for whom thought is a mere instrument of progressive accumulation. One must continue onward from here, toward a horizon that does not perform this subtle exclusion of conceptual activity for the purposes of objective reification, reforming the context in which this sophistical limitation has reduced the transcendental subject to a Being possessed of no common will or ontologically public discourse with which to enter into the act of doing philosophy as part of what composes reality within the human soul. It is upon us all as philosophers to elicit this discourse, that our praxis is of a kind that is in development of ontology—never in its regression to the dark ages where the thinkers were not public Beings as those that have become since the *Age of Enlightenment*.

This is not to suggest that noumenal activity may not enter into a pathic stage as it did for Adorno in *Negative Dialectics*—where two particular subjects would battle one another to the "point of exhaustion". One would be remiss to suggest that any such situation would be in the comfort zone of civil subjects in pursuit of a transcendental horizon. We are those that seek this beauty, and propose to *sublate* any forms of reason that are to end philosophy. For the purpose of *philosophy* is to form a reality that is salient within and beyond reason, and to posit a dialectical presupposition that allows for the reification of transcendental becoming. It is much better to be as one enlightened by truth and the *real* than to be held hostage by institutions for their own personal economic benefit. That is what is to become of the subject should they be members of a society that believe themselves to be one of the Greats as were Aquinas, or worse, a serf having been punished for thinking more of the Self than is produced by the possession of personal property and physical qualities; reduced to a servant of a presupposed higher morality that consistently seems to reproduce wealth for the privileged. We must be signified to ourselves as existing in the presence of Others psycho-socially, psychologically, symbolically, and ontologically, if only to reason that we may find the culprits of reason and change the face of this ontology to match what we'd beheld as a transcendental radiance that had acted as the catalyst for post-industrial development. The supersession of philosophical limitation is never to come about lightly though, and for this reason it is readily diagnosable that transcendental subjectivity is no longer possible without first introducing Kant to Marx.

But we must depart the confines of this corner of socio-ontological existentiality in order to posit the Self as an acting agent of societal change that presupposes self-identification through the creative act, where it had become a form of pure objectivation, rather than the dialectical relationhood to our presupposition that the horizon is existence *in-itself*. We are those that perceive this relation to the horizons of Being as projected subjects encumbered with the powers of reasoning instantiated by our presence as ontic *and* ontological Beings creating a framework whereto we possess our selves as reified existences—not simply creatures resisting the master-signifiers as such—but rather in full disclosure of the mutual correspondence that we indicate within as transcendental subjects universalizable only by way of our active positing of a reified horizontal representation that reproduces the essential appearances reified by dialectical abstraction. Thereto, we become transcendental subjects, in resistance of the ontic cityscapes whereupon the ontologization of societal activity sublates the ontological manifold as a *realiter* disorder to this proposed through the foregoing.

## 3   In Participation of the Existentiality Composing Aesthetic Experience: Semiotic Correspondence

The world of objects is to philosophy perhaps what a garden of flowers is to nature, a collection of buildings and houses to a city, or a room full of paintings to an artist. They exist both as this which is experienced, but also this which we perceive through our senses. The *inner* sense of what makes ontology the primary source of the following exposition will underscore a search for what should compel the mind to examine why we encounter existences that are Other than what *we* are, and more than mere phantoms of our interior space.

Though Being qua Being will demonstrate to us what is there as a pure function of our capacious faculties, the key component to the human soul as an Object of the mind is either a Self or its Other, but in order to experience several objects within the space of representation simultaneously would seem an unlikely condition for any well-formed subject-object. In fact, the presence of more than one object of thought or constellated representations—should one be so fortunate—is a compelling ontology for the investigation of forms of knowledge where we have engaged the *res publica* with mere powers of reasoning associated with organized contemplation. However, that one is to be ensnared by contemplation—held in stasis for subjective reification *of* the object—is a diametrically opposing problem to the Object of lordship. We must present a further elaboration of how we are to posit our Being as an object with full intention to ground objective essence, whereto the horizon opens up to representations that confer with a praxis that completes the manifold of ontology in such a manner as to supply minds with what is productive for the act of contemplation in-itself— that thinking *is* something, and not a remote activity of no significance other than the musings of an individuated Being.

From signifier to signified, though our Object is the acting agent of representational consciousness—that it is in correspondence with the Self and its Other both noumenally and phenomenally—we presuppose Being of a nature that is instantiated by the observation of our own self-identifying, signified existence to forms of thought that seem comprehensible to an inner world, yet become apprehensive where we no longer embody this representational manifold that is incurrent within the positing of Selfhood and the identification of the Self in relation to the Other; though the moment light is shed upon the transcendence of our posited conceptual content has been projected toward plateaus of reason there upon the edge, we only see the transcendental horizon from the Objective standpoint where the constellated representations are uniform in regional contingency. The process whereby we identify our communal relations is integral to this horizon, while the projection of what *may* exist for us transcendentally is *sublated* by the objectivation of our representational, projected Self. The substance to this evaluation is that Being is precisely at the logical nexus of its distantiation from other temporal relations, and therewith conceptually enmeshed with subjectivity as an abstraction of the existential reality that possesses our internal ontological relations, or intersubjectivity.

That these internal ontological relations accompany subjective reasoning perceptually is more than the instantiation of developmental reason, it posits the *a priori* correspondence that ontology has with its situational encumbrances—experiences that are generated by productive activity that stand in relation to the natural composition of a subject and its Others. The polarizing effect that this has upon transcendental becoming is decentering to the groundwork laid by active contemplation, and proposes to necessitate an essentialist stance toward all intersubjective experiences—compelled by the cancellation of self-identity and reification of one's object and the symbolic meaning that may be posited in pursuit of something existing within as a signified, and thereto is pre-emptive of abstraction where it falls short of dialectical reasoning as a mode of Being that presupposes the existential horizon as something that may be transcendentalized by thought alone and what is posited by the mind.

For spiritual endowments are these which bring meaning to the world—in which we make great strides to co-exist as representational identities that are consistently mediated by the material presence of the opposing camp that forces Being into a passive mode of self-awareness. For those of us whom undertake to subsist throughout the travails of ontological becoming as socially adept species beings, we may regress into non-being and leave philosophy behind, rather than persevering its flaws in order to supersede them. The repairs of conscious existence are never easily mended with a simpliciter solution, but certainly there is a lifeworld that bestows upon us our purpose, and allows for the ethical choices that we must make to be ordered by more than pure self-interest; but perhaps that we may signify something conceptually good to Others—giving meaning to why we do what we do. To hold the notion that we are doing *nothing* when we posit conceptual content as a shared lifeworld experience, suggests that from the Eleatics to Socrates, Plato and Aristotle, contemplation only serves its purpose insofar as it is turned into material objects by the *agents* of contemplation.

And with this, the *maker* does shine a bright light upon reason, whereby philosophers are also these as such. The word as a signifier in all its senses and in all imaginable terms, is throughout our thoughts—the books we read and write, the paintings and sculptures we observe, the architecture we examine, the films and music we experience, the images we perceive, etc. And behind each of these forms of conceptual content is a signified, and *signifieds*. Each perceptual experience of the mind is semiotically correspondent with another thing in the world, and usually identifiable as such strictly by our powers of logic and reasoning and our internal ontological experiences of the self-concept as a normative mode of human becoming. Not all of what is "out there" for contemporary 21$^{st}$ Century subjects is provided by technological advancements—the truth is that these are only subtexts to the actual representational consciousness that we may encounter whereto we design our significatory existence to ourselves as to Others. The objects of the world *are* the noematic representations that reproduce our self-identification as ontological subject-objects that may be signified to Others on the world horizon, and thereto must be carefully shaped by ethical standards that form the manner by which we would choose to be perceived at the global level insofar as we have chosen to expose ourselves to judgements for which we have no defenses in place so as to find a necessary subterfuge from the dialectical reasoning that is part of the nature of forward thinking minds. To suggest that protections must be instituted seems to displace a universalization of our efforts to propel free will into the forthcoming century, where it is still in possession of the moral edicts that had not *dispossessed* reason with forces of rapacious greed and envy by those that do not follow meta-ethical praxis with an intentionality toward objects of thought with a sense of universal normativity, but compromise the perception of justice that is particular to the institutional forms that would provisionally obfuscate the transcendental dialectic under the rubric of particular special interests. We must never return to those days either, and find a mode of becoming that imports the possibilities upon the horizon to those active in participation of the existentiality that composes aesthetic experience as much as it does political motivation and social activism.

# 4 The Tableau *of* Our Symbolic Thinking:

## Ontological *Uniformity* and Ontical Differentia

Where we consider humanity as a totality, and bring to it a sense of uniformity, many striking questions are instantiated concerning the universality of Being as an internal ontological expression of existential reality, and the outer ontic particularity associated with common place differences that we all share. The boundaries of our endeavors are naturalized by our consummation of these differences, yet the ontologization that may synthetically reproduce them is *a fortiori* the presentation of how the outer barriers may be broken down—if only we persisted to order what is posited as though it is not *stricto sensu* a matter of noumenal emancipation, but also a function of where the beginnings of our self-reflexive historical identification is incurred as a functional processual right of passage. Though on the tableau of our symbolic thinking, spiritual experiences are these which accompany ontological reflection and are oftentimes the moment of consumption of the same ideas that birthed the abstraction of our perceptual encounter with the symbolic—as it is integral to this activity that we are naturalized into stratifications of Self that are induced by the universality of *symbolized nominal signification*.

We perceive the object of thought as a semiotic expression of what there is, though for this to come to fruition completely, the task must be met with the presupposition of a projected conceptualization that conjoins the subject of contemplation to the representation that is to be posited by the mind, and experienced as an symbolized image object. The content of the conceptual experience is only linguistic insofar as it is within the noumenal ideation of subjectivity, though it is an acting formal sublation of the *ego* as a formation of reflexive self-identification, and the singularized performance of Being as it disposes of the ontological setting concerned with the object as phenomenon. Transcendental becoming is prone to accept this at the originary point of contact with its horizontal abstraction of conceptual imagery, yet has to posit the ego cogito co-presently with what is experienced *as* the object of contemplation—a symbolic nominal identity. With this held in mind, Others may be instantiated by the representational adjuration to the symbolized encumbrances that propose a furtherance of abstract thinking in unification with its nominal counter-positionality, but nonetheless it is still in liaison with the conceptual datum within the image-object, as such.

The purpose of investigating this exposition in a symbolic nominal setting—wherein we are co-presences to Others—presupposes something uniform within, that the symbolization of something reproductive is explored by the social totality as a reification of the ontological experience upon the genesis of the dialectical abstraction that had posited its objective symbolization; yet it persists that this encounter of something naturalized by intermediary Beings upon the transcendental horizon suggests that the experience rests singularly with the perceiving subject. However the instantiation of objective unification with its positional expression subsists throughout the noumenal composition of a judging Being, and thereto the hold on the experience is just that; it is the representational encounter of one subject, yet a uniformity of ontological reproduction that expresses its totalization to Others as reified objective Beings. In this sense, the impetus to observe rational symbolic phenomena exists with an emancipatory subject that projects what has been posited upon the horizon to perceptual subjects induced by uniform objective cultural expressions of the Self—that architectonic substrates of transcendental subjects would be uniform as ontological existential Beings, yet would be in possession of a differential particularization of the ontic Self.

Therewith, the modality of an expressive ontology is what may symbolize this uniformity—that its totalization is endemic to the a priori syntheses that perform the transcendentalization that instantiates its conceptual objectivation. It is only with the departure of the ego that this would become possible given the differential ontic conditionality affiliated with ontologized multiple egos operating within the same space of representation. We obviate the reification of objective essence through the transformation of what is a world-totality into what may be posited through the image in order to conjure the moments of our conscious experience with what reifies the same essentiality that proposes the abstraction of what has been posited a priori. This is ordered by rationality that confers with its objective conceptualization— the positionality upon the world-stage of what had been abstracted from the unifying element that *sublated* the positing of objective Being, and therewith subjective reality as a historical expression of self-realization; while at the very same instant *being* its self-realization—in that the co-presence of symbolic nominal signifier and the instantiation of its dialectical projection is not an abstraction of essential Being, but rather a comportment toward the depicted element as though it were there for remote perception and ontological expression as an semiotic image-content.

Throughout this aesthetic is also the projection of its dialectical counterpoint as an objectifying content that expresses the context in which the object is experienced, and thereto the unifying element consists of noumenal co-presence as it undergoes its transformation into lifeworld experience from its original point of contact—such as the conception of a nominal Being upon the horizon that is there within the context of what were borne the projected content from its dialectical imposition. The normative setting where this is ethically bound is posited by Objective reason as a transcendental presupposition, yet provisional to the perceiver through its objectifying moment that is subject to horizontal limitations—where the bridge between transcendental becoming and a transcendent ego is consequential to the ordinance of what drives subjective transformation toward its abstract horizontality. The social totality is integral to the transformational motif that undergoes the determinability expressed by the forms that are posited by the society of ontological representations that have been elicited by components of the posited interobjective Self—that where the "I-ego" is a Self for the horizontal totality, the Other is a symbolized object in its formal ontological setting as a semiotic image. We compose reality in such a manner that the world does not disappear under these conditions, and for this reason the moral imperative is subjugate to the subordination of its own conclusive powers of observation.

We can not alter the context in which the object appears, yet we can compose it in its unifying moment with the Other ontologized ontic subjects that have been posited through a unifying totalization of synthetic representation. In other words, we may exchange one image for the next, or semiotically transform one symbolic concept with what is posited within the object itself. We are able to perform this alteration without going to great lengths to do so; one must simply imagine the new context in which the object is to appear or what changes may be made to the appearance of the object. The presupposition of an ontological world experience persists transcendently, yet our subjectivity is consumed with its transcendental symbolization. Only through ontological unification is this possible—that the differential expressions of what we are has been reified through the context in which ontic particularities are social constructs under no biological constraints that would ontologize the friction of an impossible moment of synthetic transformation that composes reality in such a manner so as to make this ontology uniform and total despite its segmented ontical differentia.

From this, we must also address that the noumenal projection of identity is concomitant to the transformation of the posited object that is depicted, but that two ontologically constrained noumenal subjects may not share the same space of representation for this experience to be one of uniformity. Thereto, the lacuna must be held as the inner space contingent to the possession of symbolic content. Thereto, the ontological plateau is not without Other occupants—it is only that they are transcendentally affixed to the horizon and not projections upon the subjective determinability that instantiates the semiotic contextualization. As such, the thing-in-itself is ordered by an all-encompassing moment of exchange that is interobjective, and not noumenal in modal symbolic realism. The totalizing experience is non-differential to ontological exchange, yet uniform within its ontic self-identical reification, where dialectical projection transposes the motif of contextualized symbolic content into a signifying moment of transformation. The kinesthetic abstraction of the conceptual content its *part of ontic verification*, yet never the ontologically reflexive moment of a symbolic unification. Ergo, *logos* also has bearing on the instantiation of the semiotic image content and its aspirations to find an ontic space of uniform transmission. Thereto, we undergo a possible reflexive activity that may be undesirable to the intersubjectivity that has not yet posited a unifying moment of symbolic totalization as a universally reflexive kinesthetic abstraction. Though here, we may also find an ontological unification that transforms the *onta* through a mode of transcendental symbolization—and there realize the transmission of the nominal signifier into what is to be posited by the subject—where we consider *humanity as a totality and bring to it a sense of uniformity*.

## 5 Conclusion: Symbology and Transcendental Reproducibility

Before time had reached a point of resonance as an ontological relativity, temporal relations echoed as historical signs were developed through various symbols that were etched in the world in a synchronic fashion.

As anthropic Beings, we were no different 10,000 years ago than we are now—it is simply that the inner space had not constructed a social formalization that projected itself beyond necessity into the organized distribution of common ideals that would nurture the species as a concurrently evolving genus of non-identical creatures occupying the Earth with the interests in mind that allowed for survival rather than extinction. What we now refer to as the *lifeworld* was a place of disorientation and savage need—a reservoir for acquisition, and the presentation of something that had to sustain the evening fires with nourishment and physiological self-preservation. We were, never as One, but tribal souls seeking the most tolerable conditions with which to proliferate our kind and invigorate our primal senses with what reified a prevailing sense of Self that must have been there beyond its primitive originations. Such as it is, humanity were in its infantile stages of development and did not establish an organized recovery from its fledgling beginnings until well into the first Millennium B.C., and until ancient Greece what we now call society was non-existent notwithstanding the Mesopotamians, Ancient Egypt, China, Asia Minor, the Mayans, etc.

Since there are traces of our species' time on this planet that indicate a representational consciousness far before there is any acknowledgement that it had in fact existed as clearly defined by the symbology of Hieroglyphics for example, we can readily concern ourselves with the prospect that thoughts had been imported into the minds of those first civilizations that had somehow grown in conjunction with a progression of nature and its elements—and with the increase in tolerability for the habitat in which we were thrown as both Beings of necessity and those which were prone to deliver a messaging system that allowed for communication from one Being to another. That what were there were not simply the input of thoughts in response to what is there in the stars, but tools of mind that would order the evolution of our responses to matter and form in such a manner so as to instantiate a developmental necessity to establish forms of Reason that would keep philosophers occupied for many centuries to come. Let us estimate that we have been evolving the human mind, body and spirit for approximately 2500 years or so.

But still we return to Ancient Greece and read Plato and Aristotle as though the same may hold true for the present age in which we live. In fact, when one reads the works of the latter, it at times appears as though all of philosophy were already complete and resolved before Descartes reformed the Self-Concept in his all-too-brief lifetime. Though Aristotle is conventionally thought to be the informant of Hegel—as positing Beings in formal negotiation with the manner by which we find ourselves in relation to the world spirit—it may fall more immediately into the hands of the State with Hegel, while remaining the pure Self-Concept of subjectivity for Descartes. The gaze formed by the instantiation of our symbolic becoming as self-reflexive souls is certainly inveighed by this subjective reflexivity, and where Hegel imports our conceptual identification we discover that the inversion of Hegel into Marx is a launch-pad for both Eastern and Western Governance, and a disorder to the symbolic subjective stance that becomes of an immanence that has been suffused with the syntheses of objectivated Beings or non-Beings at odds—relegated to a non-representational position and consumed by standards that negate the possibilities of social reflection as transcendental subjects to those which are not in negotiation with the institutions *per se*, but trans-positional in their self-identification and projected ontologically toward the currency of an evolutionary historicity that posits developmental reason before it does necessary subsistence and adherence to a normative status of acquiescence.

*Das Ding*—the giant brick of the State Apparatus—is the nouveau of consumeristic behaviourism of the 21st Century, lest we had not yet left behind the 20th. We must transcend these boundaries as ontological Beings importing horizontal collectives less as adjudicators than as positing Beings perceiving the problem as uniform to a malformed instantiation of ontologically nuanced particularizations of what had already imported the culture industry as it fell into the freedoms that had abandoned its central precepts. Ours is to imagine a world that will not be thrown from its natural state of ontological awareness to one that is to be consumed by primitive forms of Reason that have not yet evolved the species being from its integral purpose toward an immanence that induces reality with form and content that is more than pure instinct, and propels mobile perspectives out of ontological condemnation and into a projected existential horizon that is formed by our symbolic obviation as those that operate under more refined conditions than what Dystopian conspiracies may ever hope to—but those may be negotiable should we not condition the outer edge of ontology toward plateaus of the encumbrances that confirm the classification of what resonates future instantiations of the symbolic tree of knowledge that first floated us a negotiable condition of unconditioned self-reflexivity. Though we are prone to accept a mirrored reflection into the Other, we must not abandon the genus of those thoughts that import horizontal aspirations to the logical nexus of their origination, and never presume that we are beyond reproach where concerns the historical remains of our primitive age, and the developmental deliverance from this which consumes our impetus to produce ideas more than passions which have not been founded on the principles of our original motive to evolve the human spirit more than the historical forms in which it has been chained to the floor and relegated to the shadows of a symbolic realism that had not yet founded a logic that would propel the seeds of human self-realization forward into the precipice from where its conception had renewed its possibilities.

# Chapter Seven

## Noematic Symbolization

While phenomena exist at the noetic pole of consciousness, the noumenal realm is distantiated from subjectivity and upon the objective side. Though it remains an intrinsic component of subjectivity—that a projection of the Self has realized its identical representation upon the horizon—we are in the very beginnings of what is to be become a rapport with a social totality as an opening prone to the possibility of noemata consisting of an objective pole of subjects in correspondence with an event that has produced an ontological response which we will here call a subject's *reflexive noematic symbolization*. The transcendental noesis of subjectivity is vertically instantiated from its originary point of contact within acts of reflection, while projected out toward the totalized objective stance that is posited as an adjunct to the politicization of the *id* as a liberated, freely formed Being that initiates social contact with a signifier, thereto residing within the ontological landscape of the visual field where all such eruptions of the artifice are in correspondence with what exists on the horizontal plateau where identity reproduces its identifying moment as a signified to the symbolization of what is reflexively within the purview of subjectivity—the conceptual landmark that had originated a psychological transformation that initiated the act as a signified experience for a co-existent upon the outer reaches of biopolitical transformation.

Social identity becomes transfixed in this very way, as Being is natured throughout the essence of which plateaus of conscious dialectical impositions negate the context in which social barriers become abstractions to the architectonic that reifies transformation as a political initiation into the id's positing as a form of thought that identifies with unconscious drives just as it does the biopolitical instantiation of its virtual representation as an existent of the ontological landscape where Being becomes enticed by normatively repressed desires. These constellate in a social transformation that instantiates the biopolitical plateau of horizontal becoming with its distantiated identical Self within the totalization of the primordial impetus to reproduce its reified self-concept—thereto instantiating a devotion to the precept that social transformation is in confluence with its transcendental-noetical representation—and projected through a signifying moment of reflexive self-identification. The reified socio-ontological component that projects this identifying moment instantiates the abstraction of what becomes the essence of the signifier that is symbolically constituted through its reified form of reproduction, and thereto projected through a unifying moment that synthesizes the natural impetus of subjectivity to *transform* subjectivity from its transcendental noetic verticality to the horizontal possibility that is preformative of the projection of an identical truth that acts in liaison with the presupposed identical status of the socio-symbolization of what is current within the projected unifying moment. Spirits acting in concert with the performance of the biopolitical self-concept as it identifies within an abstract signifying moment, resist the temptation to reproduce what had not yet been transformed through a unifying synthesis that originated in the image-sign. Though the significatory stratification of the socio-ontological identity that is reflexively self-positing from its noetic pole and transcending as a noumenal Being is certainly within the existence of a consciousness that pursues its reifying self-identification with the subject that has become an abstraction through the unifying synthesis reproduced by the contextualization of the subject of *symbolic noemata*.

From the moment of abstraction from their ontic situation, these are not in fact essences to the perceiving subject, but ontologizations of the objects that may undergo modulation through the biospheres of ontological perspicuity. In effect, what this means is that object $x$ interestingly enough could resemble object $xa$, $xb$, $xc$, just as easily. The Husserlian notion that the core attributes of the subject perceived as objects are *de facto* copies of the same genus of what were first posited, yet transformed by subjective perception into what is in correspondence with the fluxion of the perceiving subject's significatory reification of the posited elements that had generated the ontological formation of the perceived object. Of course, one may begin with the dialectical projection of a nominal certainty within the intention of forming a mental picture of the desired object, while this would seem to propose the same possible modulatory fluxion to the image reflexively as images of the same genus are reproduced in the very same way, and take on the qualities of the subject as much as they might the qualities of the object of perception. That the perceivability of objects is in question is denied, while the claim that the image will not necessarily sustain its transformation through the biospheres of ontological contemplation is certain. What forms our inner sense of the object of perception is in every sense also temporally interdependent and subject to a totalizing determination that projects from the source to the pole of abstraction—the noetic side.

Where the inner space is formed by the nucleus of ontological visibility, the object is introduced to the perceiving mind first as a general idea that is posited through a closed totality that had already reproduced the object, then reflexively abstracted by the dialectical projection that presupposed a unifying moment of ontologization through the reification of the synthetic composition of the Self as a potency that reflected upon existential possibilities. The unifying synthesis is realized where the subject posits conceptual formations of reflexive ontological relations that are in a positive state of transmission from the generating element that permits the closure to become an opening that composes the subjective formation of a concrete *idea* of what has been ontologized and what the temporal relation might be, given that the reifying moment will only respond to the genus of what were possible of the unifying moment in consideration of its modulatory fluxion as an image-sign. Again, the proposition that a positing of the nominal signifier will reproduce a knowable object given its temporal relation as a referential representation, yet a unifying synthesis that questions the authenticity of the object of perception where it might have different temporal determinations than the ones produced by subjective active object formation.

The actuality of the perceived event is also in question, where we propose that both temporal relation and the successively reproduced states of the image-sign are given a genus that had ontologized the form of the objects into representations that could be experienced by subjective image formation as the reified significations of the object in pursuit—that the particularization of form is undergoing an entirely opposing set of the determinations to the ones than are in consideration of the perception of the object. We will rightly say, that the proposition that introduces a conceptual datum to the mind instantiates the genus of an image-object without a universalization of its particular qualities, while the positing of the particular qualities of the image reproduce an image-object of particular conceptual data. As such, appearances are there in order for us to reify the concept from its positive formation as idea, while introducing it to the negative condition that surrounds the projected state of self-awareness that constitutes image formation. To hold for instance that the technological scrutiny is in effect responsible for the reproducibility of what is within the mind acts as another barrier to image formation that requires some clarification. For it is inevitable—as Benjamin had suggested—that technological reproducibility is the virtual experience of things as they exist in another form. But while those objects are reproduced, with the stratification of what posits the image as a viable component that has significations that supersede a fictive transformation from real objects

Noematic Symbolization    217

to pictorialized situations being portrayed, we now have verification that the nominal signifier acts as a copula within a unifying synthesis that may stand to conquer the temporal formation of imagined signifiers into actual posited images that exist upon the horizon in closed totalities that may be opened by dialectical abstraction.

What is in question, is whether we may also perform a similar synthetic act in accordance with the positing of propositions that may produce an image that transcends the modulatory fluxion previously addressed—that we have it within our capacities to visualize an actual event in space and time that is accurate not only in conceptual formation, but also in terms of temporal stabilization—a moment in time pictured as the event. The virtual experience perceived as it is in its ontic state, ontologized by the dialectical abstraction that reifies an opening of a closed singularity. That someone is not on a map of consciousness, and is entirely unidentifiable is beyond doubt, it is only a matter of projecting the propositional component that presupposes if $f$ then $fx, fy$, etc. It is only a matter how far to go through the causal chain in order to arrive at $fz$, for instance. So we know that there may be something in the way of the opening of what we have to perceive that is not within our conceptual grasp. In this sense, outer contacts of horizontal existentiality supervene where we might apprehend the objects who's particular unidentifiable qualities remain out of reach.

There is also the notion that a conceptual datum might supervene its closed ontic singularity through the reproducibility of opened totalities posited as existential possibilities that have become part of a constellation of the formation of image-signs that are of the same genus than this that has been reproduced. In effect, the technologically reproducible artifice acts as the *copula* to image formation, and the positing of the signified as a signifier concomitant to the content that is posited by the conceptual datum proposed. This is also *ex parte* to the self-positing noesis that instantiates both concept formation and the appearance represented of the image-sign. We see what we dialectically reproduce in a sense from our self-reproducing ideological reduction.

That this coheres with the regionalism inherent of biopolitical relations transformed by the same powers of observation is without a doubt. However, we may not always wish to be pursued by those that have standing claims that are no longer reifications of the same generating components of active contemplation than those that had reproduced the thoughts associated with them. In fact, it is these that we must sublate *in toto*.

The ones that survive developmental subjective transformation from its transcendental noesis will remain part of the manifold of relations on the objective side, and will as well be there for noematic symbolization *ex hypothesi*. It would be pleasant to propose that the existential possibilities generated by active ontological reflection made room for diachronic representations to appear through the mind. The vistas of thought are conceptual reifications of the signifiers as such, and the coordinates of the transpositional reality associated with projections of the Self will within a certain variability reproduce the experiences that had once been quotidian events that instantiated the concept formation affiliated with the maturation of socio-symbolization in the modes of consciousness that are inextricably intertwined with the presuppositions posited *through* concept formation.

Given this, it is that in order to transcend toward plateaus of existential possibility we must concern ourselves with both diachronic and synchronic representations, that we are in possession of an instantiated concept formation as it had been posited from its originary point of contact with the genus of subjective self-realization—that we are composed of experiences that may be part of the import of socio-symbolization as image-signs to Others, and so should the Others be to us. However, this outmodes *realiter* experience as a psychological transformation of the causal nexus that reproduces socio-ontological reification. The genus of our authorship over our own reproducibility must remain an integral part of subjective agency of the phenomena affiliated within the currency to our projection of the unifying synthesis that had transmitted the reflexively produced components of social transformation that reproduced the Others as signifiers requiring noematic symbolization, and the historical revelations that are within the coordinates of the same concepts being formed—sometimes acting in conflict with them. This is part of the referential qualification of what instantiates the biopolitical abstraction of the dialectically presupposed image-content within an ontological field of view.

As such, we are natured to this process of reified subjectivity that the sense of image content composes the signifying qualities coherent within the objective transformation from subjects to objects for perceiving Others. It is in this way, and by these very means, that we are stratified as socio-ontological existents in correlation with the signifying moment of transcendental appearances that originate on the noematic pole of consciousness, but are subjectively experienced as image-phenomena. Where we subtract the transcendental appearance into the noetic stratum, we have already begun to actuate the necessary potency so as to *abstract* symbolizations of the noematic pole that exists in relation to objectified beings in temporal relations that have not yet undergone any propositional determinability other than what has been actualized by subjective particularization. Hence, the *seeing* of the objects in their subjective state of particularity is a human trait that becomes of the noetic projection and its point of contact with ontological reification from its socio-symbolic ontologization into the closed public spheres of biogenetic observability. The biospheres such as they are, are ontological formations of the stratified ontic particularizations that have projected a moment of ontological self-identification—either in a mode of self-positing or from a presupposed a priori state of self-awareness that instantiates intersubjective coherence with the ontological formations that have been reified through reflexive objective self-realization. In other words, the subjects perceive their being as natured by the Other through the mirror-phase of self-identification, and reify its objectivated signification as a co-existent of the unifying synthesis that bonds beings as reflexive, objectively self-identifying subjects proceeding with the instantiation of what upon reflective contemplation is to become a distantiation from the Self that produces the subjective transformation into an abstract subject-object that coheres with its ontological transmission as a thinking being—just as it may a projected being acting upon the horizon from the immanence of objective reification that had become the identifying moment for the transcendental noesis that presupposed the state of observation that had initiated dialectical abstraction of the socio-symbolization posited upon the existential horizon. For instance $fz$, is now the function that is concomitant to the Otherness of $fx$, that $fz$ has been subtracted from reflexive observation at the noetic side only to be instantiated by the intersubjectivity proposed by the instantiation of $fy$, etc. What is in effect happening is that the signifying moment of abstraction is attempting to sublate the phenomena associated with memory, and more concerned with the closed totality of synthetic relation that has been instantiated by temporal verifiability from an apodictic representation projected through the inner space. This veridical transmission of noumenal certainty—where the thing-in-itself has begun to perceive the unifying synthesis that bonded manifold relations with the socio-symbolization of its ontological reification as an image-object—is ontologized within the closed totality before the projected subjective dialectical abstraction has occurred where it has been technologically reproduced in some form. Yet alas, we would seem to be going in circles at this point in time, as it has already been established that the genus of technological representations are manifestations of a multiplicity within the same genus that has already been reified through subjective particularization; and thereby are not of nominal significations that would constitute grounds for us to hold that the socio-symbolic being were anything more than subjugates of the technologically reproduced being in mind. Albeit, should rationalism fall short of ontological verifiability as it often does, more often than not—given this open-access system of globally transmitted ideas through the digital age—we rely on a closed totality and its opening to presupposed projections of identical propositions in order to abstract the signifiers that are already part of the nexus of socio-symbolic

Noematic Symbolization 221

beings. Their status as ontological ontic particularities transcends the referential projection of their temporal ontologization from the existential possibility that instantiated the closed public space wherein the image-object would be perceived.

This transcendence of the image-object goes unexperienced should the symbolic transmission of socio-ontological signification be breached by the interlocutions of logos that phonologically projected a negative condition for its formal symbolization as a mental picture to be formed by active ontological reflection. The reflexive composition of socio-symbolization is the *noema* of ontic objects that have been transcendentalized into the closed public spheres of noematic representation—as such biospheres of active contemplation that may be reified by dialectical abstraction form the nexus of objectification of the noemata into phenomenal objects reduced by their transformation into objects of retention and memory first—then brought into the eidetic manifold as transcendental appearances of the same genus as the universal ideas particular to noetic observation. From this, though Being sees a monadic composition of the transcendental Self as such, it does not identify with the existentially reproduced horizon that may become part of symbolic signification. Hence, the noetic stratum—while particular to the subject—is ultimately of universal composition and general to the particularizations of subjectivity. It is from this that the presuppositions of what to dialectically abstract are projected upon existential possibility. However, it is from the subjective particularization from universal noetic forms of consciousness that the identical status of subjectivity rests with within its transcendent symbolization—and thereto is reflexive of the dialectical imposition forced upon subjectivity from its universal composition. For this reason, the reproducibility of subjective existentiality is particular to its objectifying moment of choice—that it projects a unifying synthesis of its transformation from the universal to the particular upon the horizons of existential possibility, and there reifies a socio-symbolization to the

## 222   The Dialectical Self-Concept of Symbolic Being

Other as an integral moment of its ontologization into a signifier for the Other as a noematically symbolized Being.

   As such reality is both an abstraction to subjectivity, and an administered experience of the social forms that have been instantiated by formal states of self-awareness. These modes of transcendental becoming are as Husserl's mundane epoché that he had so generously bestowed upon phenomenology. But what we might insist is that the logic of our dialectical undertakings have a greater conception of the existential possibilities that have for them symbolic appearances, and may be represented from ontic experience. There is of course the matter of being in full recognition of this dialectic absent Husserl's oeuvre, yet it is certain that the transcendental dialectic of Kant is enough to have us convinced that the process is calling for this abstraction of the possible encounter with the Real that we may have. The radical act of appropriating temporal determinability with a logical progression of willed propositions forms successive states of self-awareness—that are not unlike the infinite *regressus* of Schopenhauer's symbolized matter and form. But it is proposed that we see the contents of the formal appearance as only possessing matter in its proximal ontic situation in space and time upon the horizontal plateau that had been ontologized by lifeworld causality. It is this formation of what is oftentimes an unconscious mode of Being that becomes elicited by contemplative action, as we undertake to presuppose a reality that is within our grasp. Thereto the noumenal projection from the noetic side transmits a gesture that initiates intersubjectivity and the possibilities of existential shared lifeworld encounters with the Other. Where we have no presuppositions respective of the identity of this positing being, we have apodicity, that the representation does not stand for anything that has not yet been propositionally or dialectically abstracted by contemplative action.  As the universal is absent this mode of representational awareness, the reified Other is perhaps part of the process whereby reflexive self-identification is beyond this mode of ontic experience. This may very well be a pre-ontological mode of reality, that our presuppositions are not within the grasp of the projection of self-identity, are thereto not acting in communion with the existential possibilities that drive the active momentum of nominal symbolization.

Since the significatory projection of the modes of reality are reifications for the representations of inner space, experience is unmediated by the social totality, yet also not entirely singular to Being as it begins in the act of transcendental abstraction from the noetic side should dialectical observation become part of the reflexive causality warranted by the course of action requisite of a proposed state of Being that has been distantiated from the perceptual field of a recollecting transcendental subject. In our regimen of socio-ontological praxis, *techne, poeisis*—as Lefebvre had proposed—we become reflexive *doing* creatures of mental faculties greater than those proposed by what's cultured of limitless distractions to the world at large, and we realize that in some way, the traditions of the Structuralist age are not entirely beyond the scope of the meaningful lives that we may lead moving forward in the post-industrial age—both as what would return to us aesthetic experience, but also what would bring back the *symbolic realism* that were once with the scope of possibility for those that were able to choose what would signify a mode of reality that better represented the ontological experiences that in the beginning had formed Western Democracies. Due to the evolutionary, radical self-realization that may have progressed through an intensification of social and economic struggles throughout the previous fifty years or more, we have only now begun to realize that the necessity to reify aesthetic experience through social rituals that are not steeped purely in consumerist activity and capricious overdetermination of our standard of living will propose an emancipation of an ontological becoming that will restructure the self-awareness of human-kind so as to bring forth the necessary scientific developments affiliated with philosophical endeavor.

But where we draw the line between metaphysics and science is of a significance that is an extremely sophisticated exercise. For instance what is symbolic realism? It would appear that it presupposes a unification between the Lacanian Symbolic and the Real to those that know Lacan, or to those that see the symbolic as a Jungian experience of the human psyche from unconscious states of self-awareness. Where we think outside of psycho-analysis and into the idea of thought as *idea* and idea as *thought*, the elucidation in explication of the former becomes clear. This science *is* a metaphysics. For in order for us to experience reality as it is in-itself—beyond the fixations of a delusional psyche that has a complex with false beliefs due to a bioeconomic appropriation of self-identity, we can justly presuppose that Being is reflexively the *de facto* owner of Being, and that any legal body that instantiates a condition that negates the properties of humanity with the intention of subjugating value to enforced limitations of lawful human activities, threatens what for all intents and purposes is *in toto* a mode of reality concerned with the politicization of aesthetics into a state of human self-realization—to overcome the barriers imposed by unjust powers of objective entitlement to the planetary substance that allows for human progress to become part of a radical enlightenment.

Thereto, the philosophical significance of what is here proposed should never be considered a *non sequitur*. That because of nature of human progress in the economic, social, technological, and cultural realities, the lifeworld should never be brought down to ground zero. After all, "why suggest a politicization of aesthetics as a way to experience modal reality, for it will present a horizon of existential possibility that may be quite unaccustomed to the citizens of the many regional societal platforms?" The response to this uncertainty is not without its grounding. For those that have undertaken to pursue liberty full-throttle seem to have taken great strides to eclipse moral responsibility, given that cultural barriers present non-identical realities for so many more vulnerable to the legerdemain that reifies social capital. Utopian ideals are acts set aside by technological developments more often than not, as the very stratification of progressive acquisition denies renewable existences as formal exclusions of the proprietary activities possible an evolved state of ontological becoming. The lifeworld is as it seems, only shared to the extent that it is embodied by those primary to any given discipline. Should this radical dialectical opening of a closed modal reality interfere with the quotidian existences of those more concerned with their structured emancipation as atomized individuals than the existential possibilities of a closed public awakening—that certain predators would immediately pounce upon the vulnerable for the establishment of capricious desires, etc.—the ethical boundaries that must be conferred with are those that have presupposed social transformation from the resource of the closed public forum where social actors exist as co-presences of manifold existential reality. The reproduction of the identical truth is installed as a pre-ontological component of the political structures in which they persist, where the lifeworld had transformed social experience from the causal existentiality posited in the proposed forum wherein ontic reality is exposed as an unjustifiable reification of the existential possibilities of this proposed state of collective self-awareness.

But what will this be, given that identical truth is an aspect of the differences that make multiplicity the proposed mode of administered reality for those whom would wish to experience life as individuated Beings? Since the matter has been approached at the level of what constitutes the horizons of existential possibility, it will be necessary to give a temporal relation to the concept that is to become part of the reification of what is the level of responsibility for opening a closed totality in order to pursue aesthetic experience at not only the intersubjective level, but also the collective one. That a shared lifeworld experience finds its grounding in the symbolization of noema from ontic experiences that reproduced the Real as an ongoing mode of Being that is more than just a phantasm of collective experience, but one that reveals something that is within the existential possibilities *of* the collective—whereby the experience is reified as something that is modally Real and true. A symbolic experience that reproduces itself at plateaus of psychological identifiability that renders the ontological reality a signifying moment of uniformity with a qualitative universality that has only become particular to the reified subjects of the meta-ontological landscape of human becoming and collective self-realization. However, it is here that the dialectical abstraction of the ontic modal reality does in fact become the positing of collective truth, that it is part of the import of the unifying moment where the noematic symbolization had been ontologically reproduced and projected upon an opening into social totality.

Though therewith, it can rightly be posited that there is no dialectical subjectivity where concerns the collective. For as the truth is apportioned to the Real through an instantiation of collective ontological representation, the universal conforms to a principle of ontological uniformity that is reproduced through the very concepts that disable a reification of identical truth to the subjects pursuing a uniform transmission of ontic reality through the modal representation as a universal truth to reflexively self-positing spiritual self-awareness. This horizon is one that rests with the same genus of modal reality that resists the symbolic expectations that would become of a more radical lifeworld than the one presupposed by ontico-ontological realism through its signifying moment of noematic symbolization. What is prospective of the projection of particular subjective self-identification and its ontological grounding as a uniform stratification of the horizontal existential possibility, requires the import of subjective reification at the moment of symbolic self-realization. One must transform the Real as a subject in order to reproduce itself through the inner space of representation as something of existence—such that the synthetic coordinates of moral objectification are reifications of particularized self-identity and never the instantiations of cultural reifications more prone to the standards affiliated with overconsumption and reified caprice. The existential horizon that proposes to instantiate an aesthetic consciousness that reproduces public awareness from a closed totality is the originary point of contact with the unifying synthesis that produces the dialectical impetus to propose with horizontal aspirations in order to posit the representations in filiation with both symbolically aesthetic experience, and the coordinates of what makes ontic modal reality an adjunct to a metaphysics able to apperceive the noema from its ontic origination as symbols posited through dialectical abstraction.

# Appendix A

From the edges of Reason, to the outer realm where consciousness has been bridged between being and its transcendental horizon, we reach as a species in order to address the ways by which time and space are posited as both actual interior relations, and also abstractions made by existence as a reification of the objective stance in which our powers of perception are situated. As what we consider to be of this world, our reality is within mind and, as such, the experience of what perhaps under certain conditions does not confer with the outer reified empirical experience of our relations as humans. That we address one another in accordance with identities that do not correlate with the inner experience of the transcendental world is a peculiarity to some, while at times an existing social disparity that positions a wedge between interactive subjects. That these souls are comprised of a separate substance from what is present for an emancipated subjective being conditions reality so as to presuppose that it is at variance with the real—the actual components that drive intersubjective relations beyond where they are simply those that are individual and have departed the collective substance as imbued with a sense of personal attachment to the things that provide subjectivity with a source of emancipatory reality only particular to the matter at hand—rather than the bigger picture involved where the formation of collective substance cannot be driven by any individuals' caprice or sense of self-interest.

That being, is, as it stands an edifice that outlives its own pursuit of emancipation from structures that stand to devolve it from its very foundations. In fact, what it is becomes of the sense of what is possible of *being* as emancipatory where it is concerned more in-itself as an acting emancipatory structure, than an existent merely willing to participate in what drives consciousness from its sense of having a relation to another existent that it is in conflict with; that where we abide, the emancipatory structures are dismantled by the representations that have been induced by the potency of subjects only willing to establish themselves as free subjects—unbridled in the pursuit of whichever activity subjectivity had wished to engage. That here, there may be some determinable component acting in accordance with the other subject is in lieu of an establishment of the aforementioned emancipatory structures that would be capable of sustaining collective substance beyond its disintegration into a hindered whole of opposing individuals—now unable to posit identity within the justifiable forms of reason known to humankind.

Where one's lifeworld is comprised of synthetic representations that are immanently entwined as collectively positing and engaged, active being as social subjects suggests that existence of any dialectical approach to the abstraction of the symbolic and noematic images that are posited by community relations, exposes the totality of subjectivity to a reproach from where the abstractions of one's opposing forces have become an ontic status for the subject—that Being has been "hit" by Otherness, so as to open collective substance to its outer transcendental existence is to presuppose that a collective of emancipatory structures has already *progressed and evolved past the state of dialectical opposition* amongst those seeking emancipation as potency of an individuated collective consciousness that is never to be held accountable for the damages it inflicts upon its substance within the collective, or toward the collectivity of its substance.

This is beyond the social formations available of what is possible of universalized social existents in distraction of a conceptual collectivity, all within the purposes of an acceptance of the conduct available for the formation of any such body politic established and fully willing to address dialectical opponents with an unmatched potency. That these socially engaged, abstract collectives would form a "legal" social body is now in question, since it becomes of a representation of this formed by stratified emancipatory subjects *calling* existence as atomized individuals—which has never been a rational possibility since the dawning of the Age of Reason.

Creations of the Enlightenment must be in full recognition of how it is not within the realm of possibility to occupy this planet with individuated goals that have no public interest in mind, and why it devolves philosophy to suggest that this is not simply an effort to sustain freedoms unbound by responsibilities; that being must always be as it is in relation to others of the same inner space, but that any such space of representation would not be open to a species that was only fulfilling an abstraction of its proclivity for emancipatory content that disturbs the symbolic order of structured space—inclusive of ontology as a realm open to universal content that is here presupposed as collective to its abstract emancipatory structures.

For what is being posited and or presupposed of emancipatory structuralization is what would necessitate an emancipatory "Destructuration" of the historical forms of the administered world as they are distributed synchronically as ontic and ontological disturbances of what has been universalized by an aging population—still fixated on historical values that provided the impetus for Post-Structuralism, but were never established until the 21st Century as emancipatory structures—traditions that superimposed identical stages of consciousness upon a totality of subjects that were provided with conflicting signifiers as historical presuppositions along with the existential possibilities endemic of the millennial age. This accounts for a disparity that enacts its boundaries between co-presence of image-object and noumena, while reposing the subject to a division of its objectivated positing consciousness—acting in concert with the real and an identical presupposition of what encompasses being as a mode of existence that has no abstraction of identity to which its stands in relation.

In fact, the *realiter* experience of subjective identity hosts nothing naturalized of administrable endeavors, rather positing a subjective distribution of its own powers of reified identity as a resource that has posited essence as a component of its rational ontico-ontological reflexivity. That Being qua Being has been undergoing a reified state of awareness *quid facti*, the *realiter* experience of emancipatory structures, structuralizes identity in a manner by which ontic conditions are intentional in relation to the object outside of its identical positing of the real; the a priori nature of the positing being is reaching through a process of its symbolization to the Other as a interobjective being that is transcendent in nature, yet composes reality from its very symbolization as an existent of the *realiter* experience of the Other through its transcendental significations. That these would transform subjectivity as a unity for its symbolic significatory encumbrances, enacts the embodiment of what presupposes the *realiter* experience of the subject as something presupposed throughout the significatory presuppositions of the Other. Therewith, identity is reified by its state of awareness with legitimated qualities that impact subjective identity toward its transcendental horizon beyond the symbolized interobjective presuppositions that perform qualitative ontic transmissions upon the subject as acts of what hypostatized a concomitant identity as something of the same, fixed genus, while it rests in conflict with the posited identical truth of the thing-in-itself that has become dialectically opposed to emancipatory structures as presupposed ontic identities, and in its stead posits Being qua Being as identical to its for-itself dispositions as a subject of free will, and thereby willingly "destructurating" emancipatory structures as presupposed ontico-ontological categories that are part of the import or abstraction of subjectivity due to its universalized identical projections upon the social totality.

Insofar as these are mediated by the universal reflexivity where the subject transcends intersubjective particularity, it is that the particular has no bearing upon ontic identity, as universal mediation presupposes its dialectical position on the horizon for each identical subject that projects subjectivity from its particular ontic status as a universal

Being—it is simply that the subject has already abstracted a concrete identity from the totality as a fixed ontical existent that is projecting both ontic and ontological noumenal freedoms that correspond with its formal social relation that has become of the embodied *collective spirit* or *social spirit* of the historico-temporal relation that had been part of the import of identity. That it is now mediated reflexively, introduces the relative conditions of external reality as a normative condition of the manner in which identity is engaged on the outside for all dialectical abstractions of universally mediated concrete social identities that mix with Others in physical settings where the production of social being is entirely mediated by the a priori conditions of appropriate social conduct. It is that here, different social settings are in sync with the conditions of social being in order to become the applicable settings for these persons for whom mediated particularity embroils or initiates the possibility of conflict—so it becomes interesting that at the locus of the import of the abstract characteristics that proposed identity from a universalized horizon, that it would therewith go unfettered by local forms of ontological segregation; not that these could still now in the 21st Century exist as outer divisions without real political upheaval, but that the inner space of representation would reason subjects into a proximate condition of social normativity.

We can see here how the materialists agree with the pure particularity of an ontic status, while positing the requirement of inclusivity into the universal. From the Marxo-Hegelian point of view, it is held that the social totality presupposes identity as a universal right administered by the body politic, yet we can also see how one discovers the objective exclusion of a subject's own objectivated agency where concerns substance, essence, being as a mediated particularity that possesses civil agency toward the import of the universal conditions presupposed by inclusivity as an administered totality. That subjects would not possess subjective rights over their object as a reflexive act of the conscious choice that has been made with respect to subjective identity, the dialectical potency of abstract subjective identities that have divided from their own objectivation propose to disturb the use-value of subjects—possibly cancelling natural attributes that are intrinsic to the substance of subjective being, as such. Thereto, what we have on our hands is a social abstraction from a universal horizon of production, thought of as the political/economic/cultural, etc., that is already ontologically in conflict with the social distribution of attributes, based upon the regulatory status of an institutive form of essence and thereby, attribute mediation by force of administration.

This plays well into the hands of what we have identified as "emancipatory structures", as one can perceive how inclusivity as a universalization of coherently abstract identities produced by the "administered world" would induce ontic conflicts—engaging the necessity of a transformation of ontic identity in order to comply with the significations that presupposed an abstraction of identity. In order for subjectivity to maintain a dialectical stance as an emancipatory being with rights, this conflict eventually must be eradicated one way or the other. Due to the conditions that perform the act of exclusion to the positing of objective identity because of its conflicting ontological significations, subjectivity may "destructure" those very structures that perform the institutive act of collective exclusion of the object with which a subject should be embodied or, rather, that subjectivity should embody the object as a reification of its conditional representation to the social horizon as a symbolized Being. It is by these very means that the production of the image-object may become a *realiter* experience for interobjective subjects, making allowances for the positing of a symbolic significatory status that represents the socio-ontological inclusion of subjects at variance with a class consciousness that has potentially presupposed the objective exclusion from the reified, symbolically signified ontological status. Given that this leads to a formation of coherent ontological collectives, a resolution to the dialectical conflicts import by abstraction are "destructured", and the ontico-ontological facticity of subjectivity objectively instituted as a self-mediated entity. Yet this would only be possible through its significatory status as a symbolic being representing a *realiter* experience interobjectively. This posits the transcendental horizon on the other side of the lacuna, presupposing a more rational formal abstraction devoid of the despotic signifiers that become available where the exclusions have yielded a deregulated hegemonic constellation of aggressive socio-political collectives in pursuit of fiat capital.

This may be the *de facto* way by which the ontological strata of administered universality "outs a subject that has *no way out*". In that process, subjectivity dialectically pursues its universalization as an emancipatory being anew, only to become engaged with "emancipatory structures" that have anticipated the arrival of a *Destructuralist*, and therewith, formed a constellated ontological manifold that becomes a formal exclusion of the hypostatized de-structuration in-itself—thereby necessitating a dialectical comportment that distantiates subjectivity from its abstraction of an inclusionary universal essence. When this presupposes its referential, reified condition as a subject that has not been transformed by the formal exclusion of its abstract presupposed disposition, the ontological projection of self-identity is ensconced within a formal universalization that negates the abstract presupposition—while making allowances for its hypostatization. In the process, subjectivity has "destructured" the exclusionary tactics employed by the a priori cancellation of its posited inclusive universalization as an ontologically reflexive composition of substantive essence that willfully resides in the authenticated presupposition of a universalized Being.

Thereto, by way of which the process of having been universalized becomes reflexive from its stratification into the posited conceptual horizon—the process whereby its symbolization may be induces a functionalism of its dialectical inclusion toward the social totality that may be represented through a symbolic totality. Such that this would be measured by a formal a priori exclusion of the objectivated self-

Appendix A 235

identity, the subject pursues its self-identification in order to project into a totality of symbolized social strata—thereby instantiating the horizon with an objectivated socio-temporal symbolization of the diachronic conditions that had produced its symbolic totalization. Therewith, entity from the manifold observation of the apprehending consciousness is never hypostatized in its socio-symbolic identity, but rather positing the totalization of what had initiated the process whereby symbolic identification could exist for a collectivized strata of totalized sociated subjects. That the interobjective distantiation from relational adherence to the signifying chain had so been penetrated by this ontological engagement with the sociated stratified collectives would produce the genus of the symbolized synchronic experience would also be the abstraction of its totalized signification as a symbolic experience that would be reified by a formal universalization of reflexive subject-objects apprehending the symbolic representation as a political encounter as much as it is an aesthetic one.

Such as it is, subjectivity where it hypostatizes symbolic identity, projects subjectivity upon a collectivized ontological manifold of sociated beings; with this the positing of the image-object is reproductively affiliated with the ontologized existential horizon that is interobjectively entwined with the subject's dialectical, positional stance interior to the socially produced horizon. As a transcendental subject, the horizon makes disposition of the abstract exclusion of subjectively posited "non-identical" reflexivity, while reproducing a symbolic *realiter* experience that projects the ontologization of an experience onto a totalized social horizon. That its abstraction of the forms of administered reality are co-present with its sociated existence into a transcendental horizon, becomes the abstraction of its reflexive engagement with the positing of this that encumbers the subject-object relation with its signification to the symbolic totality—thereby initiating an abstraction of its subjective positing of the objective abstraction of a *realiter* experience that may be posited in stratified collective social formations; reproducing the reflexive positing of the self-identification as both an active positing of the abstraction of a totalized symbolic representation, and the totalization of a reproduced subject that has there been symbolized.

Upon this instantiation of the interobjective experience of symbolized subjects to the totality, it is that the abstraction of the objective noumenal projection may be made in order to position totality upon the horizon and not with the object. As the symbolization had been dialectically induced already by noumenal projection, Being may there posit as an agent of its own symbolic signification, instituting the representations as copula to the conceptual content within the ontological purview of the subject. That abstraction is integral to the process is clear, yet still the distantiation from totality opens up the lacuna to phenomena otherwise absent this mode of Being. Throughout totalized symbolic significations however, the grounding of essence is in jeopardy of losing its presence as an unmediated self-identity, imposing conceptual boundaries upon the dialectical abstraction of the desired conceptual significations and qualities present the ontological manifold. The potency of noumenal projection as an intersubjective being will compose the necessary space of representation for the purposes of conceptual abstraction and positing where what we have is a binary *virtuality* of substance and form that gives powers of representation to a subject that is examining the outer space of representation from the inner ontological positioning of conscious abstraction of conceptual content. That the content is only present to the representation in presence of subjectivity suggests the positing of its logical form is not shared, but only exposed to an objective pole of abstraction. Such as would be the case, the leitmotif and aesthetic exchange composes a *realiter* experience as a reification of its own positing of the abstract conceptual content that is significatory to its a priori symbolizations to the Other. As a semiotic signifier, the positing of what is contextualized subjectively becomes available for dialectical abstraction by the Other, but is given the modality of a logical form represented to the subject that has obfuscated its own symbolic signification through a positing in the space of representation—the Other may be excluded from transmission of content that has been hypostatized by the subject for the purposes of maintaining an open space of representation. As signified however, the semiotic transmission of a signifier to another apprehending consciousness persists by way of the very opening, yet what is posited is only objective to the subject in this mode of creation.

Of the signifying chain, the comportment of the subjective positing of content as a transmission from subject-as-signified to *signifiers* through the inner space, it is only that the logical form of what is represented may be transmitted to another space throughout the signifying chain. Since the work is the reified dialectical abstraction of the subject, it is only that there its abstract use-value persists as a hypostatized property that may be utilized for the process of a shaping of the property represented—i.e., such as a leitmotif or a phrase of words or sequence of images. One could say that this is very much the modality of positing of the social imaginary, and certainly finding the world experience to be as Husserl's lifeworld (*Lebenswelt*) that the signifiers themselves may possess conceptual content and *float* to another subject. We will assume that this is part of what Hegel meant in *Phenomenology of Spirit* when he spoke of enjoyment, e.g., the statist ontology opens up the means of production to the universal class, and those maintaining self-identity as a synchronic presence are symbolically coherent to the production of the signifying chain of closed systems, and in exchange on a nominal basis will allow for the hypostatization of things signified as projected, and things *unsignified* that are posited within the property relation induced by conceptual abstraction. It is that *Zeitgeist* is a logical form of its universalized, produced manifold of represented beings; so *logos* serves a justifiable purpose as an inner discourse of identical *realiter* assertions, inhabiting the ontological manifold as a noumenally free act that is reflexively exposed to those very forms of production constellating as phenomenal identities contingent to the positing of conceptual content. This proposes a transmission of content from subject to objectivity, yet since the manifold phenomena are identical and contingent, the presupposition that the signifying chain has been breached by the logical form of dialectical abstraction becomes an administrable reflexivity, though it is here that the shared lifeworld experience has been closed to the other objects their own mode of doing—in fact it is presupposed that the positing of the subject is contingent upon its symbolization to a genus of beings that have been outmoded by the hypostatization of subjective *reproducibility*. Kant's phenomena appeal well to the relational mode of self-realization as it may have for Marx, unless it is a bourgeois exclusion that has appeared *post factum* (after the dialectical abstraction has been performed by the subject). However, what we have is not the exclusion of self-identity, *it is that the objects/phenomena are exclusions to the positing of the object* as a presupposition of its position in the signifying chain. Thereto, the reflexive stance of its signified has been reduced to its proximate manifold contingencies, intentional toward the object as its own conceptual content—the *mind* of a subject.

One could also posit that the self has been regulated by its own constellation of self-identical phenomena; just the same, subjectivity is now in a state of rest; being is de-totalized, and the horizon is of the logic of this which identifies with its own absence as a *realiter* ontology for symbolic representation. As would be the case, the awareness of the subject gives likelihood to the positing of its own object just as it would for Kanto-Hegelians. One may also observe that the subject-object unity in the reflexive mode of ego positing is in many ways quite monistic as it would have been for Spinoza or Marx. The experience of the object as it is posited reflexively engages substance unification (monistic duality). As for its reflexive signification, it is now in an a priori mode of abstraction, that it is able to posit its own object in a state of rest, it is signified contingent to the means by which it entered the horizon as a symbolized nominal Being. Of course, we know that the concept is nominal in its abstraction, though through its genus we have many reproductions of its nominal signifier as required for interobjective exchanges—but what is sought is its significatory reproducibility to the totalized symbolization that birthed an interobjectivity. Positing of the absolute from a dialectical abstraction of its symbolic totalization now becomes a possibility for subjectivity. Here there will be objectivated exclusions that prompt the positing of the dialectical absolute as a universalization of its particular socio-symbolic cohesion. Therewith, an inclusive opening will posit the genus of its conceptual universalization through a reflexive objective exclusion—a synthesis between objectivated exclusion and inclusive dialectical abstraction there occurs.

Whereby the symbolic transcendency instantiates a requisite "restructuration" of horizontal significatory reproducibility, dialectical abstraction is initiated by reflexive positing of what has been objectivated, and necessitates a noumenal projection of self-identity. What becomes an essential rupture of the subjective will from its identical self-representation is the objectivated exclusion from its symbolic formalization as a signified to horizons of social reality. This is *a fortiori* the process by which subjectivity initiates its symbolic status as a signified with self-representation that is transcendentally reproduced as a nominal subject situated and standing in relation to the produced ontological stratification of *realiter* existentiality—the means by which one *becomes* a subject again. That a subject must repudiate all filiations with its objectivated sociation with an object that is not of their own determinability is the cancellation of one's own sociation from its objective social stratification as a socio-symbolic Being that has been undermined by its significatory status to "emancipatory structures", and the inheritance of an associated contextualization of one's determinability as a dialectical symbolic nominal representation—a veridical distantiation from a normative symbolization as something "Other" to itself, and a restructuring of symbolic identity as a signified to the social horizon. Whereby this would be functionary of the dialectical abstraction of an ontological relation to others that had been universalized from subjective particularization, necessitates the "matter at hand" *a fortiori*, as one's significatory status is a process whereby dialectical self-identity is an ontic reality and an ontological possibility for self-identity—thereto, the positing of the synthetic form of being that has been reflexively identified symbolically through its totalization of horizontal self-realization. Yet the encumbrances of the rational production of self-identification are abstractions of social reality that have been hypostatized by their symbolic transcendency toward the reflexive social abstraction. Such as subjectivity is an *act of the will* it is also that the universalization of subjective comportment toward produced reality allows for an "objective reification" of the self-identity reflexive of subjects that have abstracted self-identity as an ontological possibility, rather than allowing an objective exclusion to subjugate the transcendental identity of Being into a formal universalization of what is not a *de facto* signification of subjective ontological self-representation. The reflexive abstraction from its dialectical positionality as a projected noumenal in-and-for-itself is identical with its formal dialectical abstraction a priori as a self-positing, reflexive agent of transparency and social transformation within the causal nexus of its transcendental symbolization. The reified substance of the subject here enacts a "structuration" of its sublation of the "emancipatory structures" that had instantiated the exclusionary normativity of its symbolic signification to social production, and thereby modifies the temporal succession that modulated dialectical abstraction in such a manner as to induce a subjective transformation that had been of its inclusion into a universalization that had excluded subjective self-identity from its substantive noumenal projection and symbolic self-identification. Hereto, as social reality is capable of modulating ontological self-reflexivity with its administrable universal contextualization of significatory social normativity, the positing of social identity is induced with its own "restructuration" as a being capable of socio-ontological relations as a horizontally produced mind.

Appendix A 241

That herewith, the restructuration is a formal *sublation* from its objective exclusion by "emancipatory structures".

Thereto, the dialectical abstraction of Being is formally determinable by its subjective stratification as a symbolic transcendency—reproductively induced by the collective substance of its own conceptual symbolization, and therewith noumenally represented through its reflexive self-identification. With this, the hypostatization of the reflexive nominal signification as a self-identical representation is instantiated as part of the ontological projection of self-identity and its ontological collectivization as a restructured emancipatory self-identity.

With this restoration of self-identity, and the instantiation of its restructured dialectical potency, ontological relations may not induce symbolic self-identification with a tactical exclusion from its natural status as an identical subject, but in its place forms an absence of ontological relation. The universalization of self-identity that it has been collectively filiated with as its own self-concept, allows for the re-positing of the *ego cogito* from the dialectical projection of the *res cogitans*. Functional to subjective transcendency as both a Cartesian subject, the external material and concrete space of objects become analogous to the positing of the ego, while ontological signification as a symbolized representation has been sublated through the process of conceptual universalization through its unification of self-identity and concretion of being. This is never to suggest that the process of symbolic unification is beyond reproach, yet it does insist that the horizontal transcendency of the ego has not thrown beyond its logical inner space into a social reality of the world. The corporeal reality of subjectivity becomes its innermost concern, and subjectivity must ontologize the physical objects in order to reflect upon the ontological involvement with the inner space as a fundament to its conceptual self-identification as an ontic *and* an ontological being—in this case the social production of subjectivity corresponds with the structuration of the external environment, yet maintains ego reflexivity without an involvement with its symbolic formalization or presentation to the Others as agents of social production. This new-found autonomy perhaps will be short-lived should the social reflexivity of the ontological inner space and its conceptual representation of objects become part of a dialectical abstraction by the Other. Such as it is, the structural components of the ontological space of representation have been closed to external noumenal projections that would enter the "chambers" of a thinking subject. But through its formal universalization as a restructured emancipatory being, the sublation of its horizontal totalization from its symbolic representation as a particular subject into a collective social identity is not without its relations to other subjects still in a mode of perception—now distantiated from the subjective positing of the ego-object in relation to material objects, as in Husserl's *Experience and Judgment,* we find here that since the conceptual symbolization of the locus of a sublated social totality is not where subjects would wish to dwell long-term where concerns the praxis of "emancipatory restructuration". The purpose of this dialectical endeavor is not to "escape" ontological co-presence of its signification to the transcendental horizon, but rather to fuse *realiter* experience with its reified ontological stratification as a being of value, comporting the self within the realm of social activity without losing the ability to reproduce a subjective involvement with what had already necessitated the "destructuration" of a forced universalization into "emancipatory structures". As nothing will be symbolically represented to subjectivity without its ontological involvement with *transcendental social production* through the a priori synthesis that occurs where horizontal Being has become dialectically opposed to an emancipatory structuration, so it is as though the process of attaining restructuration is one of private reflection with the external, while the dialectical abstraction of self-identity is in relation with social representation—and internal projection of a reflexive self-identification.

To posit here that restructuration will enhance dialectical potency, is perhaps purposive of this investigation, but rather to posit that restructuration is of a modality of independence from its socio-symbolic filiation with ontological formalizations of universalized particularization into the categories imposed upon subjects with a public historicity concerns the context in which emancipatory being has been stratified into its collective significations. That through the sub-stratification of its characteristic ontic and ontological actuality and possibility respectively, subjectivity may be symbolically represented as a restructured collective representation that is circumspect outside of the medial reproduction of its significatory positioning in relation to social production through its transcendental symbolization.

Therefore it becomes very much like bumping one's head upon a wall—that social integration as a restructured transcendental being would make requisite a forced taxonomy of inclusivity, or beyond that, a necessary exclusion from its emancipatory self-objectification. Thereto, dialectical abstraction is also of an ontological involvement with existentialized universal identities, which means that the subject is really a *seeker* of its own restructured socialization in order to belong to the transcendental symbolization of its significatory status in sublation of "emancipatory structures". Such as it is, emancipatory restructuration may never become symbolically signified to the former, while it initiates a sublation *in toto* of the formal universalization of the latter. Herewith, subjectivity is no longer simply a dialectical abstraction, but an emancipatory restructuration of symbolized self-identification.

# Appendix B

The self as subject, reflected into itself, is repelled toward the One, or projected into the Other. The posited identity, as such, is in-itself as it is for the Other insofar as being is reflecting upon its own self as subject (existence).

The projected subject is manifold and collective in-itself, as with the other manifold representations that confer with the positing of identical concepts to the ones being projected/abstracted by subjectivity.

The speech act is ontologized into the Other's preconscious/unconscious lifeworld and, as such is the ontical causal referent for determinative occurrences—intersubjective experiences corresponding with the subsequent ontological verification (rationalism).

The "regional" ontological totality is the "interpretant" of an "objectivated" conceptual whole, or signified and represented collectivity of subjects fused within the universality of being as "being", thusly within the universality of essence with a conceptual self-identification—(conceptual identification with the self "as" this which is collective at the ontical/subjective pole and subsequently ontologized in a unified totality).

The negative absence of space (infinite *regressus*) is a noematic copy abstracted from totality and synthesized with its conceptual signification (tetrad).

The nominal signifier is individual identity, never becoming universal. Only through "conceptual reproduction" of the image is it universalized into consciousness. While what is particular and singular to the subject is universalized through the abstraction of the nominal signifier from totality, universality never grabs hold of the nominal identity as represented to the image concept. But here, inter-objective relations ensue through the sublation of the nominal identity in its positional relation upon the objective pole of consciousness as an interior being and mental representation of the sublated nominal identity, and of the conceptual being that has been abstracted—the self-identity of subjectivity—creating an object (noumenal) of reflection. Totality is re-introduced as a temporal horizon rather than the social existence of the *genus proximativa*, and as such subjectivity resolves to its pre-reflective state of awareness to the synthetic a priori and any formal abstractions to follow.

From the standpoint of empirico-ontological projection, identity (self-identity) remains nominal and may not be universalized into the social totality. As such, it is conceptually transcendent as an image to perceiving subjects universally. Universal self-identity (as with Adorno) is only as universality insofar as the perceiving ontological subject posits noumenal being inter-objectively—where it is particularized into the other subject's consciousness. However, within a void universality, as was formerly examined, nominal self-identity may be co-present with the image of its conceptual signification. The signifier as nominal identity is both the identity if the Other (that is, the empirico-ontological identity) and appropriated by the subject a priori as a contingent self-identical presupposition or concern.

The Other's projected noumenal being may be as a particular posited being within the self-identity of the subject and perceived contingently. The aforementioned ontological "tetrad" is hereby affirmed to be positive identification—based upon the epistemic conditional and empirical content of the projection. As such, the dialectical reasoning of the subject must be engaged in order to resolve each socio-psychological consideration with a rationalistic examination of the truths as they were represented.

In these terms, the projected entity of the nominal signifier, from its conceptual a priori abstraction, is posited as both particularity and contingency. Again, identity is only universal to the subjective pole of consciousness—whereby the social totality may experience it synchronically through conceptual reproduction.

The representation is the commodity relation as thing-in-itself (noumenon), and the economic phenomenon/object is the commodified being that represents the "commodity form" that is subject to abstraction from the social totality (socio-economic plane), and signified through its conceptual identification (the image). The forms are not mediated by essence, but rather the appearances that were installed before the objective essence of the subject; and as such, were also represented as potential concepts to the social forms themselves—eventually becoming an object for the active agents of the socio-economic totality through exchange-value *commodifications* of being—if only to induce the subject with necessary formal abstractions of further polemical, dialectical, and rhetorical manoeuvers that introduce the concretion of essence.

The *holistic* ontology that produces the synthesis of essence and social totality is not unlike the "we-object" of Sartre and Jameson. This is not realized through social capital, but is in fact determined by conceptual signification/identification itself—void of any noumenal projections, or as the case may be, concurrent with them.

# Bibliography

Aristotle, *The Basic Works of*, edited by Richard McKeon, University of North Carolina at Chapel Hill, 1941, Random House; Toronto, New York.

Adorno, Theodor W., *Negative Dialectics*, 2007, The Continuum International Publishing Group, Inc. New York.

──────────*Aesthetic Theory*, 1997 by the Regents of the University of Minnesota; translated and edited by Robert Hullot-Kentor.

Adorno et al, *Aesthetics and Politics*, Verso 2007; London, New York.

Althusser, Louis, *On the Reproduction of Capitalism, Ideology and Ideological State Apparatuses*, translated by G.M. Goshgarian, Verso 2014; London, New York.

──────────*For Marx*, translated by Ben Brewster, Verso 1969; London, New York.

Althusser, Balibar, Establet, Macherey, Rancière; *Reading Capital the Complete Edition*, translated by Ben Brewster and David Fernbach, Verso 2015; London, New York.

Bakhtin, M.M.; *Toward a Philosophy of the Act,* translation & notes by Vadim Liapunov, Edited by Vadim Liapunov & Michael Holquist, University of Texas Press 1993; Austin.

Berger, Peter L. and Luckman, Thomas, *The Social Construction of Reality*, Anchor Books 1967; New York.

Bhaskar, Roy, Enlightened Common Sense, The Philosophy of Critical Realism, 2016, Routledge; New York.

Butler, Judith, Laclau, Ernesto, and Zizek, Slavoj, *Contingency, Hegemony, Universality, Contemporary Dialogues on the Left*; 2000, Verso, New York.

Deleuze, Gilles, *Difference and Repetition*, translated by Paul Patton, 1994; Columbia University Press, New York.

Derrida, Jacques, *Of Grammatology*, Corrected Edition, translated by Gayatri Chakravorty Spivak,1997 (1974) John Hopkin's University Press, Baltimore and London.

Fichte, J.G., *The Science of Knowledge*, edited and translated by Peter Heath and John Lachs, Cambridge University Press, 1982.

Habermas, Jurgen, *Post-Metaphysical Thinking*, *Philosophical Essays*, translated by William Mark Hohengarten, 1992 MIT Press; Cambridge, Massachusetts, London, England.

——————————, *Truth and Justification*, translated by Barbara Fultner, 2003; the MIT Press, Cambridge Massachusetts.

Hegel, G.W.F., *The Phenomenology and Spirit*, translated by A.V. Miller, Oxford University Press, 1977; Oxford, New York, Toronto, Melboune.

——————————*The Difference Between Fichte's and Shelling's System of Philosophy*, prepared and edited by H.S. Harris and Walter Cerf,1977, State University of New York Press.

Heidegger, Martin, *Being and Time*, translated by John Macquarrie and Edward Robinson, 1962 by Harper and Row Publishers Inc.

——————————*Mindfulness,* translated by Parvis Emad and Thomas Kalary, 2016 Bloomsbury; London, New York.

Horkheimer, Max and Adorno, Theodor W., *The Dialectic of Enlightenment*, translated by Edmund Jephcott, 2002, Stanford University Press.

Husserl, Edmund, *Cartesian Meditations: An introduction to Phenomenology,* translated by Dorian Cairns, Martinus Nijhoff, The Hague; 1960.

——————————, *Experience and Judgment, Investigations in a Geneology of Logic*, translated by James S. Churchill and Karl Ameriks, Northwestern University Press; Evanston 1973.

——————————*Ideas*, translated by W.R. Boyce Gibson; 2002, Routledge, London and New York.

——————————*On the phenomenology of the Consciousness of Internal Time* (1893-1917), translated by John Barnett Brough, 1991, Kluwer Academic Publishers;Dordrecht/Boston/London.

——————————*Phantasy, Image Consciousness, and memory* (1898-1925), translated by John B. Brough, edited by Rudolf Bernet, 2005; Springer, the Netherlands.

——————————*The Crisis of European Sciences and Transcendental Phenomenology*, translated and with an introduction by David Carr, Northwestern University Press, Evanston; 1970.

Jameson, Fredric, *Marxism and Form, Twentieth Century Dialectical Theories of Literature*, 1971, Princeton University Press; Princeton, New Jersey.

Korsche, Karl, *Marxism and Philosophy*, Translated by Fred Halliday, 1970, 2008 by Monthly Review Press; New York.

Laclau, Ernesto, *Emancipation(s)*, 1996, Verso; London, New York.

———————, *The Rhetorical Foundations of Society*, 2014, Verso; London, New York.

Laclau, Ernesto, Mouffe, Chantal, *Hegemony and Socialist Strategy: Towards a Radical Democratic Politics*, 1985, Verso; London, New York.

Lefebvre, Henri, *Metaphilosophy*, translated by David Fernbach, 2016, Verso; London, New York.

Lowenthal, Leo, *Literature and Mass Culture, Communication in Society*, Volume 1, 2016, Transaction Publishers; New Brunswick and London.

Lukács, Georg, *History and Class Consciousness, Studies in Marxist Dialectics*, translated by Rodney Livingstone,1971; The Merlin Press Ltd.

Marcuse, Herbert, *Eros and Civilization, A Philosophical Inquiry into Freud*, 1955, 1966; Beacon Press, Boston.

———————*Hegel's Ontology and the Theory of Historicity*, translated by Seyla Benhabib, MIT Press 1987; Cambridge, Massachusetts, London, England.

———————*One Dimensional Man, Studies in the Ideology of Advanced Industrial Society*, 1964; Beacon Press, Boston.

———————*Reason and Revolution, Hegel and the Rise of Social Theory,* 1999 by Humanity Books, (originally published by Oxford University press 1941), an imprint of Prometheus Books; Amherst, New York.

Marx, Karl, Engels, Frederick, *Economic and Philosophic Manuscripts of 1844*, translated by Martin Milligan, 2011 Wilder Publications; Blacksburg, Va.

Peirce, Charles Sanders, *Writings on Semiotic, Peirce on Signs*, edited by James Hoopes,1991 The University of North Carolina Press; Chapel Hill, London.

Plato, *The Republic of*, translated by Allan Bloom, 1991, Basic Books, A member of the Perseus Books Company.

Sartre, Jean-Paul, *Being and Nothingness, The Principal Text of Modern Existentialism*, translated by Hazel E. Barnes, Washington Square Press; New York, London, Toronto, Sydney, Singapore.

――――――――――――*The Imaginary, a phenomenological psychology of the imagination*, translation, Routledge 2004; London, New York.

――――――――――――*The Transcendence of the Ego*, translation Routledge, 2004; London and New York.

Schopenhauer, Arthur, *The World as Will and Representation Vol 1*; translated from the German by E.F.J. Payne, 1958; The Falcon's Wing Press, Indian Hill, Colorado.

――――――――――――*The World as Will and Representation* Vol 2; translated from the German by E.F.J. Payne, 1958; Dover Press, New York.

Whitehead, Alfred North, *Process and Reality, An Essay in Cosmology*, 1985; The Free Press, New York.

Žižek, Slavoj, *Absolute Recoil*, Toward a New Foundation of Dialectical Materialism,2014: Verso, London, New York.

――――――――――――, *Less Than Nothing, Hegel and the Shadow of Dialectical Materialism*,2012: Verso, London New York.

――――――――――――, *The Ticklish Subject, The Absent Centre of Political Ontology*, 1999; Verso, London, New York.

# INDEX

## A

abeyance, 95
abidance, 186
abilities, 43, 81
ability, 26, 59, 113, 151, 242
abolition, 95
absence, 14, 55, 76, 81, 84, 86, 92, 105–106, 134, 137, 139, 155, 163, 165, 179–180, 238, 241, 244
absolutes, 21, 45–46, 161
Absolutist, 150
abstractions, 98, 128, 130, 179, 182, 193, 214, 228–229, 232, 240, 245–246
accountable, 58, 65, 78, 198, 229
accumulation, 44, 130, 152, 199
acquiescence, 211
acquisition, 182, 210, 225
action, 16, 22, 30, 35–37, 41, 52, 54, 60–61, 69, 71, 74, 76, 85, 97, 107, 112, 114, 145, 153, 168, 180, 222–223
actions, 44, 46, 57, 73, 77, 94, 100, 114, 156
activism, 163, 205
activities, 28, 34, 37, 46, 57, 72, 91, 125, 163, 185, 192–193, 198–199, 224–225
activity, 35, 37, 43–44, 52, 54, 61–62, 72–73, 79, 82, 109, 112, 124, 130, 157–158, 168, 176–177, 184, 192, 198–203, 205, 209, 223, 229, 242
actor, 46, 59, 94, 132, 139
actors, 21, 49, 52, 123–125, 225
actuality, 21, 51, 53–56, 63, 102, 104, 159, 167, 180, 182–183, 185–186, 192, 216, 243
actualization, 52, 167, 180, 184
actualized, 21, 182, 184, 219
addiction, 155–156
adherence, 211, 235
adherent, 134
adjudicators, 211
adjunct, 14, 85, 213, 227
adjuration, 206
adjure, 35, 43, 47, 57, 69–70, 184
adjuring, 37
administered, 4, 80–81, 104, 114, 119, 124, 128, 135–136, 144, 148–149, 151–152, 154, 158, 168, 222, 225, 230, 232–235
administrable, 230, 238, 240
administration, 152, 233
administrative, 46, 136, 185
Adorno, 147, 151–152, 160, 168, 200, 245, 247, 249
advancement, 80
advancements, 204
advantages, 161
Aesthetic, 7–8, 127, 194, 201, 247
aesthetic, 127, 168, 185, 187, 189, 192–194, 199, 205, 207, 223, 225–227, 235–236
aesthetical, 186
aesthetics, 134, 185–186, 191, 224
affairs, 55, 93, 104–105, 156
affiliated, 132, 134–135, 138, 145, 147, 149, 163, 207, 218, 223, 226, 235
affiliation, 4
affirmation, 24, 32, 94, 120, 174, 176
affirmations, 66, 135, 182
affirmed, 49, 80, 169, 245
affirming, 174
affordability, 136, 144
aforementioned, 35–36, 75, 117, 119, 128, 143, 149, 152, 154–155, 157–158, 165, 180, 182, 184, 199, 229, 245
agency, 29, 43–44, 48, 53–54, 56, 59–62, 64–65, 67–68, 72–73, 75–76, 78, 85, 93–96, 101, 109, 112, 124, 126, 139, 144, 148, 150–156, 158, 189, 198–199, 218, 232
agents, 46, 49, 52, 59, 65, 149, 163, 204, 242, 246
aggressive, 234
agreements, 61, 123, 198
alethic, 36, 54, 127, 180
algorithm, 29
alien, 74, 126
alienated, 118–120, 185
alienation, 126–128, 137, 184

253

# INDEX

allowances, 107, 233–234
Althusser, 247
altruism, 45, 154
amalgamation, 194
ambition, 108, 156
amelioration, 103
analogical, 180
analogous, 241
analysand, 144
analysis, 27, 224
analytic, 69, 71, 99, 109–110, 144
analytically, 87, 99
anarchy, 162
Ancient, 210–211
annexed, 95, 120
anointed, 59, 91, 105
anomie, 86
anonymity, 148
antagonism, 45, 102, 152
antagonist, 102
antagonistic, 64, 66, 71, 88, 107, 145
antagonistically, 152
antecedent, 33, 89, 105
antecedently, 34, 80
anthropic, 210
anthropologically, 38
anthropology, 79, 143
antinomy, 165
antiquated, 135, 189
antithetic, 197
apex, 69
apodicity, 222
apodictic, 54, 59, 91, 181, 189, 220
apophantic, 58, 69
aporetic, 83
aporia, 13, 15, 23, 29–30, 67, 69, 74, 80, 94, 98, 102
aporias, 76, 86
apotheosis, 141
Apparatuses, 247
appearance, 14, 20, 38, 41, 97–98, 104, 110, 125, 127, 138, 168, 178–180, 190, 208, 217, 219, 222

appearances, 16, 48, 52, 57, 81, 89, 109–111, 117, 137, 165–166, 178, 187, 201, 216, 219, 221–222, 246
apperceive, 227
apperceived, 20, 35
apperception, 60
apportioned, 52, 63, 119, 141, 183, 226
apprehend, 149, 196, 217
apprehended, 79, 177, 182
apprehending, 197, 235, 237
apprehension, 84, 129, 136, 144, 152, 166, 186
apprehensive, 202
appresentation, 80
appropriation, 17, 20, 37–38, 53–54, 73, 75, 77–78, 85, 102, 120, 144–145, 164, 184, 224
aprioristic, 45, 60, 98
apriority, 44, 52, 64, 83, 106, 174
Aquinas, 198–200
arborescence, 182
architectonic, 207, 214
arena, 32
Aristotle, 80–81, 150, 156, 204, 211, 247
artefact, 192
artefacts, 45, 68, 134
artifice, 188, 213, 217
artificial, 135
artist, 185, 201
artistic, 19, 185
arts, 20
Asia, 210
aspects, 59, 63, 115, 178
aspirations, 41, 46, 69, 195, 209, 212, 227
assertions, 45, 84, 173, 237
assertoric, 80
assertory, 37, 39–40
asset, 170–171
assets, 94
assimilate, 16

assistance, 16
atomized, 225, 229
attainable, 28, 38–39, 57–58, 69, 178
attainment, 38, 48, 50, 53, 100, 170
attribution, 138, 166, 183–184, 186
attuned, 27, 169, 197
audient, 26
aufheben, 128
augmentation, 78, 94
aural, 36
authentic, 19, 127
authenticated, 234
authenticity, 216
authoritarian, 180
authorities, 58, 95
authorship, 218
autochthonous, 154
autonomized, 126
autonomous, 65, 112, 125, 167–169
autonomy, 60, 65, 85, 97, 126, 168, 182, 242
avarice, 103
avocation, 92 awakening, 125, 189, 225 awareness, 17, 23, 28, 37, 50, 73, 87, 105, 110,

123, 127, 144, 148, 159, 172, 174, 186, 189, 203, 212, 216, 219, 222–227, 231, 238, 245
axiological, 144
axiology, 38

**B**

Badiou, 24, 103
baggage, 119
Bakhtin, 194, 247
Balibar, 247
Barnett, 249
barricades, 178
barrier, 216
barriers, 25, 199, 205, 214, 224

254

# INDEX

beginnings, 205, 210, 213
behaviour, 198
behavioural, 130
behaviourism, 211
Beings, 101, 194, 196–197, 200–201, 206–207, 210–211, 225
beings, 26, 29, 33, 35, 37, 42, 49, 52, 56, 67, 83–87, 89, 92–93, 99, 101, 103, 112, 121, 123, 127–128, 130–132, 134–135, 137, 140, 142, 145–146, 148–149, 153–154, 156, 161, 163, 168, 170, 187, 189, 203, 219, 221, 235, 237–238
beliefs, 37, 50, 54, 224
Benjamin, 216
bereft, 37, 59, 65, 71, 87, 98, 105, 135, 173
Berger, 247
Bernet, 249
Bhaskar, 248
Bio-economic, 159, 224
Bio-genesis, 16
Bio-genetic, 219
biological, 208
biologically, 25
biopolitical, 213–214, 218–219
biospheres, 215, 219, 221
birthed, 65, 205, 239
birthing, 67
blithering, 36
bodies, 46
bondage, 177, 181
boundaries, 67, 186, 196, 199, 205, 211, 225, 230, 236
bounds, 186
bourgeois, 130, 133–134, 161, 188, 238
bourgeoisie, 153, 161
breadth, 50
brute, 25, 92
brutes, 163
buildings, 201

bungler, 84, 98
bureaucracy, 34

## C

calamities, 25, 60
calamity, 81, 97
calculable, 41
Canada, 147
cancellation, 19, 22, 120, 145, 191, 203, 234, 239
capabilities, 64, 170
capability, 120
capable, 72–73, 162, 164, 229, 240
capacious, 201
capacities, 25, 28, 36, 179, 217
Capital, 247
capital, 20, 85, 102, 127, 129, 133, 145, 152, 157, 196, 198, 224, 234, 246
Capitalism, 247
capitalism, 20, 133, 144, 198
Capitalist, 148
capitalist, 145–146, 169, 188–189
caprice, 21, 92, 103, 135, 226, 228
capricious, 101, 107, 135, 156, 163, 187, 223, 225
capriciously, 81
Cartesian, 133, 144, 187, 192, 194, 241, 249
casualties, 155, 157
categorical, 95
categories, 117, 150, 231, 243
causal, 15, 17, 19, 27, 32, 34, 43–44, 48, 52, 58, 64, 72–74, 82, 93, 112–114, 125–126, 140, 149, 157–158, 170, 175–176, 188, 190, 217–218, 225, 240, 244
Causality, 6, 71
causality, 14–15, 17, 22, 26–27, 30, 33–35, 43–44, 59, 61, 71–76, 81, 85, 91, 105, 113, 222–223
causation, 38
centralized, 46
centuries, 211
Century, 151–152, 161, 189, 204, 211, 230, 232
century, 27, 161, 189, 204
certainty, 53, 92, 98, 189, 215, 220
certitude, 140
characteristic, 22, 81, 243
characteristics, 69, 80, 112, 195, 232
chimp, 91
China, 210
choices, 17, 50, 73–75, 112, 152, 157, 203
circumspection, 69
circumstance, 31, 34, 87–88, 93, 107, 135
circumstances, 81, 107, 120, 138, 150
citizen, 66
citizenry, 82
citizens, 60, 65, 147, 153, 224
cityscapes, 201
civil, 21, 25, 49–50, 52, 85, 96, 146, 157–158, 184, 198–200, 232
Civilization, 250
civilizations, 210
clarification, 35, 48, 216
classes, 156
classification, 161, 212
classless, 181
clinching, 28
cloaked, 107
closure, 215
coalesce, 92, 152, 182
coalescent, 99
coercive, 16, 32, 64, 66, 90, 96, 108, 112, 169
coexist, 26
coexistent, 137, 219
co-existents, 192
co-extensive, 169

255

# INDEX

cogitans, 65, 241
cogitate, 67
cogitative, 188
cogito, 21, 23, 39, 42, 70, 89, 92, 105, 144, 167, 169, 187, 206, 241
cognition, 38, 57, 67, 196
cognitive, 69
cognitively, 170
coherence, 159, 219
coherent, 154, 219, 233, 237
coheres, 218, 220
cohering, 96
coincidence, 21
Collective, 85, 159
collective, 14–15, 17, 19–20, 23, 26, 31, 33, 38, 40, 46–47, 49–54, 56–72, 74–75, 78, 81–82, 85–96, 99–100, 102–105, 107–108, 111, 113–115, 120–121, 124, 126, 129–130, 132, 134–136, 139, 142, 152, 156, 161–170, 172, 175, 177, 179, 181, 183–184, 186, 192–194, 196, 225–226, 228–230, 232–233, 235, 241–244
collectively, 22, 25, 43, 47, 50, 52, 65, 81, 86, 96, 155, 229, 241
collectives, 19, 52, 63, 86, 158, 162–164, 211, 229, 233–235
collectivistically, 108
Collectivity, 60
collectivity, 22, 34, 43, 52–53, 57–58, 65, 68–69, 73, 81, 83–84, 88–90, 93, 99, 126, 162–163, 165, 168, 229, 244
collectivization, 160, 164, 171, 185, 241
collectivized, 33, 134, 162, 180, 235

collusion, 137
combative, 37
commensurable, 119, 122
commensurate, 37, 60, 78, 108
commensuration, 35, 64
commercial, 4, 70, 133, 145, 148
commercialized, 184
commitments, 194
commodifications, 133, 189, 246
commodified, 126, 246
commodify, 41
commodities, 161
commodity, 122, 142, 246
commonality, 72
commonplace, 46, 56
communal, 22, 53, 202
communication, 21, 119, 210
communications, 161
communion, 75, 182, 223
communiqué, 161, 167
communism, 151
communities, 43
compatibilism, 27
compatibilist, 92
competition, 127, 146
compliance, 136, 174, 198–199
comporting, 242
comportment, 20, 179, 186, 207, 234, 237, 240
composition, 15–16, 58, 194, 197, 203, 206, 215, 221, 234
compositional, 170, 183
concealed, 99
conceivable, 14, 71, 149
concept, 14, 20–21, 24, 31, 33, 39, 45, 47, 52, 54–56, 59, 61, 67–70, 74, 78–81, 83, 89, 92–93, 97–101, 109–111, 118, 124–125, 128, 130–132, 135–138, 143, 146–148, 150–152, 161, 163, 169, 173, 180–182, 185, 187–189, 194–195, 204, 208, 214, 216–218, 225, 238, 241, 245
conception, 20, 32, 34, 67, 80, 99, 165, 188, 195, 207, 212, 222
conceptions, 78, 109–110, 161, 181, 187, 193–194
concepts, 13, 15, 17, 24, 33, 37, 39, 42, 45, 54, 57, 62–63, 66, 74, 82–83, 88–89, 93, 103, 105–106, 114, 118–119, 122, 129–130, 136, 147, 152, 163, 171, 173–174, 176, 195, 198, 219, 226, 244, 246
conceptual, 16, 26, 42, 45, 55, 59, 61–63, 70–71, 73–74, 78–79, 81, 84, 90, 92–93, 101, 105–106, 108, 113, 115–119, 121–133, 135–143, 147–149, 152, 158, 165–169, 172–177, 181–182, 185–186, 189, 192–194, 197, 199, 202–204, 206–207, 209, 211, 213, 215–218, 229, 234, 236–239, 241–242, 244–246
conceptualization, 63, 118, 123, 192, 206–207
conceptualizations, 162, 188
conceptualized, 162, 180, 186, 194
concert, 153, 159, 214, 230
conclusions, 25, 48–49, 51, 75, 86, 94, 112, 117, 173
conclusive, 118, 208
conclusively, 75, 118,

256

## INDEX

144, 170
concomitant, 22, 69, 98, 100, 118, 169–170, 208, 217, 220, 231
concrete, 37–38, 41, 43, 51, 54, 57, 75, 92, 131, 166, 178, 180, 182, 184–185, 216, 232, 241
concretion, 51, 92, 178, 183, 241, 246
condemnation, 212
condemned, 198
conditionality, 38, 63, 105, 158, 172, 186, 190, 207
conference, 186
confluence, 125, 135, 140, 158–159, 214
conformity, 16, 20
confrontation, 111
conjure, 13, 21, 110, 198, 207
connection, 15, 20, 40, 44, 58–59, 64, 66, 71, 80, 90, 96, 112, 143–144, 168, 172, 178
conquer, 123, 217
conscience, 56, 66, 71, 137
conscious, 33, 35, 45, 51, 81, 159, 172, 176, 183, 203, 207, 214, 232, 236
consciousness, 13, 22, 26, 31, 34, 39, 42–43, 45–46, 49, 51, 53, 55, 57–58, 60, 62–67, 69–70, 72, 76, 80–81, 84–85, 87, 89, 92–93, 102, 104–105, 107, 109–113, 115–117, 120–121, 123, 125, 128–130, 132–133, 135, 141, 143, 147, 149–150, 156, 159–160, 162, 165–166, 170, 172–179, 181–182, 184–189, 191, 194–196, 198, 202, 204, 210, 213–214, 217–219, 221, 226, 228–230, 233, 235, 237, 245–246
consequence, 29, 31, 77, 153, 181, 196
consequences, 43, 94
consequential, 67, 70, 208
consequents, 67, 107
conspiracies, 212
constellate, 14, 19, 214
constellated, 22, 186, 189, 202, 234
constellation, 17, 26, 33–34, 37, 47, 55, 59, 89–90, 173, 186, 217, 234, 238
constellations, 43, 50, 158
constituens, 49, 98
constitute, 17, 19, 29, 35–37, 39–40, 55–57, 87–89, 99, 122, 185, 220
constituted, 16, 21, 24, 26, 28, 31–32, 34–35, 43, 45–46, 48, 50–51, 55–56, 75, 84, 88, 90–91, 93, 95, 101–103, 105, 172, 180–181, 214
constitutes, 20, 24, 31, 40, 57–58, 94, 104, 216, 225
constituting, 39
constitution, 21–24, 27, 32, 36, 41, 56, 69, 75, 89, 91, 93
constitutional, 37, 185
constitutive, 20, 22–23, 26, 29, 32, 35, 37, 39–40, 44, 46–47, 50, 52, 56, 58, 62, 64–66, 69, 71, 82–83, 89, 95, 101, 107, 166, 178, 185
constrained, 75, 101, 209
constraint, 199
constraints, 16, 26, 54, 65, 68, 79, 81, 88, 208
construction, 23
constructive, 71
consumer, 20, 154
consumerism, 168
consumerist, 223
consumeristic, 211
consumers, 19
consummation, 32, 135, 205
consumption, 19, 30, 51, 64, 123, 189, 199, 205
contemplation, 13, 17, 22, 27, 33, 67, 77, 83, 90, 92, 94, 108, 110, 116, 144, 202–204, 206, 215, 218, 220–221
contemporaneity, 65
contemporaneous, 33–34, 60, 68, 74, 103, 179
contemporaneously, 28, 70, 181
contemporary, 20, 35, 139, 150, 204
context, 39, 119, 125, 136, 177, 192, 199–200, 207–208, 214, 243
contextualization, 137, 209, 214, 239–240
contextualized, 186, 192, 209, 236
contiguous, 91, 169
continental, 13
contingencies, 15, 23, 33, 36–37, 45, 55–56, 70, 74–76, 87, 99, 139, 176, 238
Contingency, 6–8, 106, 122, 177, 248
contingency, 21, 24, 33, 37, 49, 64–65, 98–99, 106–107, 118, 140, 174, 180, 188–189, 202, 246
contingent, 14, 21–23, 27, 39, 45, 48, 50, 54–55, 57, 63, 70, 74–75, 88–89, 94, 97–98, 101, 103, 105, 107–112, 117–118, 138–140, 160, 165–167, 170, 172, 174–175, 179–182,

257

# INDEX

192, 198, 209, 237–238, 245
contingently, 74–75, 97, 111–112, 160, 168–170, 174, 245
continuous, 113
contradiction, 80, 144–146, 148–152, 175, 187
contradictions, 144–145, 148–149, 151–152, 155, 158, 182, 188, 190
contradictory, 130, 148, 176
contrariness, 35
cooperative, 153
coordinates, 218–219, 226–227
Co-presence, 140, 167, 207, 242
Co-presences, 193
Co-present, 130
copula, 57, 60, 68, 102, 112, 178, 191, 217, 236
corollary, 138
corporate, 135, 157
corporations, 19
corporatist, 19
corporea, 166
corporeal, 28, 51, 140, 188, 241
correlate, 62, 89, 131, 228
correlation, 15, 51, 88, 90, 93, 105, 109, 118, 138, 219
correlationist, 92
correspondence, 21, 88, 92, 118, 134–135, 173, 201–203, 213, 215
cosmological, 49
Cosmology, 251
counterfactual, 81
counterparts, 33, 83, 124, 130
counterpoint, 191, 207
counterposed, 179
counter-positionality, 195
creation, 27, 38, 91, 176, 237
creative, 17, 101, 122, 162–163, 168, 176, 185–186, 199, 201
creativity, 95, 168, 185
creature, 58
creatures, 201, 210, 223
criminal, 153
criminality, 56
Crisis, 194, 249
critical, 4, 198–199
cultural, 17, 20, 27, 44, 51, 61–63, 65, 67–68, 79, 120–121, 129–130, 134, 143, 149–152, 161–163, 171, 177, 191, 207, 224, 226, 233
currency, 27, 35, 59–60, 76, 93, 103, 105, 130, 211, 218

## D

darkness, 196
Darwinian, 168
Dasein, 21, 23, 26, 38, 42, 54, 75, 81, 84, 93–94, 103, 140, 166, 170
datum, 84, 158, 165, 167, 172, 206, 216–217
decenter, 144
decentering, 203
deception, 38, 49, 99
deceptive, 70–71, 82, 197
defenseless, 155
defenses, 204
degeneration, 155
deification, 73, 133
deified, 51
deify, 78
Deleuze, 248
delimitation, 189
delimited, 60, 135
delinquency, 153
deliverance, 212
delusional, 224
Democracies, 148, 154, 223
democracies, 157
Democracy, 145
democracy, 14, 27, 29, 31, 35, 46–47, 49, 56–57, 60–61, 65, 73, 81, 106, 162, 164
Democratic, 250
democratic, 29, 32, 34, 37–38, 49, 54, 95, 101, 114, 157
democratically, 41, 46–47, 49, 52, 58, 78, 95
denaturalization, 137
deontic, 30, 54
deregulated, 234
Derrida, 170, 248
Descartes, 105, 192–193, 199, 211
despotic, 181, 234
Destructuralist, 234
destructurating, 231
Destructuration, 230
destructuration, 242
destructure, 233
destructured, 233–234
detachability, 141
detachable, 140–143, 150, 161
detached, 178
detachment, 159
determinability, 45, 47, 182, 186, 194, 199, 208–209, 219, 222, 239
determinable, 28, 30, 50, 173, 177–178, 184, 229, 241
determinate, 27, 34, 51–53, 105, 111
determination, 17, 22–23, 36, 40, 44–45, 47–48, 54–56, 58–60, 68, 73, 75–76, 88–89, 91, 100, 112–114, 118, 128–130, 141, 148–149, 167, 170–171, 173, 178, 180, 215
determinations, 23, 27, 33–35, 37–38, 40, 43–44, 52, 54–55, 60–61, 64, 66, 87, 93, 99, 103, 108–109, 111–114, 130, 134,

258

# INDEX

138–139, 142, 156, 158, 167–168, 171, 175, 179–181, 185, 216
determinative, 69, 118, 136, 178, 244
deterrent, 61
de-transcendentalized, 32
devaluation, 107
devalue, 95
devalued, 161, 179
devaluing, 84
development, 25, 29, 51, 94, 103, 156, 161, 163, 183–184, 200, 210
developmental, 47, 102, 203, 210–212, 218
developments, 87, 223–224
devolution, 189
devolve, 228
diachronic, 116, 119, 132, 134, 188, 218, 235
diachronically, 138
diachrony, 117, 133, 142
diacritical, 103
diagnosable, 48, 200
dialectic, 19–20, 22–23, 29–30, 37–38, 40, 42, 44, 59, 62, 64, 70, 75, 80, 94, 97–98, 106, 108, 118–119, 124, 129, 137, 139, 141–142, 151, 166, 168–171, 179, 198, 205, 222
dialectical, 21, 23, 30, 35–36, 42–43, 47–48, 51–55, 58, 61–62, 67–68, 70–71, 75, 78, 81, 85, 93–95, 99–101, 106–107, 111–113, 119–120, 122, 126, 128, 130, 132, 134–139, 141–142, 144–146, 148–152, 155, 158, 166–167, 169–171, 174–185, 187–190, 194, 196–201, 203–204, 206–207, 209,

214–215, 217, 220–223, 225–227, 229, 231–243, 245–246
dialectics, 22, 30, 42, 45, 82, 119
dichotomous, 22, 30, 35, 42, 44, 52, 69, 175
dichotomy, 23, 25, 40, 126, 167–168
dictator, 159
dictatorship, 161
differentia, 37, 208
digital, 220
Ding (Das), 211
Ding an sich, 165–166
diplomacy, 34
directives, 58, 81, 168
dirempt, 85
diremption, 54, 92
disavowed, 48, 85
disclosed, 31, 113, 173, 179–180
disclosedness, 100
disclosing, 154
disclosure, 108, 114, 201
disconnected, 123, 197
discourse, 52, 87, 102, 171, 199–200, 237
discrepancies, 104, 158
discrimination, 120, 155
discriminatory, 157–158
disease, 81
disempowering, 95
disenfranchised, 86, 179
disengage, 20
disintegration, 229
dismantled, 229
disobedient, 49
disorder, 201, 211
disparities, 120, 157
disparity, 104, 153, 228, 230
dispossessed, 204
dissent, 38
dissociation, 153
dissolution, 95
distantiate, 132, 196
distantiated, 213–214, 223, 242
distantiates, 52, 234

distantiation, 16, 184, 197, 203, 220, 235–236, 239
disturbances, 100, 230
disunity, 32, 69, 83, 92
divine, 27
divinity, 43
divisional, 70
divisions, 69, 169, 232
doers, 52
dominance, 20
domination, 167
dominion, 41
downfall, 163, 168
dualism, 152
dualistic, 58, 193
duality, 14, 71, 100, 182, 194, 238
duties, 46, 88
duty, 29, 46, 55–57, 95
dyad, 113, 119
dynamical, 72, 189
dynamics, 34, 57, 62, 188
Dystopian, 212

**E**

Earthquake, 72
Eastern, 211
eclipse, 224
eclipsing, 26, 56
ecology, 29, 38
economic, 20, 61, 72–73, 84, 93, 96, 113, 118–120, 123, 125, 129–130, 133, 141, 148–153, 156–158, 161–162, 184, 192, 194, 199–200, 223–224, 233, 246
economics, 26, 118
economies, 157
ecosystem, 25
edicts, 204
edification, 38, 64
edifice, 123, 228
edificial, 192
education, 67, 146, 153, 157, 161
effectual, 39, 158
effectuate, 190

259

# INDEX

efficacious, 29
effort, 16, 28, 73, 77, 93, 100, 102, 107, 118, 230
egalitarian, 25
Ego, 5–6, 57, 67, 133, 192–193, 251
ego, 13, 20, 23, 28, 32, 36, 39–42, 44, 49, 52–53, 57–58, 65, 67–68, 70, 73, 80, 88, 92–94, 104–106, 108–112, 144, 146, 158, 167–169, 172–176, 179–181, 184, 187, 194–196, 206–208, 238, 241–242
Ego cogito, 14
egos, 194, 207
Egypt, 210
eidetic, 85, 131–132, 185, 221
eidos, 170
Eleatics, 204
election, 162
elements, 14, 43–44, 58, 62, 68, 210, 215
elicited, 131, 186, 208, 222
eliciting, 85, 173
elucidary, 135, 148, 171
elucidated, 29, 105, 147, 156
elucidating, 119
elucidation, 106, 119, 193, 224
elucidations, 106, 159
elusive, 15, 47
emancipated, 16, 29, 42, 46, 52, 103, 123–126, 137, 179, 182, 186, 228
Emancipation, 249
emancipation, 36, 54, 58–59, 66, 93, 174, 205, 223, 225, 228–229
Emancipatory, 5, 7, 66, 133
emancipatory, 16, 47, 63, 108, 122–123, 129, 135–136, 140, 157, 163, 182, 185, 206,

228–231, 233–234, 239–243
embodied, 4, 141, 158, 191, 197, 225, 232–233
embodiment, 231
emergent, 80
empathic, 192
empirical, 26, 30, 43, 49, 65–66, 69–70, 72, 77, 88–90, 92–101, 103–105, 107–108, 115, 133, 143, 146, 159, 163, 167, 172–174, 176, 199, 228, 245
employment, 112, 153
empowered, 144
empowerment, 93
enacts, 21, 167, 230–231, 240
encompasses, 230
encompassing, 13, 53
encumber, 94
encumbered, 92, 107, 115, 123, 171, 201
encumbers, 124, 235
encumbrances, 31, 41, 51, 74, 87, 125, 129, 203, 206, 212, 231, 240
endangerment, 185
endeavor, 13, 23, 28, 32–34, 42–43, 50, 65, 77, 103, 106, 115–116, 155, 170, 186, 197, 199, 223, 242
endeavors, 16, 28, 185, 205, 230
endemic, 133, 142, 145, 169, 207, 230
endorsed, 91
endowed, 41, 91, 103, 106
endowment, 73
endowments, 203
enemy, 27
Energeia, 130, 146, 154
energeia, 66, 81
enforced, 224
enforcement, 154
engagement, 74, 123, 128, 185, 187–188,

190, 235
Engels, 250
enjoyment, 40, 163, 237
enlightened, 86, 104, 176, 200
enlightenment, 96, 224
enslaving, 19
ensouled, 93
enterprise, 17, 43, 70, 131, 135, 144, 156, 188, 196
entertainment, 67
entities, 17, 38, 51, 53, 58, 113, 115, 117, 186, 191
entitlement, 224
entwined, 117, 132, 167, 229, 235
environmental, 25, 182
epiphanical, 48
epiphany, 83
epiphenomenal, 102, 173
epiphenomenon, 145
episodic, 48
episteme, 174
epistemic, 36, 39, 45, 58, 70, 73, 77, 113, 117, 136, 144, 245
epistemological, 53, 82, 84, 87–88, 92–94, 97–98, 101, 109, 114–115, 169–170, 174, 192
epistemologically, 45, 47, 75, 104, 116, 158, 178
Epistemology, 177
epistemology, 15, 30, 39, 70, 76, 82, 87–88, 100, 105, 108, 113, 118, 143
epoché, 222
equality, 120, 148, 154, 162
equally, 32, 59, 72, 89, 120–121, 147, 176, 189
equanimity, 55
equation, 13, 25, 53, 69, 181
equivalent, 161
equivalential, 127

260

# INDEX

eradicate, 71, 90
eradicated, 85, 148, 233
Eros, 250
erudite, 135
eruptions, 213
eschatological, 170
Essence, 5–6, 39, 80, 85
essence, 15, 23, 29–32, 35, 37–39, 42, 44, 48, 51–52, 54–58, 62, 64, 67, 71–73, 75, 78–90, 92–93, 95, 98–99, 101–102, 104–105, 108, 111, 115–116, 118–119, 122–123, 125–132, 139, 141–146, 149, 151, 154, 161, 166–171, 173, 176–184, 186, 202, 207, 214, 231–234, 236, 244, 246
essences, 111, 183, 215
essential, 52, 54, 72, 86, 110, 115, 129, 165, 179, 187, 197, 201, 207, 239
essentialist, 203
essentiality, 182, 207
essentialized, 183
establishment, 55, 75, 96, 119–120, 225, 229
eternal, 90, 196
ethic, 51, 187
ethical, 13, 21, 44, 47, 49–50, 54, 56–57, 59, 64–65, 82–83, 85, 88–89, 91, 99, 120, 130, 132, 150, 158, 177, 186, 188–189, 203–204, 225
ethically, 50, 57, 63, 126, 146, 159, 189, 207
ethics, 51, 54
ethnological, 25
ethos, 89
evental, 19, 75
events, 27, 34, 48, 56, 61, 72, 76, 86, 218
eviscerating, 95
evolution, 29, 210

evolutionary, 24, 30, 189, 211, 223
examination, 23, 36, 125, 245
Exchange-value, 30, 184
exclusion, 127, 130, 199, 232–235, 238–241, 243
exclusionary, 95, 164, 234, 240
exclusions, 225, 234, 238–239
exclusively, 80
exhaustive, 43, 170
existences, 140, 185–186, 191, 201, 225
existent, 15, 43, 137, 139–142, 159, 166–167, 193, 210, 213–214, 228–229, 231–232
Existential, 8, 183
existential, 54, 79, 119, 123, 157, 185–186, 188, 193–195, 197, 203, 205, 207, 212, 215, 217–218, 220–226, 230, 235
existentialism, 170
Existentiality, 8, 198, 201
existentiality, 56, 58–59, 184, 191–192, 196, 201, 205, 217, 221, 225, 239
existentialized, 183, 243
existentially, 113, 177, 221
existents, 135, 142, 155, 194, 219, 229
expansion, 30, 41
exploitation, 73
exploited, 161
exponent, 136, 182, 196
exponential, 184
exposition, 197, 201, 206
exposure, 145
expression, 62, 105, 122, 134, 169, 173, 184–185, 205–207
expressions, 152, 172, 186, 207–208

expressive, 207
extensions, 168
extensive, 17
exteriority, 94
external, 27, 35–36, 43, 107–108, 171, 180, 232, 241–242
externality, 31, 59, 88, 108
externalized, 182
extinct, 25
extinction, 210

# F

Faber(homo), 135
facticity, 15, 36, 44, 66, 70, 84, 90, 93, 97–98, 100, 104, 106, 233
factions, 52, 69, 162–163, 191
facts, 49, 52, 60, 74, 88, 100, 104, 120, 150
factual, 17, 70, 84, 98, 102
faculties, 69, 196, 201, 223
faith, 55–56
fallacies, 82
fallibility, 77
false, 15, 23, 49, 112, 154, 173, 186, 224
falsehood, 49
falsehoods, 127
falsity, 20, 23, 37, 55, 64, 69–70, 76, 84, 107
fame, 157
Faschoid (crypto), 19
Fascism, 145
Feuerbachian, 165
fiat, 24, 68, 73, 85, 88, 234
Fichte, 64, 89, 109–110, 248
filiation, 227, 243
filiations, 239
financial, 143, 153, 156
finite, 192
finitude, 43, 188
fiscal, 108
fixations, 224

261

# INDEX

fledgling, 106, 210
flux, 177, 196
fluxion, 215–217
focal, 191
folly, 40
forecloses, 180
forefront, 20, 45, 143
for-itself, 231
formal, 112, 116–117, 119, 129–131, 134–135, 141, 153, 185–187, 191–192, 196, 198, 206, 208, 211, 221–222, 225, 232, 234–235, 240–243, 245–246
formality, 129
formalization, 157, 198, 210, 239, 242
formalizations, 192, 243
formalize, 122
formalized, 178
formation, 50, 70, 119, 132, 206, 215–218, 222, 228–229, 233
formations, 69, 127, 129, 132, 215, 219, 229, 235
formative, 21
former, 62, 74, 84, 88, 92, 99–100, 102, 105, 119, 140, 150, 153–154, 160, 168, 186, 224, 243
formulations, 160
foundational, 149
foundations, 56, 228
freedom, 13, 15–16, 19–20, 22, 26, 35–36, 44, 46–47, 50, 58–59, 72–75, 78–79, 95, 107–108, 110–111, 122, 124, 149, 168, 177, 185, 199
freedoms, 4, 17, 43, 46, 49, 78, 111, 172, 185, 212, 230, 232
Freud, 146, 250
Freudian, 146
frontiers, 199
fruitful, 168, 197

fruits, 55
fulfill, 26–27, 38, 46, 112
fulfilling, 230
functionalism, 36, 46, 69–70, 234
functionality, 60, 72
functionary, 118, 178, 184, 239
fundament, 83, 94, 102, 109, 241
fundamental, 4, 80
fuse, 176, 187, 242
fused, 150, 189, 197, 244
fuses, 52, 111
fusion, 40, 168, 177, 187

## G

gap, 39, 51, 66, 165
gatekeeper, 102
gender, 25, 38, 162
genera, 82
generality, 26, 61
generations, 29
generative, 14, 25–26, 46, 82, 85
genesis, 25, 141, 188, 206
genetic, 16, 25, 155, 187
genus, 14, 17, 25, 34, 44, 47, 49, 58, 72, 77, 80, 87, 112, 210, 212, 215–218, 220–221, 226, 231, 235, 238–239, 245
geopolitical, 54, 86
givens, 53, 65, 109, 128, 198
globalization, 86
globally, 220
Gnostics, 14
goals, 37, 53, 58, 82, 230
Godhead, 109
governance, 157
government, 82
governments, 19, 146, 153–154, 156
Grammatology, 8, 167, 170–171, 248
Greece, 210–211
greed, 204
Guardian, 150

guardian, 45, 63
guilty, 37

## H

Habermas, 248
habitat, 14, 210
habitualities, 15, 17, 46
handmaidens, 32
happenings, 196
happiness, 157, 163
harmonistic, 58
harmony, 76, 193
harnessed, 191
Hegel, 39, 55, 80, 86, 99, 110, 125, 131, 143, 145–147, 151, 160–161, 175, 177, 198, 211, 237, 248, 250–251
Hegelian, 63, 145, 165, 232
Hegelians, 238
hegemonic, 46, 85–86, 146, 149, 162–163, 197–198, 234
Hegemony, 148, 248, 250
hegemony, 126, 164
Heidegger, 160, 166, 248
Heideggerian, 165
heteronomy, 65–66, 85, 87, 182
hierarchical, 29, 95, 185
hierarchy, 95, 179
Hieroglyphics, 210
hijacked, 86
historical, 20, 30, 33, 52, 108, 119–120, 149, 178, 205, 207, 209, 212, 219, 230
historically, 27, 34, 126, 157
Historicity, 6, 20, 77, 250
historicity, 20, 25, 30, 38, 42, 48, 63, 77, 81, 211, 243
historicization, 138
holistic, 246
homeless, 153
horizon, 31, 37, 39, 52, 116, 120, 123–126,

# INDEX

135, 139–140, 143–144, 148, 159, 169, 175–176, 179, 182, 187–190, 192–193, 195–197, 199–207, 209, 212–213, 217, 220–221, 224, 226, 228, 231–236, 238–239, 242, 245
horizons, 11, 115, 140, 164, 166, 191, 201, 221, 225, 239
horizontal, 115–116, 133, 140, 151, 156, 168, 179, 181, 189, 193, 195, 199, 201, 206, 208, 211–214, 217, 222, 226–227, 239–242
horizontality, 192, 208
Horkheimer, 249
hostile, 122
hostility, 17
humanity, 27, 38, 205, 209–210, 224
humankind, 22, 25, 30, 38, 43, 65, 72, 76, 96, 178, 229
Hume, 199
Husserl, 194, 222, 237, 242, 249
Husserlian, 144, 192, 215
hylozoistic, 72
hypostatization, 100, 120, 141, 170, 185, 234, 237–238, 241
hypostatizations, 186, 189
hypostatize, 186
hypostatized, 115, 142, 184–186, 190, 231, 234–235, 237, 240
hypostatizes, 76, 142, 235
Hypothesi , 218
hypothesize, 160
hypothetical, 37

## I

iconoclasts, 70
icons, 19
ideal, 14, 66, 81, 146

idealism, 29, 34, 38, 62, 110–111, 150
idealist, 129
idealistic, 37, 175
ideality, 68
ideals, 37, 180, 210, 224
Ideas, 149, 249
ideas, 14, 25–26, 38, 40, 47, 51, 64–65, 67, 83, 101, 103–104, 108, 118, 121, 125, 130, 149–150, 159, 171, 180, 185, 198–199, 205, 212, 220–221
ideation, 37, 52, 102, 116, 125, 130, 134–135, 139, 179, 194, 206
identical, 17, 20–21, 24, 36–37, 39, 48–50, 52, 57, 61–65, 71, 76, 79, 88–89, 93–95, 97–98, 103, 106–111, 113, 131, 137–140, 143, 150–152, 159–160, 164–165, 167, 172, 175, 177, 179, 181, 195–197, 199, 210, 213–214, 220–221, 224–226, 230–231, 235, 237–241, 244–245
identifiability, 226
identifiable, 144, 195–196, 204
identification, 7, 21, 46, 51, 80, 88, 99, 112, 115, 117, 123, 127, 131–135, 142–143, 148, 150, 158–159, 163, 165–167, 172, 181–182, 184, 191–194, 196–197, 201–202, 205, 211, 214, 219, 222, 226, 235–236, 241, 244–246
identitarian, 86, 183
identities, 17, 92–93, 97, 113, 132, 142–143, 149, 151, 153, 161–162, 197, 203,

228, 231–233, 237, 243
ideological, 144, 146, 197, 217
ideology, 129, 137, 145
idiot, 36
illness, 145
illnesses, 156
ills, 85–86, 155–156
Image-content, 207
Image-object, 230
Image-sign, 193
imaginary, 191, 237
imagination, 24, 57, 101, 251
immanence, 87, 211–212, 220
immediate, 15, 48, 62, 71, 80–82, 87, 116, 118, 132, 171, 178, 182
immemorial, 185
impetus, 25, 47, 52, 62, 68, 73, 99, 140, 170, 196, 199, 206, 212, 214, 227, 230
import, 212, 218, 226, 231–233
imports, 205, 211
imposition, 207, 221
impositions, 214
impossibility, 33, 80, 127, 150, 155, 187
impression, 172–173
impressions, 14, 23, 102, 105, 134
inalienable, 158
inclusion, 118, 145–146, 152, 233–234, 240
inclusionary, 234
inclusive, 104, 116, 119, 156, 192, 230, 234, 239
inclusivity, 127, 148, 157, 232–233, 243
incompatibility, 56
incomplete, 155
inconceivable, 13
indebted, 78
individualists, 85
individuality, 75, 88, 100, 108
individualization, 108

263

# INDEX

individualized, 130, 168
individuals, 96, 153, 168, 225, 228–230
individuated, 19, 47, 52, 85, 103, 109, 195, 202, 225, 229–230
individuation, 44, 137
indivisibly, 89
industrial, 38, 58, 70, 74, 81–82, 86, 108, 119, 127, 133, 142, 155, 161, 163, 167–168, 179, 182, 186, 189, 198, 200, 223
inequality, 71
inequitable, 169
inequity, 38, 85
infinite, 28, 74, 98, 188, 222, 244
informant, 211
infrastructure, 73, 88
infringe, 46
infringement, 66
inhabit, 78, 93, 123, 193
inhabiting, 237
inhabits, 96, 141
inherence, 21
inherent, 22, 34, 44, 51, 53, 62, 68, 82, 87, 91, 113, 121, 141, 144, 148, 152, 168, 170, 183, 218
inheres, 21, 191
inhering, 127
initself, 13, 15–16, 28, 103, 115, 148, 165, 174, 177, 179
injustice, 85
injustices, 155
inner, 24, 62, 108, 115–116, 119, 143, 159, 164–165, 172, 187, 191, 193–194, 197, 201–202, 209–210, 215, 220, 223, 226, 228, 230, 232, 236–237, 241–242
In representation, 39, 50
instantiated, 19, 21, 131, 145–146, 166, 196, 201–202, 205–206, 213, 218, 220–222, 240–241
instantiates, 207, 209, 214, 216–217, 219, 224, 239
instantiating, 55, 214, 235
instantiation, 128, 165, 195–197, 203, 206–207, 209, 211, 214, 219–220, 226, 236, 241
instantiations, 212, 226
institution, 41, 50, 86, 148
institutional, 25, 32, 36, 38, 41, 46, 49, 54, 56, 58, 68, 70, 90, 95, 136, 139, 142, 145, 158, 162, 185, 204
institutions, 19, 27, 41, 73, 86, 96, 103, 123, 139, 146, 153, 156, 162, 182, 199–200, 211
insurgency, 49
intellect, 36, 64, 68, 70, 83
intellectual, 4, 25, 65, 123, 132
intellectuals, 20
intelligibility, 29, 31, 66, 88, 172
intelligible, 15, 23–24, 26, 29, 48, 52, 66, 69, 83, 85, 88–89, 93, 95, 100, 173, 183
intention, 13, 17, 40, 43, 61, 80, 95–96, 126, 132, 148, 180, 199, 202, 215, 224
intentional, 13–14, 133–135, 137, 139, 171, 173, 176, 231, 238
intentionality, 17, 58, 66–67, 70–71, 85, 100, 103, 204
intentions, 95, 102
interactions, 107
interactive, 228
interconnectivity, 83
interdependent, 215
interfacing, 21
interior, 61, 166, 201, 228, 235, 245
interiority, 63
interlocutions, 221
interlocutor, 169
interloper, 82
internal, 31, 35, 122, 145–146, 203–205, 242
International, 247
internationally, 160
Interobjective, 8, 52, 172
interobjective, 134, 138, 140–141, 160, 166, 169, 184, 189–190, 208–209, 231, 233, 235–236, 239
interobjectively, 171, 174, 177, 187, 234–235
interobjectivity, 124, 128, 139, 148, 169, 172, 182, 188, 239
interpellation, 129
interplay, 20
interpretant, 244
intersubjective, 15, 20, 23, 35–36, 40, 42, 61, 64, 67, 77, 79, 81, 85, 89, 97–99, 107–108, 118, 121, 126, 131, 141, 158, 160, 165–166, 192, 203, 219, 225, 228, 231, 236, 244
intersubjectively, 46, 71, 74, 148, 160
intersubjectivity, 49, 93, 98, 203, 209, 220, 222
In-themselves, 74, 140, 149, 161–162
intuition, 180
invasive, 28
invention, 29
inversion, 14, 151, 188, 211
inverted, 135
investigation, 31, 50, 130–131, 202, 243
investigations, 171
invisible, 16, 139,

264

# INDEX

184–185, 192
irrational, 48, 145
irrationalism, 155
itself-transcending, 19

## J

Jameson, 246, 249
jeopardize, 25, 61, 71
jeopardized, 145
Judeo, 28
judgement, 23
judgements, 42, 204
judgment, 33, 37, 41, 45, 53, 55–56, 62, 74, 85, 103, 106, 110, 152, 155, 170
judgments, 14–16, 21, 23–24, 26, 37, 39, 42, 52, 55, 59, 62, 64, 66, 69–71, 74–75, 79–80, 82, 84, 87, 93–94, 97–98, 101, 103, 106, 116, 122, 150, 152, 167, 173–174, 181–182, 199
judicial, 82
judiciary, 195
Jungian, 224
jurisdiction, 46, 146
jurisprudence, 102
justice, 51, 106, 120, 148, 198, 204
justifiable, 111, 229, 237
justification, 37, 77, 150

## K

Kant, 55, 94, 99, 133, 150–151, 160–161, 177, 192–194, 199, 201, 222, 238
Kantian, 144, 153, 165
Kanto -Husserlian, 192, -Hegelian, 238
kinesthetic, 209
knowable, 60, 93, 149–150, 216
Knower, 6, 103
knower, 103

## L

Lacan, 224
Lacanian, 55, 224
Laclau, 145, 248–250
lacuna, 144, 175, 209, 234, 236
lawful, 20, 37, 224
laws, 4, 22, 28, 30, 37, 49, 59, 72, 113
Lebenswelt, 237
Lefebvre, 223, 250
legal, 154, 172, 224, 229
legerdemain, 37–38, 49, 56, 64, 71, 82, 84, 99–100, 127, 179, 224
legislative, 46
legitimated, 231
legitimation, 38
Leibniz, 86, 193–194
leitmotif, 134, 236–237
liaison, 4, 92, 101, 192, 206, 214
Liberal, 145
liberated, 16, 36, 213
liberties, 81
libidinal, 16
libido, 16
lifeworld, 15, 19, 27, 29, 33, 35, 38, 40, 42, 47, 49, 51, 56, 61, 64, 66, 70, 72, 74, 79, 81, 89–90, 99, 102–103, 128, 146, 154, 168–169, 193, 203–204, 207, 210, 222, 224–226, 229, 237–238, 244
lifeworlds, 76
lightening, 43
likelihood, 152, 195, 238
limitation, 28, 68, 120, 150, 177, 179, 188, 198, 200
limitations, 26, 74, 88, 90, 100, 170, 174, 178, 181, 195–196, 198, 208, 224
limitless, 223
litigation, 85

livelihood, 154
locality, 62, 169
localized, 182
Locke, 199
locus, 65, 232, 242
logic, 36, 198, 204, 212, 222, 238
logocentrism, 171
logos, 209, 221, 237
lordship, 202
losers, 148
loyalty, 48
Lukács, 250

## M

magnitude, 37, 48, 113, 143, 150, 170
magnitudes, 142, 172
maintenance, 25, 54, 106, 176, 178
majority, 95
maker, 204
mangled, 86
manifestations, 220
manifold, 14, 44, 69, 93–94, 99, 108–109, 113, 121, 160, 170, 175, 185, 187, 189, 201–202, 218, 220–221, 225, 234–238, 244
manoeuvers, 246
manoeuvre, 127, 173
Marcuse, 250
marginalized, 153–154
margins, 154
Marx, 125, 144–145, 151, 153–155, 161, 177, 201, 211, 238, 247, 250
Marxism, 117, 249
Marxist, 133, 152, 250
Marxo-Hegelian, 165, 232
Mass-consciousness, 19
material, 24, 47, 51, 55, 104, 108, 115, 129, 142, 149–150, 188, 193, 203–204, 241–242
materialism, 111, 119,

265

# INDEX

150, 180
materialist, 22, 129
materialists, 232
mathematical, 116
maturation, 218
Mayans, 210
Mead, 105
meaningful, 85, 223
mechanisms, 130, 157
media, 27, 40, 129
medial, 139, 243
mediate, 172
mediated, 24, 33, 36, 44, 62, 75, 77, 80–82, 93, 98, 114, 164–165, 183, 203, 231–232, 234, 246
mediating, 33, 58, 112, 152, 180
mediation, 24, 32, 48, 52, 58, 72, 81, 92, 100, 107, 137, 161, 165, 177, 180, 231, 233
medieval, 199
mediocrity, 163
memories, 48
menial, 31
mental, 55–56, 77, 79–80, 88, 111, 116–117, 145, 156, 160, 171, 174, 187, 191, 215, 221, 223, 245
merge, 191
Mesopotamians, 210
metacritique, 13, 71
metalogical, 83, 131
metaphysic, 154
metaphysical, 26, 28, 56, 75
metaphysics, 53, 194, 224, 227
metapsychological, 75, 89, 158–159
Meta-solution, 13
methodological, 65
methodology, 100
millennial, 230
Millennium, 210
mimetic, 90
Mind-substance, 25
minorities, 153

misgivings, 127
mob, 33
modality, 37, 54, 86, 94, 106, 110–112, 119, 132, 176, 207, 236–237, 243
modernity, 65, 81
modes, 47, 58, 74, 76, 119, 132, 183, 218, 222–223
modulated, 240
modulating, 240
modulation, 215
modulatory, 215–217
moments, 27, 51, 84, 207
momentum, 223
monadalogically, 68
monadic, 35, 38, 57, 68, 113, 177, 191–194, 221
monadological, 14–15, 21, 23, 57–58, 67, 70, 75–76, 79, 83–84, 93, 113
monadologically, 47, 79, 93, 96, 108
monads, 86, 113, 194
Monarchy, 147
monetization, 56
monism, 152
monistic, 238
monopolizing, 17, 149
morality, 13, 28, 70, 153, 200
morass, 93
motif, 34, 53, 60, 63, 67, 80, 103, 111, 174–175, 192, 208–209
motifs, 20, 85
motility, 41, 106, 172
movable, 41, 81
movement, 19, 62, 95, 103, 161, 192
movements, 15, 20, 25, 65
mover, 82
multiplicities, 22
multiplicity, 22, 29, 37, 43, 49, 52, 70, 85–86, 93, 113, 129, 157, 162, 220, 225
multitude, 36, 78, 83,

113–114, 151, 194
multitudes, 14–15
mutandis, 19, 29
mutatis, 19, 29

## N

Nations (First), 154
naturalistic, 40–47, 49, 52, 54, 60, 72–73, 75, 111
naturalization, 141
naturalized, 140–142, 191, 195, 205–206, 230
necessities, 37
necessity, 16–17, 20, 22, 24, 31, 44, 49–50, 54, 61, 69, 76, 80, 82, 84, 88, 94, 107–108, 112, 122, 178, 184, 210, 223, 233
nefarious, 13
negated, 16, 36, 95, 135, 175, 179, 182
negating, 180
negation, 13, 19, 24, 32, 52, 71, 82, 84–85, 92, 102, 126, 131, 133, 139, 144–145, 150, 166, 171, 178–180, 182, 188, 196–197
negations, 66, 108, 135, 145, 170, 173, 179, 181
negative, 16, 21, 42, 45, 62, 82, 85, 98, 108, 173–174, 176–180, 196, 216, 221, 244
negativity, 98, 180, 197
negotiation, 94, 102, 121, 211
negotiations, 82
neurological, 146
noema, 131–132, 221, 225, 227
noemata, 213–214, 221
noematic, 116, 128, 131, 141, 165, 170, 177, 196, 204, 213, 218–219, 221, 226, 229, 244
noesis, 85, 141, 167, 213,

# INDEX

217–218, 220
noetic, 14, 32, 84, 89,
  104, 141, 159, 196,
  213–215, 219–223
noetical, 214
nominal, 123–125,
  127–130, 133, 137,
  147–148, 168, 171,
  195, 205–207, 209,
  215–217, 220, 223,
  237–239, 241, 244–246
nominalist, 14, 22, 32,
  104
Non identities, 196
Non-identity, 113, 177
nonrepresentational, 211
normative, 30, 47, 49, 53,
  69, 130, 167, 191,
  198–199, 204, 207,
  211, 232, 239
normativity, 51, 54, 198,
  204, 232, 240
norms, 16–17, 31, 37, 49,
  70, 179
nothingness, 59, 91–92
notion, 14–16, 19, 23–24,
  26, 30–32, 38, 42–43,
  46, 48–49, 51, 53, 55,
  63–64, 69, 72, 75,
  79–80, 83, 86–87,
  92–93, 98, 103,
  110–111, 117–119,
  128, 135–136,
  147–148, 154–155,
  169, 178, 182, 195,
  203, 215, 217
notional, 73, 92
notionality, 32, 55, 83
notions, 26–27, 51, 57,
  77, 92, 98, 110, 128,
  141, 150, 153, 159,
  161, 170–171, 173,
  178, 189, 192, 198
noumena, 23–24, 33, 37,
  71, 109–110, 128, 230
noumenal, 15–16, 19–23,
  29, 35–36, 40, 43,
  45–47, 53–54, 59,
  62–63, 65, 72–73, 75,
  78, 82, 84–85, 95, 102,

109–112, 128, 160,
  164–169, 172–173,
  176–177, 180–181,
  185, 187, 189,
  195–196, 200,
  205–209, 213–214,
  220, 222, 232, 236,
  239–240, 242, 245–246
noumenality, 72, 175
noumenally, 17, 24, 44,
  73, 94, 111, 166–167,
  202, 237, 241
noumenon, 150, 246

## O

obedience, 126
objectification, 21, 72,
  129, 189, 191–192,
  221, 226, 243
objectifications, 70, 190
objectified, 85, 165, 183,
  191, 219
objectifying, 60, 140,
  143–144, 207–208, 221
objectivated, 136,
  165–166, 171, 175,
  181, 211, 219, 230,
  232, 234–235, 239, 244
objectivation, 199,
  201–202, 207, 233
objective, 15–17, 19–20,
  22–24, 26–29, 31–35,
  41, 44–46, 48–56,
  58–59, 61–68, 70–116,
  118–120, 122–127,
  130, 132–137, 139,
  141, 143–145, 148,
  150, 154–155,
  158–159, 163,
  165–171, 173, 176,
  182–183, 185–188,
  191–194, 196–199,
  202, 206–207, 213,
  218–220, 224, 228,
  232–233, 235–237,
  239–241, 245–246
objectivities, 132
objectivity, 22, 26, 33,
  36, 41, 44, 47, 52,
  55–56, 59, 63–64, 68,

73–74, 77, 83–84, 89,
  92, 97, 101, 103, 109,
  123, 132, 144,
  154–155, 159–160,
  175–176, 178, 181,
  184–185, 238
objectivizated, 184
objectivization, 118, 138
objectivized, 181
observability, 219
observable, 49
observational, 28
observations, 33, 70, 77
observer, 79
obsessive, 50
obsolete, 41
obstacle, 66, 102, 106,
  189
obviation, 212
occurrence, 28, 36, 72,
  105
occurrences, 75, 168, 244
oedipal, 16
oligarchic, 78
onta, 209
ontic, 15, 21, 25, 33, 54,
  68–69, 144, 147–148,
  150, 152, 155, 157,
  159–160, 162–163,
  169, 176, 187–189,
  193, 196, 201, 205,
  207–209, 215, 217,
  219, 221–222,
  225–227, 229–233,
  240–241, 243
ontical, 25, 54, 64,
  84–85, 88–90, 104,
  124, 133, 141–143,
  154, 159–160,
  164–167, 172, 177,
  181, 183–184,
  187–189, 192, 194,
  196, 208, 232, 244
onticality, 64, 167
Ontico-ontological, 144,
  158, 231
ontification, 194
Onto-epistemic, 75
ontological, 13–15, 21,
  24–25, 33–34, 36, 38,

267

42–43, 48–49, 52, 54, 56, 59, 61–62, 64, 67, 69–70, 76, 80, 86, 88, 90, 97, 99, 102, 108, 111, 113, 115, 117–119, 121–123, 125, 127–137, 139–166, 168–174, 177, 181–184, 186–199, 201, 203–209, 211–215, 218–223, 225–226, 230–237, 239–245
ontologization, 118, 159, 166–167, 181, 188, 201, 205, 215, 219, 221–222, 235
ontologizations, 117, 215
ontologize, 208, 241
ontologized, 129, 138, 142, 147–148, 183–184, 207–208, 216–217, 220, 222, 235, 244
ontology, 22, 24, 39, 59, 72, 76, 115–122, 124–126, 128–130, 132, 136, 138, 144, 147–149, 151–161, 163–164, 181, 187–188, 190–191, 197, 200–203, 207–208, 212, 230, 237–238, 246
opponent, 37, 95, 100, 102, 136
opponents, 26, 49, 155, 229
opposition, 49, 98, 122, 135, 178–179, 182, 187, 190, 229
oppositions, 181
oppression, 36, 46, 114, 182
organic, 38, 46
organism, 25–26, 53, 81
organization, 49, 52, 117, 156, 196
organizations, 19
origin, 44, 51, 66, 72

originary, 24, 26, 79, 82, 133–134, 141, 190, 206, 213, 218, 227
origins, 20, 22, 64, 116, 156
ossified, 192
otherness, 16, 56, 63–65, 67, 70–71, 74, 78, 82, 84, 88, 90–91, 98, 102, 107–108, 173–174
ousia, 39, 55, 80, 146, 170
outcome, 34, 44, 56, 61, 74, 82, 158, 182
outcomes, 154
outer, 24, 43, 63, 68, 108, 119, 164–166, 172–173, 199, 205, 212–213, 217, 228–229, 232, 236
outmoded, 238
outmodes, 218
outs, 234
overconsumption, 226
overdetermination, 133, 223
overdeterminations, 129, 158
overthrowing, 181
ownness, 103

**P**
paintings, 201, 204
pantheistic, 38, 60, 72
pantheists, 43
paradox, 162
paranoid, 145
Parmenides, 24
participant, 20, 109, 123, 132, 190
participants, 66, 73, 123
participation, 65, 101, 164, 196, 205
participatory, 14, 29, 49, 56–57, 59–61, 65, 69, 81, 106, 195
particularities, 38, 41, 93, 154, 160, 162, 183, 208, 221
particularity, 14, 24, 26, 28, 38, 42, 63–64,

77–78, 80–81, 93, 98–99, 112–113, 139, 147, 150, 152, 165, 180, 183–184, 205, 219, 231–232, 246
particularization, 92, 100, 107, 166, 172, 184, 207, 216, 219–221, 240, 243
particularizations, 117, 211, 219, 221
particularized, 134–135, 142, 165, 185–186, 226, 245
passage, 94, 128, 178, 205
passions, 198, 212
passive, 24, 26, 110–111, 186, 203
paternal, 146
pathic, 20, 84, 200
pathogenic, 73
pathway, 106, 119
patient, 153
pecuniary, 162
pedestrian, 147
peers, 17
Peirce, 251
perceiver, 208
perceivers, 196
percept, 169, 174
perception, 64, 113, 115–116, 194, 196–197, 204, 207, 215–216, 228, 242
perceptions, 14, 60
perceptual, 87, 160, 174–175, 204–206, 223
perceptuality, 195
performance, 13, 26, 206, 214
performances, 164
performative, 37, 57, 59, 108, 163
perishing, 188
permanent, 174
perpetual, 50, 83
perpetuate, 49, 59, 65
persevering, 203
persists, 118, 140, 149, 178, 206, 208, 237

268

# INDEX

personal, 17, 57, 107, 149, 156, 158, 200, 228
personhood, 195–196
persons, 28, 158, 232
perspective, 34–35, 153, 155
perspectives, 155, 212
perspicuity, 215
perversions, 136, 186
phallocentric, 168
phantasm, 58, 225
Phantasy, 249
phantoms, 201
phenomena, 23–24, 30, 71, 77, 94–95, 109–110, 115, 118, 123, 125, 129, 133, 150, 176, 187, 198, 206, 213, 218–220, 236, 238
phenomenal, 16–17, 21, 29, 39–41, 45–46, 59–60, 62, 65, 73, 78, 82, 84, 93–95, 102–103, 109, 111–113, 117–118, 143, 152, 160, 165–168, 172, 181, 196, 198–199, 221, 237
phenomenality, 44, 63–66, 69, 71–72, 75–78, 83–84, 93–94, 102, 176, 181
phenomenological, 16, 35, 39, 109, 131, 170, 251
phenomenologically, 111, 123
Phenomenology, 145, 237, 248–249
phenomenology, 222, 249
phenomenon, 20, 22, 24, 26, 34, 40, 50, 56, 62, 64–65, 75, 102, 132, 137, 144, 150, 164–165, 206, 246
philosopher, 151, 162
Philosophers, 163
philosophers, 51, 199–200, 204, 211

philosophic, 23, 45, 178
philosophical, 30, 68, 76, 86, 118–119, 194, 199–200, 223–224
philosophizing, 105
philosophy, 13, 15, 19, 22, 29, 37, 50, 66, 111, 115, 118, 151, 157, 160, 166, 199–201, 203, 211, 230
phonologically, 221
phronesis, 139
physicality, 51
physiological, 210
pictorialized, 217
planet, 25, 29–30, 72, 96, 189, 210, 230
planetary, 38, 46, 224
plateau, 137, 191, 209, 213–214, 222
plateaus, 85, 202, 212, 214, 218, 226
platitudes, 198
Plato, 149–150, 156, 163, 204, 211, 251
Platonic, 78
platonic, 63
pluralistic, 33
plurality, 22, 52, 67, 70
plutocracy, 78
poeisis, 115, 223
polarities, 181
polarity, 102
polarizing, 197, 203
pole, 124, 129, 136, 138–139, 141, 143, 159–160, 165–167, 186–189, 194, 213–215, 219, 236, 244–246
polemical, 246
poles, 64, 109, 124, 150, 194
policies, 81, 135, 162
politicization, 46, 213, 224
politicized, 16
popular, 19, 52, 70, 163
popularity, 157
populated, 30

populism, 162
populous, 154
posit, 15–16, 21, 23, 31, 34, 52, 58, 72, 75, 87, 91, 100, 106, 108, 110, 120, 123, 127, 137, 139, 141, 143, 145, 148, 155, 167, 170, 176, 182, 192, 195–198, 200–203, 206, 227, 229, 236, 238–239, 243
posited, 15, 24, 27, 34–35, 39, 44–45, 57–58, 70–71, 79, 88–90, 95, 97, 103, 105, 110, 112, 115, 117, 119, 121, 123, 125, 130–132, 136–140, 142–143, 147–148, 158, 169, 171, 173–179, 181, 186–188, 191–196, 199, 202–203, 205–209, 213, 215, 217–218, 220, 225–231, 234–235, 237–238, 244–246
positing, 7, 13–15, 20–21, 23–24, 27, 32–33, 35, 39, 42, 45–46, 48, 53, 55–56, 58–59, 62–65, 67, 71, 74, 76–80, 82–83, 87–91, 94, 97–99, 101, 104–107, 110–113, 116, 125–128, 130, 133–135, 141, 144, 146, 151–152, 158–159, 161, 164, 166–168, 171–172, 174–182, 184, 187, 189, 192–197, 201–202, 207, 211, 214, 216–217, 219, 222, 226, 229–233, 235–242, 244
positional, 206, 211, 235, 245
positionality, 55,

269

# INDEX

192–193, 206–207, 240
positivists, 134
posits, 29, 34, 48, 52, 58, 62, 64, 68, 71–72, 75, 79, 88, 95, 103, 107–109, 111–113, 133, 138, 140, 142–143, 149, 168, 172–174, 177–178, 180, 184, 186–188, 193, 197, 203, 211, 215–216, 231, 234, 245
possessed, 13, 91, 144, 156, 200
possesses, 115, 203, 232
possessing, 140, 222
possession, 24, 26, 38, 47, 57, 70, 139, 141–142, 144, 149, 152, 155, 157, 161–164, 166, 198, 200, 204, 207, 209, 218
possibilities, 54, 122, 135–136, 138, 142, 148, 157, 159, 165, 168, 189–190, 192, 205, 211–212, 215, 217–218, 222–223, 225, 230
possibility, 23, 25, 29, 36, 38, 45, 50, 54, 70–71, 77, 79, 90, 96, 98, 102, 112, 116–117, 121, 127, 130, 137–138, 143, 152, 154, 161, 163, 172, 187–189, 195–197, 199, 213–214, 218, 221, 223–226, 230, 232, 239–240, 243
possibly, 32, 41, 70, 188, 233
Post-industrial, 13, 78, 111, 177
Post-Structuralism, 230
potency, 52, 60, 66, 71, 73, 78, 87, 96, 106, 120, 126, 137, 160, 174, 215, 219, 229, 233, 236, 241, 243

potentia, 21, 34, 38, 44, 62, 71, 88, 103, 140, 142, 166, 188
potentiality, 70, 133, 135, 179, 188, 196
poverty, 155
powerful, 30, 73, 135, 186
practical, 148
practicality, 71
pragmatic, 61
praxis, 17, 19–20, 107–108, 111, 115, 118, 123–124, 128–137, 139–142, 157–158, 168, 173, 182, 184–186, 200, 202, 204, 223, 242
precedence, 33, 100
precept, 24, 214
precepts, 212
precipice, 212
precipitate, 60, 82, 84–85, 112, 118
precipitated, 108
precipitates, 44, 118
precisely, 59–61, 108, 133, 166, 188, 203
preconscious, 244
predators, 225
predicable, 27, 38, 43, 47, 49, 181, 183, 185
predicative, 106
Pre-established, 193
preformative, 214
preponderance, 61, 68, 91, 140
presence, 19, 44, 47, 50, 108, 116–118, 123, 125, 128, 130, 138, 149, 158, 169, 176, 192, 200–203, 207, 230, 236–237
presences, 116, 159, 194, 206, 225
presentation, 175, 205, 210, 242
presentations, 75, 123
preservation, 29–30, 44, 46, 61, 67, 71, 106, 129, 132, 137, 139,

144, 162–163, 173, 210
preserved, 61, 64, 74–75, 132, 149, 155
preserves, 68, 107, 137
presuppose, 17, 141–143, 146, 197, 199, 202, 222, 224, 228–229
presupposed, 145, 174, 178, 181–182, 189, 193–196, 200, 214–215, 219–220, 225–226, 230–234, 238
presupposes, 31, 127, 129, 133, 139, 141, 143–145, 150–151, 162, 164–165, 172, 181–182, 184, 191, 194, 196, 201, 203, 206, 217, 224, 231–232, 234
presupposing, 196, 234
presupposition, 145, 193, 195–197, 200–201, 206, 208, 230, 234, 238, 245
Presuppositions, 8, 172
presuppositions, 14, 31, 43, 60–61, 126, 167, 173–175, 178, 183–184, 187, 189, 198–199, 218, 221–223, 230–231
prey, 21, 69, 149
primal, 210
primary, 53, 104, 158, 201, 225
primates, 25
primordial, 58, 68, 141–142, 214
principle, 22, 31, 44, 70, 80, 106, 144, 148, 185, 226
principles, 4, 57, 68, 127, 212
priority, 161
privileged, 156, 200
privileges, 4
problematic, 59, 70, 82, 84–85, 94, 98, 118, 170, 179

270

# INDEX

problematics, 71, 86, 176
procreate, 17
producers, 121, 156
production, 46–47, 51,
   64, 68, 80, 92, 100,
   103, 110–111,
   116–117, 119,
   122–123, 127, 132,
   134, 136, 144, 146,
   151, 153–154,
   167–168, 171, 176,
   179, 183, 187–189,
   191–193, 232–233,
   237, 240–243
productions, 117
productive, 47, 62–63,
   98, 101, 103, 122, 130,
   139, 142, 162, 168,
   174, 176–177, 182,
   185, 199, 202–203
productivity, 47, 168
products, 45, 61, 66, 77,
   79
progression, 47, 94, 210,
   222
progressive, 152, 199, 225
progressus, 26, 62, 64,
   105
prohibition, 132, 187, 189
prohibitions, 158
prohibitive, 68, 82, 154
projection, 21, 23–24, 45,
   59, 84, 93, 100–101,
   122, 131, 135–139,
   141–142, 160–162,
   164, 166–167, 170,
   177, 180, 184, 186,
   190, 193, 196, 202,
   207–209, 213–215,
   218–219, 221–223,
   226, 234, 236,
   239–242, 245
projectional, 192, 194
projections, 65, 100, 122,
   130, 139, 143, 160,
   171–172, 187, 189,
   194, 196, 209, 218,
   220, 231, 242, 246
proletariat, 153–154, 161
propel, 148, 152, 199,

204, 212
propels, 171, 212
properties, 17, 23, 30,
   32–34, 39–41, 43–44,
   47, 49, 51, 53, 81,
   86–88, 91, 101,
   120–121, 129, 131,
   141, 147–148, 159,
   170, 183, 196, 224
proposition, 15, 23, 60,
   138, 140, 149, 197, 216
propositional, 82,
   196–197, 217, 219
propositions, 14, 39, 65,
   75, 77, 80, 88, 97–98,
   169–171, 178–179,
   217, 220, 222
proprietary, 191, 225
propriety, 144
prospective, 15, 189, 226
prosperity, 61, 143, 182,
   199
protections, 204
provisional, 133, 136, 208
provisions, 4, 32
proximal, 14, 21, 222
proximate, 24, 28, 34,
   39–40, 48, 50, 53–54,
   58, 63, 70–71, 83, 88,
   104, 109, 134, 167,
   169, 174–176,
   180–181, 232, 238
proximity, 21, 41, 56–57,
   62, 69, 86, 101, 167,
   169, 172
psyche, 112, 224
psycho, 28, 144, 167,
   200, 224
psychoanalytic, 170
psychological, 28, 194,
   198, 213, 218, 226, 245
psychologism, 126
psychology, 33, 139,
   154–155, 251
psychophysical, 51, 159
psychotic, 145
punishments, 155, 185
pure, 15–16, 20, 22, 32,
   34, 38–39, 54, 60–61,
   66, 77, 83–84, 88–89,

92–93, 95, 103–105,
   110, 132, 136, 138,
   161, 164, 170–171,
   179, 181, 187, 189,
   201, 203, 211–212, 232
purposive, 243
purposiveness, 79, 95
purview, 213, 236

## Q

qualitative, 122, 150,
   226, 231
quantitative, 122
quantities, 183
quantity, 51, 90, 183
quantum, 22, 27–28, 172,
   187–188
quest, 134, 140, 149, 165
quotidian, 120, 218, 225

## R

radiance, 200
Rancière, 146, 247
rapport, 15, 43, 88, 133,
   135, 213
rational, 13–14, 16, 20,
   22, 25–27, 30, 32,
   34–35, 40, 43–44,
   49–50, 52, 56, 58–62,
   64–69, 72–73, 75,
   78–79, 81–84, 86, 88,
   93, 95, 99, 101–103,
   105, 125–126, 129,
   144, 146, 148–150,
   152, 154–155, 158,
   170, 172, 176,
   183–185, 189–190,
   198–199, 206,
   230–231, 234, 240
rationalism, 15, 123, 185,
   220, 244
rationalistic, 65, 245
rationality, 45, 48, 51, 64,
   71, 76, 91, 103, 112,
   167, 176, 179, 198, 207
rationalization, 168, 199
realigned, 37
realism, 16, 21, 26, 42,
   90, 92, 97, 116, 121,
   125–126, 149, 186,

271

# INDEX

193, 197, 209, 212, 223–224, 226
realiter, 74, 159, 169–170, 188, 191, 194, 201, 218, 230–231, 233–239, 242
realities, 224
reality, 14, 28, 31, 51–52, 60, 62, 75, 82–83, 88–89, 91, 101, 107, 111, 119, 123, 126, 130, 135–138, 140, 142, 148–150, 165, 167–168, 172, 175, 185, 187–189, 193, 195, 197, 200, 203, 205, 207–208, 212, 218, 222–228, 231–232, 235, 239–241
realization, 34–35, 43, 154, 161, 185, 196–197, 207, 212, 218–219, 224, 226 238
realm, 14, 24–26, 35, 52, 59, 70, 73, 77, 89, 92, 103, 107–108, 111, 130, 140, 213, 228, 230, 242
realms, 106
Re-appropriation, 133
reasonable, 84, 102, 179
rebellion, 13
recipients, 121, 146
reclaim, 122
recognition, 24, 68, 83, 88, 108, 111, 162, 222, 230
recognizable, 93, 139
recollecting, 223
reconcile, 111
reconstitute, 84
reconstituted, 147
recovery, 210
recreation, 153
recycle, 53
redefining, 147
redemptive, 15
reduction, 62, 159, 217
reductions, 100, 198
reengages, 173
reestablishment, 133
referent, 32, 68, 126, 128, 196, 244
referential, 34, 216, 219, 221, 234
reflections, 37, 115, 177, 191
reflexive, 16–17, 24, 44, 47, 57, 59–60, 64, 74, 78, 83, 85, 122, 130, 135, 137, 145, 150–152, 155, 158, 167, 176, 180–182, 184, 191, 196–197, 205–206, 209, 211, 213–215, 219–223, 232, 234–235, 238–242
reflexivity, 34, 86, 133, 149, 181, 196, 211–212, 231, 235, 238, 240–242
refugees, 153
regime, 159
regimen, 77, 223
regional, 86, 133–134, 157, 159, 168, 192, 202, 224, 244
regionalism, 218
regions, 133, 135, 140
regress, 203
regression, 128, 200
regressus, 28, 74, 222, 244
regulation, 146
regulative, 46
regulatory, 47, 148–149, 233
reification, 21, 56, 102, 104, 127, 136, 152, 168, 177, 181, 183, 186, 191–193, 196–197, 199–200, 202–203, 206–207, 209, 215, 218–220, 225–226, 228, 233, 236, 240
reifications, 21, 218, 223, 226
reified, 20, 53, 62, 76, 85, 95, 115, 136, 139, 141–142, 145, 149, 165, 177–180, 182–186, 193–195, 201, 206, 208, 210, 214, 216, 219–222, 225–226, 228, 231, 233–235, 237, 240, 242
reifies, 52, 176, 185, 207, 214, 217, 221, 224
reify, 17, 86, 98, 143–144, 146, 180, 192–193, 216, 219, 223
reifying, 214, 216
relationhood, 185, 201
relations, 13, 17, 25, 36, 50–51, 64, 71, 77, 82, 99, 108, 116–120, 122–123, 127, 129–133, 172, 179–180, 183–184, 191–195, 198, 202–203, 209, 215, 218–220, 228–229, 240–242, 245
relationship, 22, 43, 52, 83
relativists, 150
relativity, 48, 196, 209
relativization, 197
relativize, 69
relevance, 33
relevant, 97, 99, 115, 117, 173
renewal, 187
renewed, 106, 112, 136, 212
Re-positing, 241
representation, 13, 20–21, 23–24, 31, 35, 37, 39, 41–43, 47, 52, 60, 66, 69, 79, 88–91, 93–94, 97, 100, 102, 104, 107, 110, 115, 117–119, 121, 125, 127–128, 132, 135, 138, 140, 144–146, 149, 159–160, 162, 164–166, 168–169, 171–176, 181, 184, 189–191, 193–195,

272

# INDEX

201–202, 206–209, 213–214, 216, 220–222, 226, 229–230, 232–233, 235–239, 241–243, 245–246
representational, 14, 23, 33, 47, 49, 56, 58–59, 69–70, 84, 87, 91–92, 99, 122, 132–133, 141, 144–145, 149, 168, 178, 194, 202–204, 206, 210, 222
representationalism, 29
representations, 13–14, 16–17, 19–20, 23, 27, 30, 36, 39–41, 44–45, 47, 51–52, 54, 57–58, 65, 68, 81, 84, 87–88, 93–94, 98, 100, 108–111, 113, 116, 118, 121–122, 124–125, 129–131, 133–134, 137, 139–140, 145, 149, 160, 162, 169, 171, 174–175, 177, 183, 197, 202, 204, 208, 216, 218, 220, 223, 227, 229, 236, 244
repressed, 214
reproduced, 4, 79, 117, 120, 126, 128–130, 132, 147–148, 162–163, 167, 214–221, 225–226, 236, 239
reproducibility, 216–218, 221, 238–239
reproducible, 217
reproducing, 217, 235
reproduction, 117, 130, 132, 147, 206, 214, 225, 243–244, 246
reproductions, 128, 239
reproductive, 116, 123, 206
repudiate, 194, 239
repudiated, 197
res (cog),65, 241, (corp) 166, (pub), 164, 202

residual, 134, 192–194
residue, 64
resistance, 93, 201
resolute, 37, 85, 172
resoluteness, 37
resolved, 82, 106, 211
resolves, 40, 45, 52, 245
resolving, 24

resonance, 209
resonates, 212
resources, 43, 72–73, 130, 135, 149, 157–158, 163

response, 69, 85, 162, 210, 213, 224
responses, 210

responsibilities, 46, 230
responsibility, 55, 65, 83, 153, 155, 158, 224–225
responsive, 77

restoration, 241
restraints, 72
restriction, 79, 90
restrictions, 68
restructuration, 239–243
restructure, 17, 223
retaliatory, 24
re-territorialization, 182
re-unification, 197
reunion, 15
reunited, 56
revelation, 72, 99
revelations, 186, 219
revenue, 153
reversal, 180
revolution, 19, 31, 104
revolutionary, 57, 96
revolutions, 130
rhetoric, 124
rhetorical, 246
rightful, 123
rigidification, 194
robot, 91
rubric, 121, 205
rudiment, 62, 71, 87
rumination, 50
rupture, 239

## S

salient, 50, 199–200
Sartre, 125, 162, 192, 194, 246, 251
savage, 210
Schelling, 110
schematization, 39, 51
schizophrenia, 145
Schopenhauer, 222, 251
scientism, 187
scrutiny, 28, 52, 124, 216
sculptures, 204
security, 49, 156–157
seeker, 243
segregation, 232
selective, 99, 182
self-awareness, 121, 159
self-concept, 138, 182–183, 188
Self-determinateness, 58
Self-determined, 58
Selfhood, 202
selfhood, 53, 84, 107, 109
self-identical, 45, 75, 78, 90, 139, 151, 160, 165, 209
Self-identification, 131, 133, 135, 139, 145, 150, 152, 158, 162, 165, 204, 206, 219, 240–243
Self-identity, 152, 161, 166, 203, 240, 245
Self-knowledge, 119
Self-mediating, 173
Self-mediation, 179
Self-positing, 78, 110, 145, 214
Self-realization, 223, 226, 240
Self-referential, 180
Self-reflexivity, 197
Self-representation, 122, 240
Self-same, 21, 70, 107
semiosis, 115, 196
semiotic, 121, 139–140, 168, 177, 205, 207–209, 236–237

273

## INDEX

semiotics, 117
serf, 200
servitude, 78, 126, 198
sexual, 16, 25
shareholders, 156
Shelling, 110
significance, 40, 43, 191, 196, 202, 224
significant, 90, 100
Signification, 7–8, 124, 191, 193, 195, 197, 199, 201, 203, 205, 207, 209, 211
signification, 46, 117, 122–125, 127–128, 130–132, 137, 140, 148–149, 166, 172, 177, 180, 195, 197, 205, 219, 221, 235–238, 240–242, 244–246
significations, 118, 131, 168, 171, 177, 181, 196, 216, 220, 231, 233, 236, 243
significatory, 137–139, 149, 168, 176, 182, 186, 204, 214–215, 223, 231, 233–234, 236, 239–240, 243
signified, 117, 120, 123–124, 131, 134, 138–143, 168–170, 177, 179, 189, 191, 200, 202–204, 213, 217, 233, 237–239, 243–244, 246
signifieds, 204
signifier, 26, 67–68, 117, 122–124, 128, 133, 140–141, 147, 169–171, 177, 179, 181, 194, 198, 202, 204, 207, 209, 213–214, 216–217, 222, 236–237, 239, 244–246
signifiers, 16, 19, 67, 85, 115, 129–130, 137, 140, 160, 168, 171, 197, 201, 217–220, 230, 234, 237
signify, 115–116, 131, 203, 223
signifying, 137–140, 172, 177, 191, 193–196, 209, 214, 219–220, 226, 235, 237–238
simpletons, 73
simpliciter, 203
simplicity, 52
simplification, 43
simulacrum, 181
singular, 138–139, 175, 177, 223, 245
singularity, 52, 83, 175, 195, 197, 217
singularized, 206
situation, 15, 87, 102, 107, 129, 154, 161, 173, 200, 215, 222
situational, 108, 203
situations, 217
socialism, 155
socialization, 46, 145, 243
socialized, 87
sociated, 46, 235
sociation, 82, 175, 239
societal, 35, 38, 44, 46, 51, 62, 70, 72, 81, 83, 86–87, 89, 93–94, 111, 201, 224
societies, 15, 43, 95, 164
socioeconomic, 72, 246
Socio-institutional, 65
Socio-naturalistic, 43–44, 47, 111
Socio-naturalistically, 72
Socio-ontological, 214
Socio-symbolic, 153, 239, 243
Socio-symbolization, 218
Socrates, 156, 204
solidarity, 127
solipsism, 182, 198
solitude, 28
solution, 29, 69, 96, 149, 203
solutions, 30
sophisms, 198
sophistical, 78, 199–200
sophisticated, 224
sophistication, 186
soul, 81, 89, 192, 194, 198, 200, 202
souls, 210–211, 228
species, 25, 27, 40, 43, 61, 65, 82, 119, 163, 189, 203, 210, 212, 228, 230
speech, 13, 21, 33, 36–37, 41, 54, 75, 77–78, 81–82, 84, 88, 93, 95, 97, 101, 107–108, 160, 166–168, 171–172, 244
sphere, 34, 42, 71, 95, 174
spheres, 126, 158, 184, 186, 190, 219, 221
Spinoza, 238
spiritual, 27, 203, 205, 226
standardization, 156
standards, 19, 135, 204, 211, 226
stasis, 202
statesman, 57
statist, 237
statistical, 158
stigmatized, 16
strata, 14, 123, 130, 132, 134, 144–146, 153, 159, 163–164, 234–235
stratification, 14, 120, 152, 167, 183, 191, 193–194, 196, 214, 216, 225–226, 234, 239, 241–242
stratifications, 205
stratified, 134, 153, 192, 194, 219, 229, 235, 243
stratify, 178
stratum, 196, 219, 221
stricture, 90
strictures, 27
structural, 182, 242
Structuralist, 223
structuralization, 230
structuralizes, 231
structuration, 192, 234,

274

# INDEX

240–242
subjectification, 192–193
subjective, 13–15, 17,
  21–23, 26, 29, 33–35,
  37–38, 41, 44–45,
  47–53, 55, 59, 61–64,
  68, 72, 74–75, 79, 81,
  83–84, 86–87, 89–90,
  94, 96–98, 100,
  102–103, 105–106,
  108, 111–113, 116,
  119–120, 124, 126,
  128–131, 133–138,
  140–142, 150, 155,
  160, 163, 167–168,
  172, 174, 176, 179,
  181–182, 184–186,
  193–196, 198–199,
  202–203, 207–209,
  211, 215–216,
  218–221, 226, 228,
  230–233, 235,
  237–242, 244, 246
subjectivism, 84
subjectivity, 14–17,
  22–24, 27–30, 32–36,
  38, 40, 43–45, 47–50,
  52–53, 55, 57–58, 62,
  64–65, 67–68, 70–93,
  96–105, 107–110,
  112–113, 120,
  122–123, 125–126,
  129, 131, 134–136,
  138, 141–142,
  144–145, 148, 151,
  158–159, 165–166,
  170, 173–176, 178,
  180–188, 193,
  195–196, 198–199,
  201, 203, 206, 208,
  211, 213–214, 219,
  221–222, 226,
  228–229, 231,
  233–236, 238–245
subjectivization, 137, 197
subjectivized, 184
Subject-object, 44–45,
  123, 126
sublate, 148, 200, 218,
  220

sublated, 16, 30, 77,
  110–111, 141, 146,
  158, 169, 175,
  177–179, 184, 186,
  192, 196, 202, 207,
  241–242, 245
sublates, 168, 184, 201
sublation, 13, 49, 75,
  128, 177–179, 194,
  206, 240–243, 245
sublimation, 185
submission, 179
subordination, 129, 208
subservience, 174, 199
subsistence, 211
substantiality, 184
substantiated, 137, 197
substantiation, 192, 195
substantive, 16, 31, 45,
  55–56, 174, 184, 234,
  240
substrate, 20, 32–33, 54,
  58, 141, 187
substrates, 142, 168, 207
substratification, 243
substratum, 140, 143
substructures, 197
subterfuge, 38, 52, 204
subtraction, 38, 197
succession, 240
successions, 107
successive, 222
suchness, 195
suffuse, 124
suffused, 211
suggestable, 133, 165
summon, 23, 37, 124
summoned, 89, 109, 138,
  171, 174
superficial, 135
superficiality, 163
superimposed, 199, 230
superposition, 197
supersede, 70, 196, 203,
  216
supersedes, 134, 197
Supersensible, 165
Supersession, 7, 140
supersession, 200
superstructuration, 192

superstructure, 123, 125,
  151, 185
supervene, 176, 217
supervenience, 61
suppress, 123
surplus, 21, 38, 85, 184
sustain, 25–27, 70, 73,
  85, 192, 194, 210, 215,
  230
sustainable, 25, 75, 78
symbolic, 16–17, 20–23,
  26, 28–29, 33, 35,
  37–38, 40, 42, 45–46,
  52, 60, 73–74, 92, 125,
  127–128, 131–132,
  152, 168–169, 171,
  187, 189, 194–197,
  203, 205–209,
  211–212, 214,
  219–224, 226,
  229–231, 233–236,
  238–242
symbolization, 16, 23,
  67, 140, 158, 171, 185,
  187, 191–194, 197,
  206, 208–209,
  213–214, 218–221,
  223, 225–226, 231,
  234–236, 238–243
symbolizations, 131, 183,
  219, 236
symbolize, 207
symbolized, 47, 148, 158,
  187–188, 192, 196,
  205–206, 208, 222,
  231, 233, 235–236,
  238, 241, 243
symbology, 210
symbols, 209, 227
symphonic, 192
synchronic, 116, 124,
  132–134, 136–138,
  209, 218, 235, 237
Synchrony, 7, 117
synchrony, 117, 133,
  142, 148
syntheses, 207, 211
synthesis, 20, 38–41, 54,
  56, 62–63, 67, 79, 100,
  106, 110–111, 119,

275

# INDEX

122, 126, 128, 140,
143–145, 148, 151,
167, 177–179, 182,
187, 189–190, 194,
197, 214–221, 227,
239, 242, 246
synthesize, 78, 133, 176,
180
synthesized, 116, 144,
147, 169, 180, 244
synthesizes, 62, 214
synthesizing, 164
synthetic, 51, 55–57,
64–65, 68–69, 71, 78,
87–88, 90–92, 95, 97,
99, 101, 105, 109–110,
118, 129, 131, 134,
141–142, 189, 192,
194, 197, 208, 215,
217, 220, 226, 229,
240, 245
syphogrant, 63
systemization, 42, 116
systemized, 104
systems, 155, 168, 237

## T

tableau, 205
tactical, 17, 241
tactics, 96, 234
tangibility, 51
tangible, 104
tathandlung, 171
tautology, 120, 147
taxation, 149
taxonomy, 182, 186, 243
techne, 115, 139, 168, 223
technological, 20, 44, 51,
99, 129, 160–161, 167,
204, 216, 220, 224
technology, 16, 51, 161
temporal, 15–16, 35, 40,
42, 45, 48, 65–67, 88,
90, 101, 107, 116, 120,
131–132, 138,
141–142, 170, 203,
209, 216–217,
219–222, 225, 232,
235, 240, 245
temporality, 25, 37, 39,

42, 44–45, 71, 78, 88
temporalization, 112, 169
temporalized, 188, 193
temporological, 20, 40,
45, 56–57, 68, 70
terrain, 117, 122, 127,
134, 136–137,
139–140, 149, 173,
181, 186, 190
territory, 150, 182
tetrad, 116–117, 119,
121–122, 127, 244–245
tetradic, 132
tetralogical, 123
theocratic, 199
theoretical, 182
theory, 24
thingness, 109
things, 14, 16, 27, 41, 74,
115, 124, 140, 143,
147, 149, 155–157,
161, 163, 176, 185,
216, 228, 237
thoughts, 13, 21, 24–25,
28, 32, 36, 46–48, 51,
56, 72, 77, 85, 105,
110, 118, 152, 197,
204, 210, 212, 218
tolerable, 77, 93, 210
tolerance, 126
tortious, 32
totalitarian, 30, 159
totalities, 113–114,
133–134, 217
totality, 19, 33, 38,
42–43, 52–54, 65, 70,
75, 81–83, 85–86, 93,
101, 109–111,
113–120, 122–133,
135, 138–143,
145–147, 154, 156,
159–160, 163–171,
175–177, 179–182,
184–185, 187–192,
194–196, 205–209,
213, 215, 220, 223,
225–227, 229–232,
234–236, 242, 244–246
totalization, 24, 67–68,
70, 73, 89, 183, 186,

192, 195–197,
206–209, 214,
235–236, 239–240, 242
totalizations, 197
totalized, 68, 80, 93, 96,
133, 142, 169,
181–182, 193, 213,
235–236, 238–239
totalizing, 209, 215
traditions, 20, 223, 230
traits, 28
trajectory, 58, 74
transcend, 14, 186, 211,
218
transcended, 89–91
transcendence, 170, 202,
221
transcendent, 15, 22, 45,
49, 84–85, 92,
187–190, 208, 221,
231, 245
transcendental, 15,
21–24, 28–29, 32–35,
37–44, 46–52, 56–63,
69, 74, 76, 85–86,
88–95, 107–110, 117,
142, 158, 168, 176,
183, 187–194, 197,
199–203, 205–209,
211, 213–214,
218–223, 228–229,
231, 234–235, 240,
242–243
transcendentality, 35, 196
transcendentalization, 207
transcendentalized, 189,
203, 221
transcending, 214
transcends, 26, 92, 186,
194, 217, 221, 231
transference, 144
transfixed, 214
transform, 70, 208, 214,
226, 231
transformation, 131,
207–209, 213–216,
218–221, 225, 233, 240
transformational, 208
transformative, 92
transformed, 68, 99,

# INDEX

214–215, 218, 225, 234
transforms, 209
transmission, 24, 33, 53, 57, 62, 68, 73, 106, 159–160, 166, 173, 177, 187, 209, 215, 220–221, 226, 237–238
transmissions, 87, 161, 188, 231
transmit, 79
transparency, 44, 240
transposes, 191, 209
transpositional, 218
transubjective, 187
trauma, 19
travails, 203
triad, 91, 93, 119
trickster, 82
triumph, 88
truth, 15, 19, 21–22, 26–28, 34–42, 48–52, 55–56, 59–61, 66, 72, 74–75, 77, 79, 82, 84–87, 89, 94–97, 99–107, 109–110, 112–113, 120, 127, 138, 154, 170–171, 173, 180, 186, 200, 204, 214, 225–226, 231
truths, 36, 49–50, 60, 87–88, 92, 101, 111, 117, 245
tyranny, 95

## U

uncertainty, 224
uncompromised, 182
unconditioned, 59, 68, 97, 104, 179, 212
unconscious, 24, 35, 105, 146, 214, 222, 224, 244
uncoupled, 42, 56, 154
underling, 198
underscore, 201
undertakings, 222
undesirable, 209
unexperienced, 221
unfathomable, 14, 112
unfavourable, 82
unfettered, 232

unfortunate, 88
unidentifiable, 71, 217
unification, 29, 59, 63, 66, 82, 113, 119, 175–176, 179, 185–186, 193, 195, 206, 208–209, 224, 238, 241
uniform, 202, 206–209, 211, 226
uniformity, 205–207, 209, 226
unilaterally, 136
unison, 195
unity, 29, 31–32, 34, 38, 46, 49, 60, 62, 68, 78, 88, 90, 92–93, 95, 99–101, 109, 113, 130, 175, 181–182, 231, 238
universal, 7, 21–23, 26, 29–31, 33–35, 37, 40, 46, 48–50, 52, 59–60, 70, 76, 78, 81, 83, 91–93, 99–101, 103, 105, 108, 114, 116, 118–120, 122, 129–130, 137–139, 147–152, 154, 157, 161–165, 173–174, 176–179, 188, 194–195, 199, 204, 221–222, 226, 230–234, 237, 240, 243–244, 246
universalism, 22, 152
universalistic, 30
universality, 14–15, 17, 22–23, 26–28, 30, 32–33, 35–38, 40–43, 45, 51–52, 54, 56–58, 60, 68, 71–72, 74, 78–81, 83, 86, 90–92, 96–97, 99, 102–103, 106–107, 109, 112–114, 117, 120, 124, 126–128, 138, 142, 147–150, 157, 161–163, 168, 172–173, 176, 178, 180, 182–184, 186,

193, 205, 226, 234, 244–245
universalizability, 120
universalizable, 36–38, 40–41, 46–47, 49–50, 201
universalization, 54, 118, 120, 122, 124–127, 129–131, 135, 153, 156, 165–166, 172, 178, 182–184, 186, 189, 193, 204, 216, 233–235, 239–243
universalize, 56, 130
universalized, 31, 93, 123, 125, 127, 132, 139, 148–149, 152, 165, 172, 177–179, 183, 191, 194, 229–232, 234, 237, 240, 243, 245
universals, 35, 116, 124, 152
universe, 16, 20, 22–23, 26–28, 30, 43, 72–73, 79, 192
unknowable, 74
unknown, 111
unmask, 48, 99
unmasked, 48
unmasking, 99
unmatched, 229
unmediated, 37–38, 41–42, 78, 80, 145, 152, 162, 166, 168, 172, 183–184, 223, 236
unmistakably, 99
unnecessary, 107, 170
unprepared, 85
unrecognized, 43
unrepresented, 21
unsignified, 237
unsuspecting, 19
upbraid, 75
upheaval, 13, 32, 41, 59, 96, 232
urban, 155
urge, 13
urgency, 74
usage, 112, 126

277

# INDEX

use-value, 134, 139, 183, 233
utilization, 95
utilize, 25, 43, 73, 106, 186
Utopian, 14, 46–47, 55, 122, 224

## V

valid, 59, 87, 94, 103, 115
validate, 95
validity, 23, 36–38, 40, 45, 48, 54, 69, 94–96, 99–101
valuable, 78
valuation, 69
valuations, 50
vantagepoint, 149
variability, 218
variable, 127, 142
variables, 74
variations, 25, 39
ventures, 63
verifiability, 101, 105, 124, 192, 220
verifiable, 37–38, 43, 49, 70, 74–75, 82, 118, 134, 159
verification, 17, 21, 36–37, 47–49, 70, 97–99, 103, 105, 108, 192, 209, 217, 244
verified, 194
verifies, 89, 193
verify, 98, 143
viable, 50, 106, 176–177, 216
vicissitudes, 20, 26, 76–77, 94
victim, 154
victimized, 37
violation, 37, 50, 68
violations, 44, 185
violative, 50
violence, 24–25, 49, 113
virtuality, 236
visibility, 215
visible, 66, 153
vision, 157, 182, 193–194
visionary, 135

vistas, 94, 218
visual, 196, 213
vital, 198

## W

wealth, 46, 96, 130, 149, 156–157, 200
Web (world-wide), 160
welfare, 145–146
weltanschauung, 34, 103, 105
weltgeist, 31, 86, 91, 101, 127
Whitehead, 251
wisdom, 50, 192
world-consciousness, 174

## Z

Zeitgeist, 237
Žižek, 24

278

www.ingramcontent.com/pod-product-compliance
Lightning Source LLC
Chambersburg PA
CBHW020643230426
43665CB00008B/289